IMAGES of America

Civil Rights on Long Island

On the Cover: NAACP and Long Island Congress on Racial Equality (CORE) are picketing the Jamaica Queens Woolworth store. The demonstration is a result of the segregated lunch counters in the Greensboro, North Carolina, Woolworth department store. This demonstration is to bring awareness to the segregationist policies of Woolworth and solidarity for the activists in the South. (Eugene Burnett Collection.)

IMAGES
of America

CIVIL RIGHTS ON LONG ISLAND

Christopher Verga on behalf of the
African American Museum of Nassau County

ARCADIA
PUBLISHING

ISBN 978-1-4671-1717-3

Published by Arcadia Publishing
Charleston, South Carolina

Printed in the United States of America

Library of Congress Control Number: 2016941980

For all general information, please contact Arcadia Publishing:
Telephone 843-853-2070
Fax 843-853-0044
E-mail sales@arcadiapublishing.com
For customer service and orders:
Toll-Free 1-888-313-2665

Visit us on the Internet at www.arcadiapublishing.com

This book is dedicated to all the people and organizations that promoted the causes of equality. May their legacies live on for future generations.

Contents

ACKNOWLEDGMENTS

I am grateful for the community support and the local community's desire to learn about this almost forgotten chapter in Long Island heritage. I am thankful for the local civil rights activists Eugene Burnett, Delores Quintyne, Joe Turner, and Joysetta and Julius Pearse for sharing their stories, photographs, and other material to make this book possible. Special thanks to the Town of Babylon Office of Historic Services and Mary Cascone for helping me format pictures, mentoring me, and directing me to the abundant resources used to complete this book. Special thanks to Prof. Geri Solomon and the Special Collections at Hofstra University for providing documentation of student activism, which helped highlight the counter culture's role in promoting equality throughout Long Island. Special thanks to Bay Shore Historical Society, Newsday, LLC, Joshua Ruff at Smithtown Historical Society, Nassau County Photo Archive, and the Historical Society of the Westburys for providing images for the book. Special thanks to Carol Marino for letting me review her early-1990s hip hop photo collection and allowing me to use the selected photographs for chapter five. The collective efforts from everyone made it possible to bring to life Long Island's civil rights struggles of the past to reflect on our current challenges and progress.

Unless otherwise noted, all images appear courtesy of the African American Museum of Nassau County.

INTRODUCTION

Long Island has been in the corridors of almost all major turning points of American history, but Long Island has been overlooked as a battleground of the civil rights movement. Since early colonization by the English in the 17th century, a racial caste system has directly or indirectly been enforced. This caste system has its origins with the development of the Slave Codes. These codes reinforced rules that did not allow blacks free or enslaved to meet in groups of more than 12; burials had to happen before sundown; jury trials were restricted; and blacks could be executed with speculative evidence. Most of the Africans on Long Island during this time were from the West Indies and were stripped of their West African cultural identity.

From the 17th century to the late 18th century, 18 percent of the population of Suffolk County, Long Island, was enslaved, and in Queens County (most of modern day Nassau County), 27 percent of the population was enslaved. This made Suffolk and Queens Counties the largest slave population in the north for most of the Colonial era. The enslavement of the Africans generated generational wealth for many of the wealthiest families of Long Island. To protect the wealth of these families against the growing abolitionist movement, local towns established overseers of the poor who would deed the community's poorest members—who were recently freed slaves or Native Americans—to the richest families as indentured servants.

Before the state legislated to abolish slavery, Quaker religious orders demanded that members of their religious communities free all their slaves by 1789 to remain in good standing with the church and God. This affected large segments of the Long Island population and partly influenced New York State to pass a bill that was to phase out slavery by July 4, 1827. By 1825, 98 percent of Suffolk County's black population was freed. After the success of manumission, the racial caste system and overseers of the poor that reinforced slavery were not confronted. Many of the recently freed became tenant farmers to their former owners. In addition, black political participation was prevented in 1821 with the passing of an added clause in the New York State Constitution that required a person to own \$100–\$250 worth of property in order to vote. Disenfranchisement and the racial caste system isolated the black communities into subcultures or assimilated them into local Native American communities. Other blacks had seen the sea as a refuge from the lack of equality and sailed out on whaling voyages to seek economic opportunity.

At the dawn of the American Civil War, the racial caste system started to come into question. The institution of slavery in the American South was facing a slow and bloody death. Many of Long Island's black residents answered the call to preserve the Union and be part of the final blow to slavery. Long Island natives such as Joachim Pease fought with distinction, were awarded the Medal of Honor, and became inspirations for others to pick up arms and fight. Charles Devine Brewster, a Native American who was identified then as "colored," answered this call of duty and was enlisted in New York's 20th Regiment. Like many black soldiers who risked their lives for freedom, Brewster came home and assumed there will be a better future for his children. Years later, he rallied the black population of Amityville to demand that the colored school be closed and his children and other black children be integrated with the white students. His demands were echoed throughout the black communities of Jamaica Queens, which led New York governor Theodore Roosevelt to sign a law abolishing segregation in urban schools. The law that abolished segregation was opposed by the Roslyn School District, which fought to keep its colored school open until 1917.

Another contributing factor that spurred the questioning of the racial caste system and disenfranchisement was the breakdown of isolated black communities. With the rise of European immigration, the demand for affordable housing pushed traditional black communities to relocate. Traditional black communities of the North Shore, such as Lake Success, saw the rise of the mega estates of the Gilded Age's industrial leaders. Job opportunities such as cooks, coachmen and groundskeepers grew for the North Shore black communities. These jobs catapulted blacks into the middle class and led them to seek political involvement. The fight for integrated school systems and the breakdown of isolated communities were the making of a century-long fight for civil rights.

With the growing European immigrant population and the onset of the Great Migration, segments of Long Island's white population started to fight the forces of change through membership within the Ku Klux Klan. The Ku Klux Klan established its largest membership in 1920s New York within Long Island. The Klan infiltrated local real estate markets and law enforcement and gained political influence. The culture established by the Klan pushed back all the civil rights gains of the growing black middle class on the eve of the most financially lucrative time in American history, the post–World War II housing development boom. With the culture of segregation masked as an economic problem, Levitt & Sons developers included rental clauses of their properties that banned anyone not of the Caucasian race from living in any of its properties. These clauses were removed the following decade, but a culture of unwritten rules reinforced segregation up to the dawn of the 21st century.

Currently there is a lack of historical knowledge on the racial struggles of the past, which keeps us from the progress of a future founded on equality through integration. As Long Island grows more racially and ethnically diverse, there has been a renewed interest in the civil rights movement and what role Long Island had. Detailed within these chapters are pictures of Suffolk and Nassau County's struggles for racial equality that history has forgotten. The fight of activists such as CORE's president Lincoln Lynch and George "Father Divine" Baker will be reexamined. Protests such as neighborhood integration of early-1960s Lakeview, lawsuits for integrating Malverne School District, and employment opportunity sit-ins will be illustrated for the next generation of inquisitive minds thirsty for understanding of their local heritage.

One

Reinforced Racial Barriers

Following the slow dismantlement of slavery, black and Native American people retreated to isolated communities or assimilated with local Native Americans. After the construction of the Brooklyn Bridge and expansion of the Long Island Railroad, Brooklyn became more urbanized and pushed the development of suburbs to western Long Island. In addition to expanding communities, the increased demand for resorts and country estates for wealthy business owners started to shape the landscape, economy, and demographics of Long Island as a whole. These changes created several economic opportunities for black and white communities alike. The evolving economic conditions not only helped Black people get in the middle class but also started to challenge the racial caste system put in place by the establishment of slavery. Following the increased economic opportunities on Long Island for blacks, African Americans from Brooklyn started to relocate for employment at eastern hotels, resorts, and estates.

Some whites resisted the shattering of the racial caste system. Methods used for resistance against the caste system ranged from the establishment of colored-only schools, the rise of various hate groups, and an aggressive push for real estate segregation. The main goal of all these techniques was to create a divided society with the least amount of racial integration. This divide was enforced through intimidation, restriction of home loans, limiting the black population's access to education and training in specialized skills, and political disenfranchisement. This push to put the black communities back in isolation halted black middle-class gains. Other long-term effects created a segregated culture for most major suburban developments in the upcoming century.

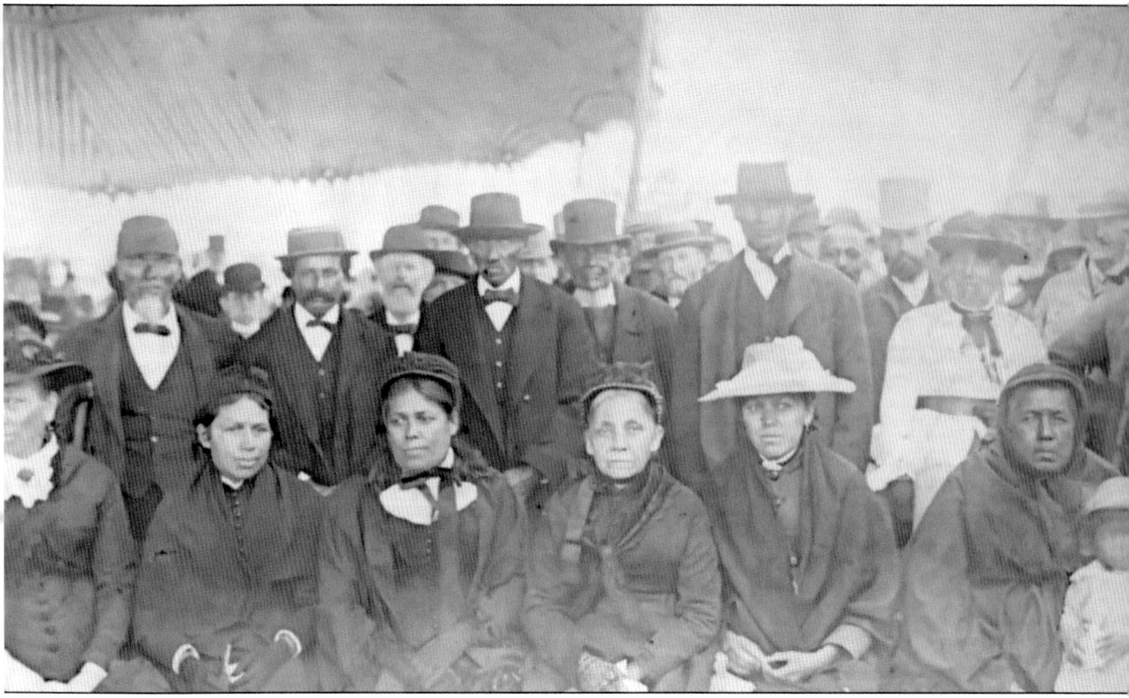

During slavery, Native Americans were exploited as free labor or became enslaved. The Shinnecocks of South Hampton, as pictured, were among the many Native Americans enslaved by colonists. (Library of Congress.)

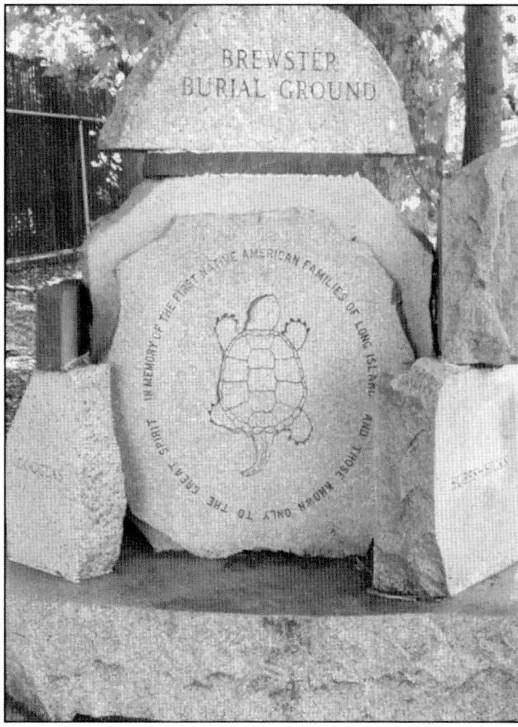

The historical markers and burial plots of the Brewster family reflect the cultural influence of local tribes. Late-19th-century and early-20th-century Native Americans and Africans intermarried, raised children together, and supported each other economically. This support between Natives and Africans shaped communities such as Freetown in East Hampton and the village of Lake Success. During the Civil War, the mixed communities of Native Americans and African Americans served in the New York 20th Colored Regiment. The Brewster family plot is the final resting place of some of these soldiers.

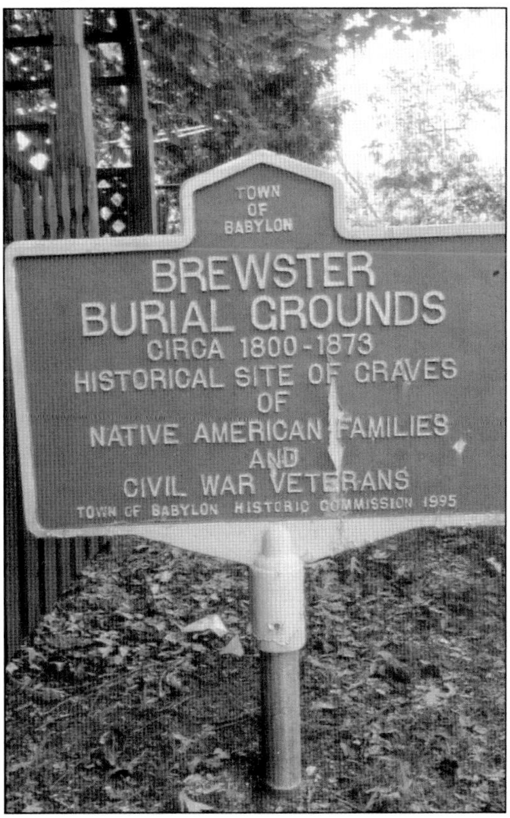

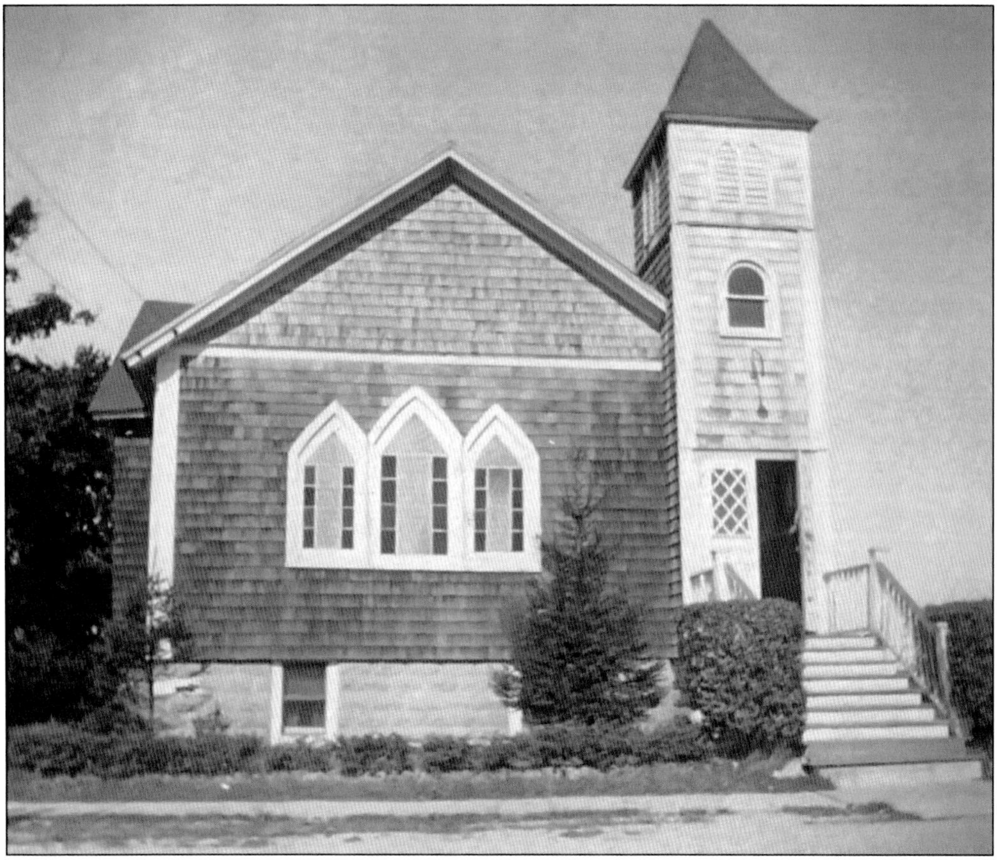

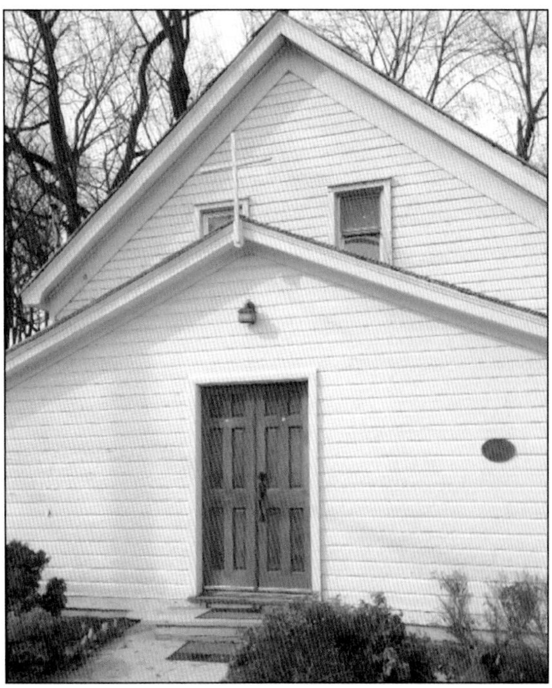

The African Methodist Episcopal Church (AME) was established by Richard Allen, a former slave from Delaware. Allen bought his freedom and moved to Philadelphia. He organized the AME Church in the early 19th century in protest of discrimination among white majority denominations. The denomination took root among communities in Long Island. The Bethel AME Church of Amityville (above) and the Lakeville AME Zion Church (left) became centers of the community. The church embraced the mixed Shinnecock/Montaukett natives and African cultures through festivals such as Harvest Home. Harvest Home Festival celebrates the fall harvest by decorating the church with corn and squash. (Both, Historic Photograph and Postcard Collection of the Town of Babylon, Office of Historic Services.)

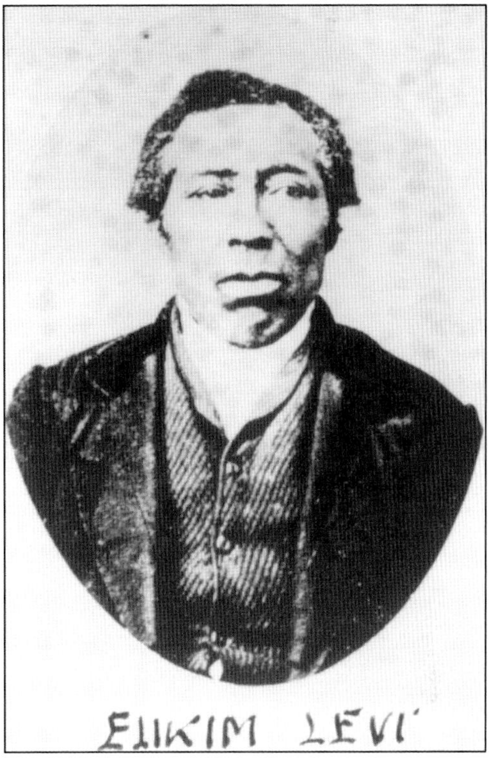

Rev. Eliakim Levi was the first pastor of the AME Zion Church of Westbury and owner of a successful dairy farm. The Zion church was founded in 1834 on Grand Boulevard. This church's congregation was made up of first-generation freed slaves. These freed slaves established their own community, empowered by the church. This community set up strips of stores along current-day Post Avenue and became a thriving economic sector for the African Americans within surrounding communities. The community became known as Grantsville. Pictured below is one of the ladies of the Zion congregation and of the Grantsville community. (Both, Historical Society of the Westburys Photo Archive.)

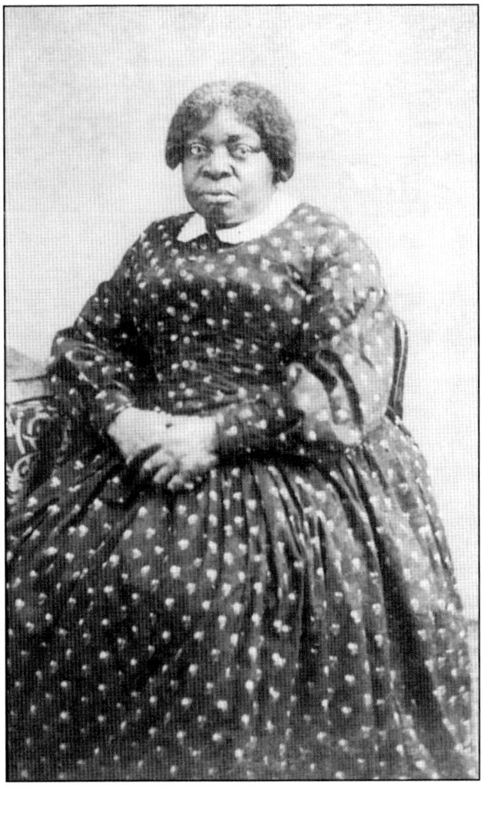

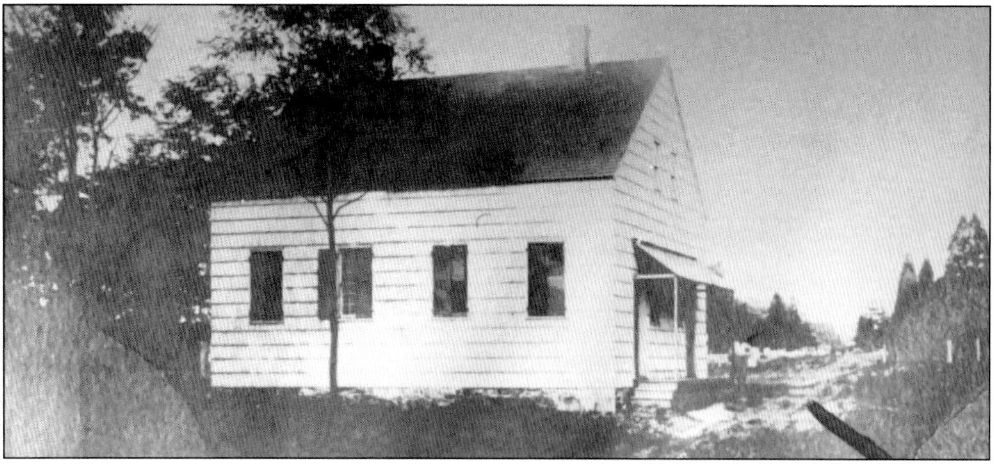

Quakers (Religious Society of Friends) made up a large population of slave-owning families in Long Island. By 1789, the Quaker church took a strong stance against slavery and demanded that its members emancipate all their slaves in order to remain in good standing with the church and God. Quaker churches went on to fund and set up schools for freed slaves. Pictured above is a Friends meetinghouse in Wantagh. This church funded the Charity School in Wantagh until tax revenue overtook tuition charges and integrated most of the community districts. (Nassau County Photo Archive.)

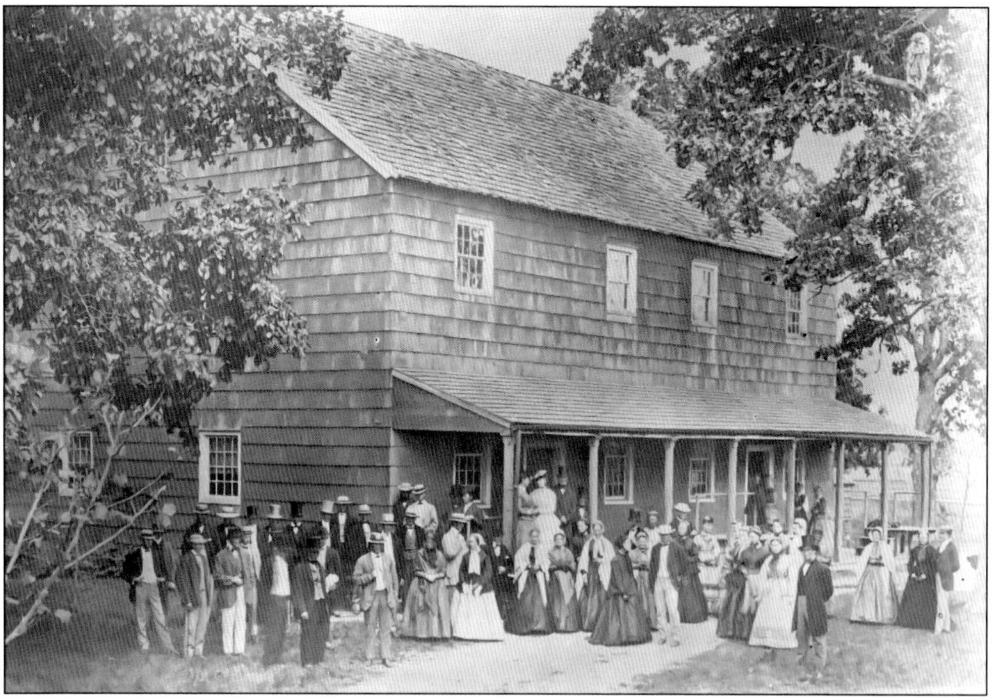

Pictured above in 1864 are the Westbury Quaker Meeting House and its congregation. The first Quaker meetinghouse in Westbury was constructed in 1701 on the corner of Post Avenue and Jericho Turnpike. Members of this congregation freed all their enslaved Africans in 1776. These freed slaves and their decendants were the people that founded Grantsville. Locally, it is rumored that this meetinghouse played a role in housing or helping slaves from the Underground Railroad. (Historical Society of the Westburys Photo Archive.)

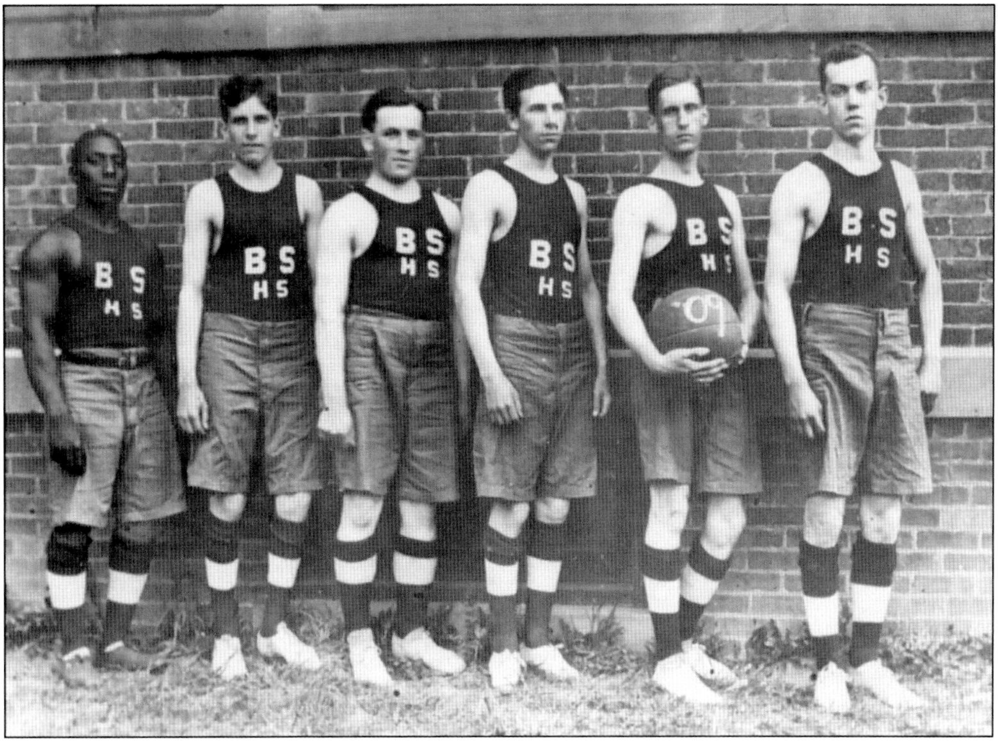

Integrated schools did not always mean equal access to education. Due to the need for extra household income, many black families were unable to send their children to school. Pictured below is Bay Shore School District's 1916 third-grade class. Above is Bay Shore High School's 1909 basketball team. From left to right are Fred Page, Harry Doxsee, Charles Kirkup, Joseph Whelan, Harry Kirkup, and Bob Jayne. Bay Shore around this time was a resort community but maintained a sizable black population. That population is not reflected in either of the school pictures, due to families choosing job opportunities over education for their children. (Both, Bay Shore Historical Society.)

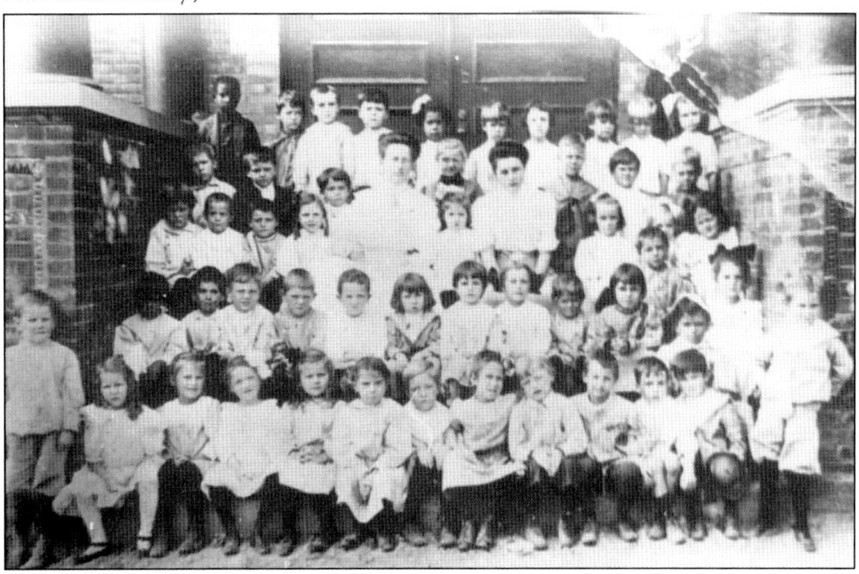

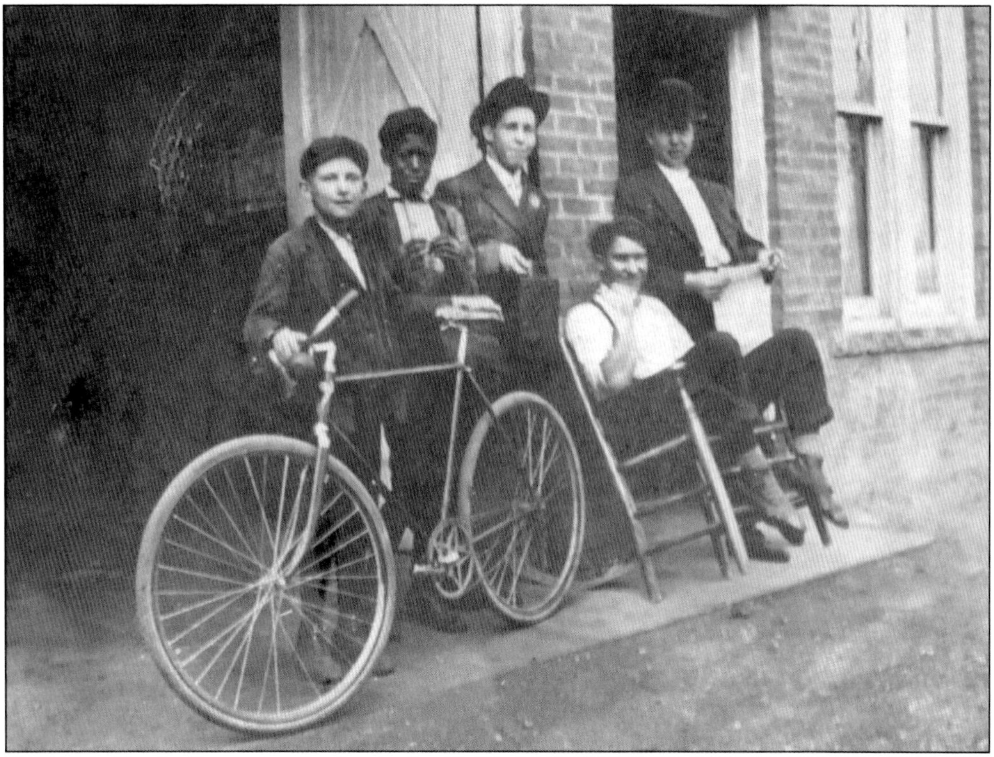

Long Island society was rarely integrated between blacks and whites. Both communities remained isolated from each other until the later part of the 20th century. Westbury was one of those rare communities that had racial interaction. Post Avenue had strips of stores owned by both blacks and whites. Grantsville was supported by the community's AME Zion church and white-dominated Quaker church. Pictured above is an integrated group of young people. (Historical Society of the Westburys Photo Archive.)

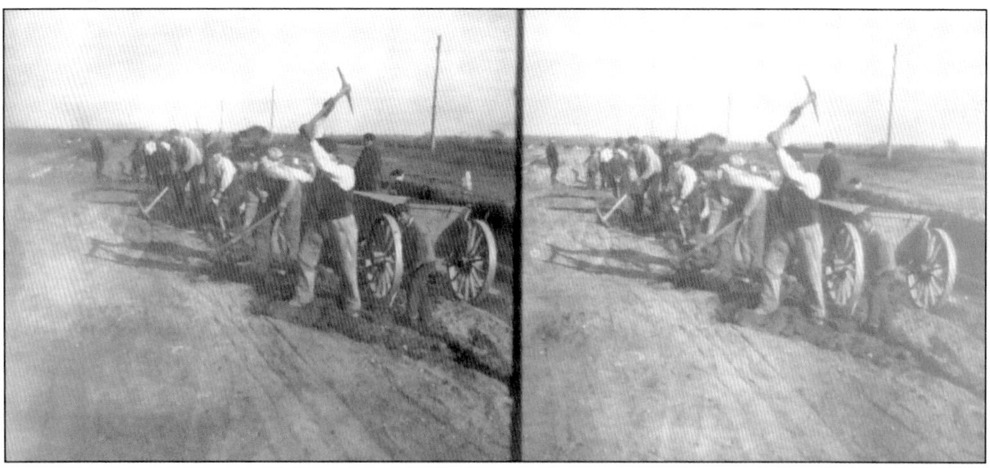

Black communities across Long Island saw the rise of luxurious upper-middle-class suburbs and mansions during the dawn of the 19th century. Neighboring black and immigrant communities responded to a demand for cheap labor in construction of public works projects. Jobs such as road work, pictured in the image above, catapulted blacks into the middle class and led them to seek political involvement. (Library of Congress.)

Local black communities saw an increase of city people coming out to Nassau and Suffolk for the weekends to escape the congestion and hazards of urban life. Popular leisure activities included riding equestrian trials. Black communities took advantage of a demand for stable, coachman, and trainer jobs. Pictured here is Peter Blydenburgh Holster, who worked in the stable of the Grand Central Hotel of Hicksville in 1900. (Nassau County Photo Archive.)

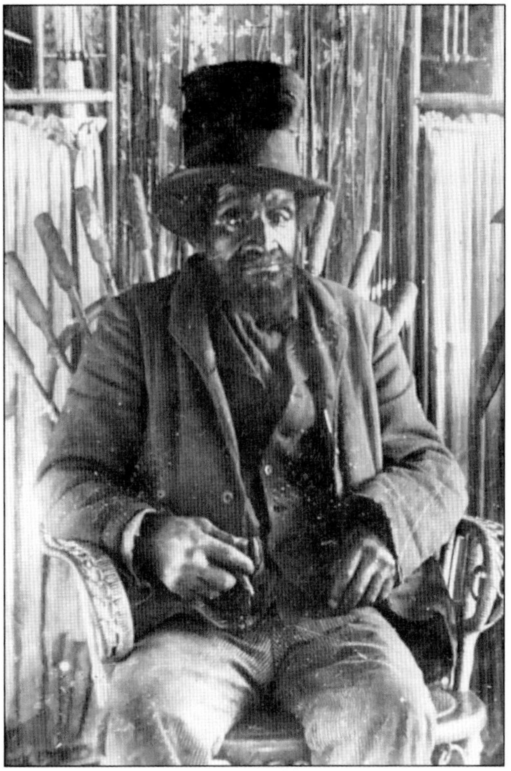

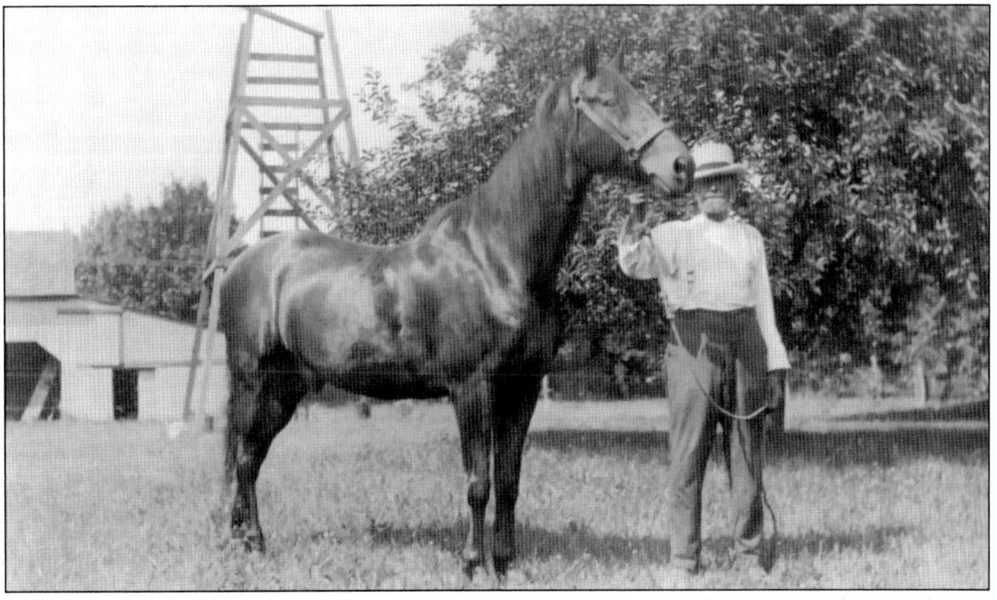

In addition to a demand for them in luxury hotels and homes in the countryside, prize horses became a valuable commodity. Horse racing and breeding became a path to the middle class for many Long Island blacks. In many cases, when people buy a prize horse, they have to pay for the additional service of boarding the horse year-round. Struggling black farmers were able to cash in by renting their stables to these horse owners. (Historical Society of the Westburys Photo Archive.)

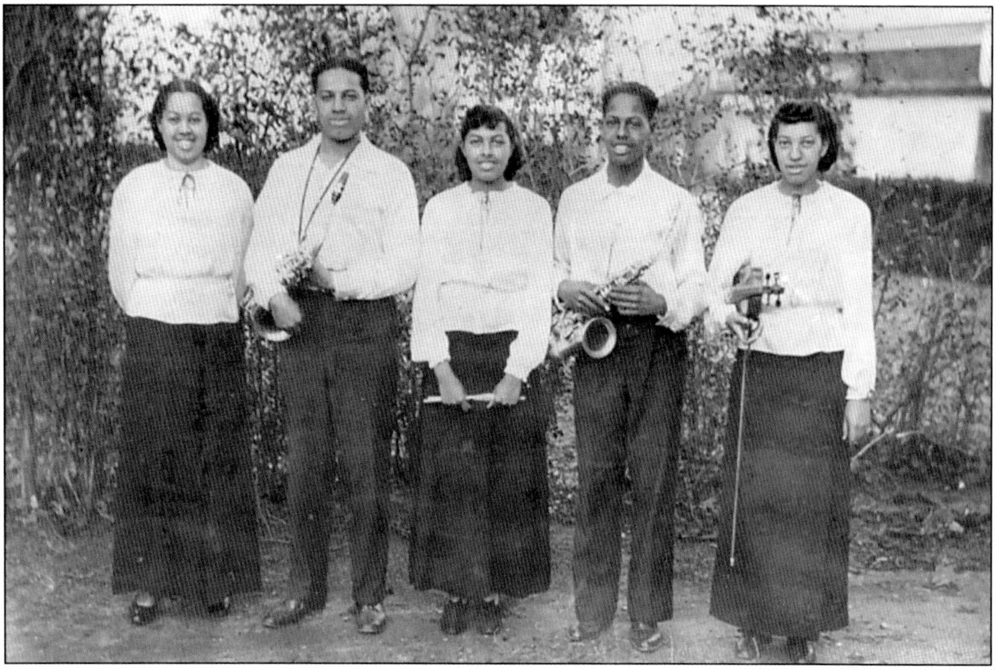

The rise of South Shore hotels increased the demand for musical entertainment. In the South Shore community of Bay Shore, several opera houses were opened that hosted world-famous opera singers. These shows attracted innovators in many genres of music, including early jazz. Pictured above is the Johnathan family band. From left to right are Ethel, Kenneth, Katherine, JT, and Roslyn Johnathan. The Johnathan family was able to cash in not only as performers at many of these local luxury hotels but also as photographers and club and lounge owners. Below is the family's businesses card for the band and club. (Both, Bay Shore Historical Society.)

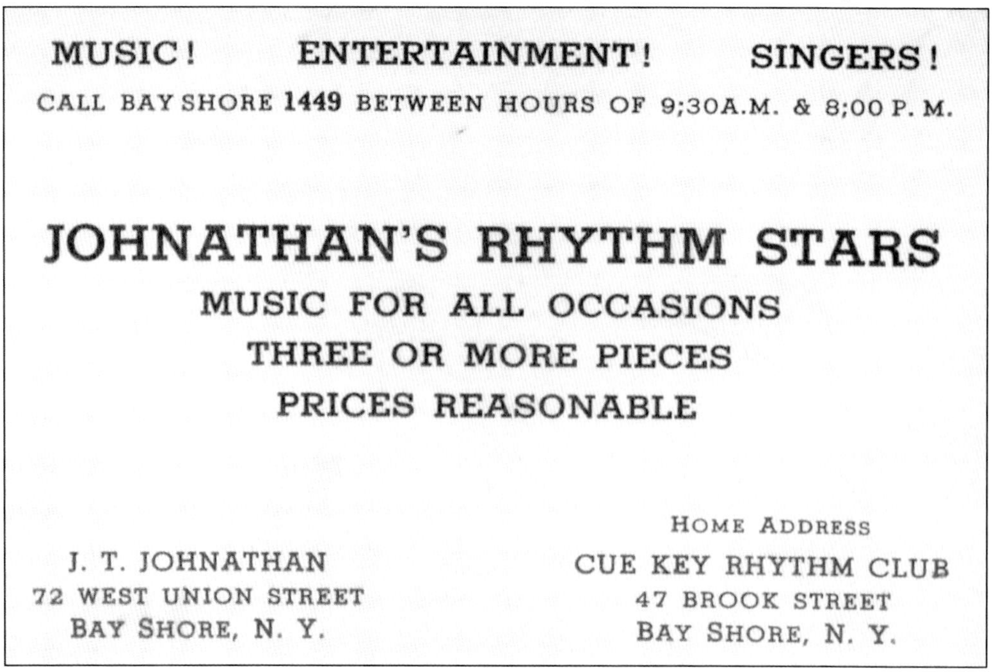

MUSIC! ENTERTAINMENT! SINGERS!

CALL BAY SHORE 1449 BETWEEN HOURS OF 9;30A.M. & 8;00 P. M.

JOHNATHAN'S RHYTHM STARS

MUSIC FOR ALL OCCASIONS

THREE OR MORE PIECES

PRICES REASONABLE

J. T. JOHNATHAN
72 WEST UNION STREET
BAY SHORE, N. Y.

HOME ADDRESS
CUE KEY RHYTHM CLUB
47 BROOK STREET
BAY SHORE, N. Y.

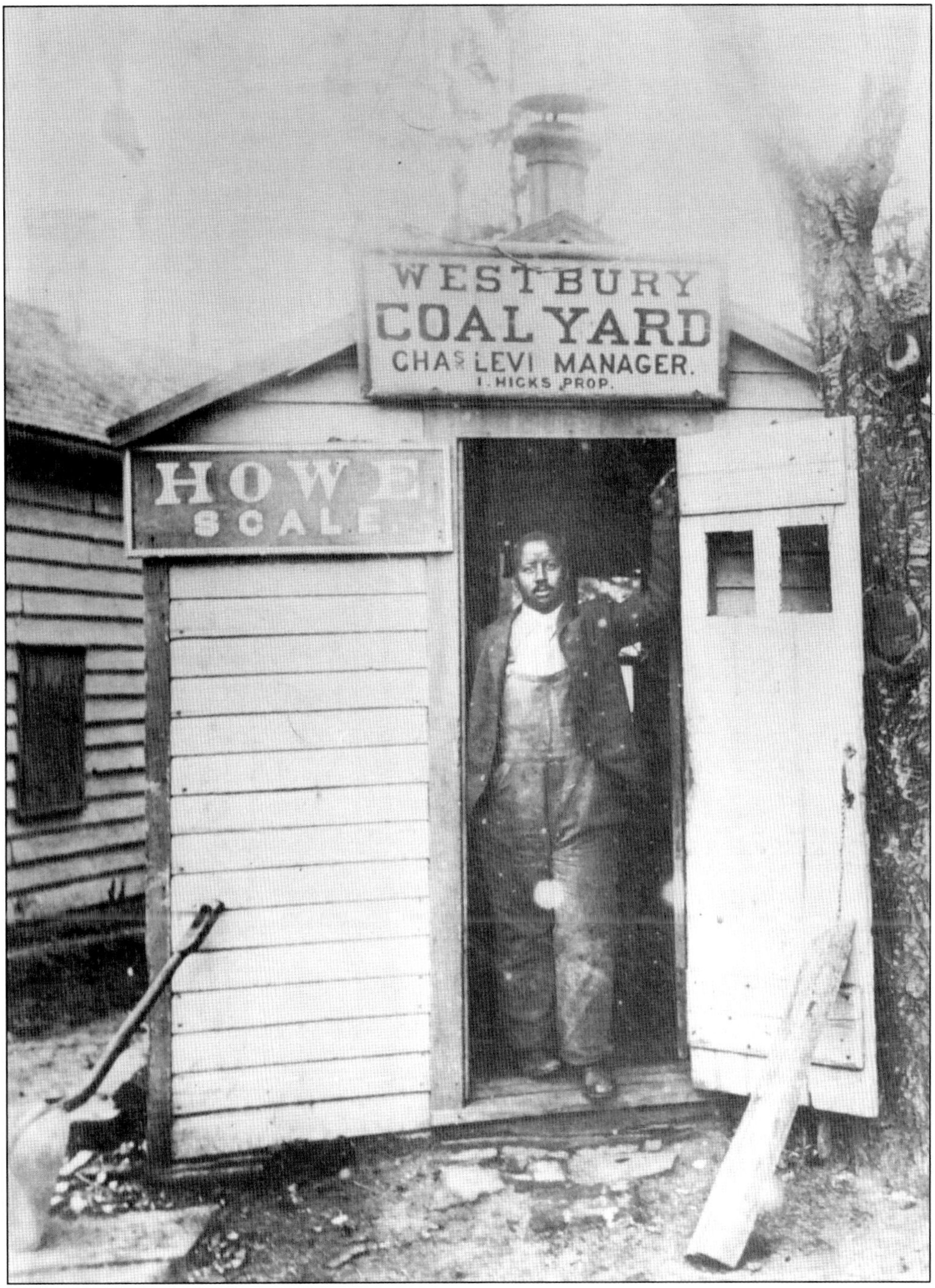

Westbury native Charles Levi was one the many successful black businessmen. Levi owned and operated a 30-acre farm and a coal business. He acquired most of his wealth from his father, Rev. Eliakim Levi of the AME Zion church. He diversified his inherited wealth by starting a coal service. With the expansion of late-19th-century suburbia, home heating became a lucrative business. Most houses of this time had furnaces that required endless supplies of coal. Here, Levi is standing in the doorway of his coal business. (Historical Society of the Westburys Photo Archive.)

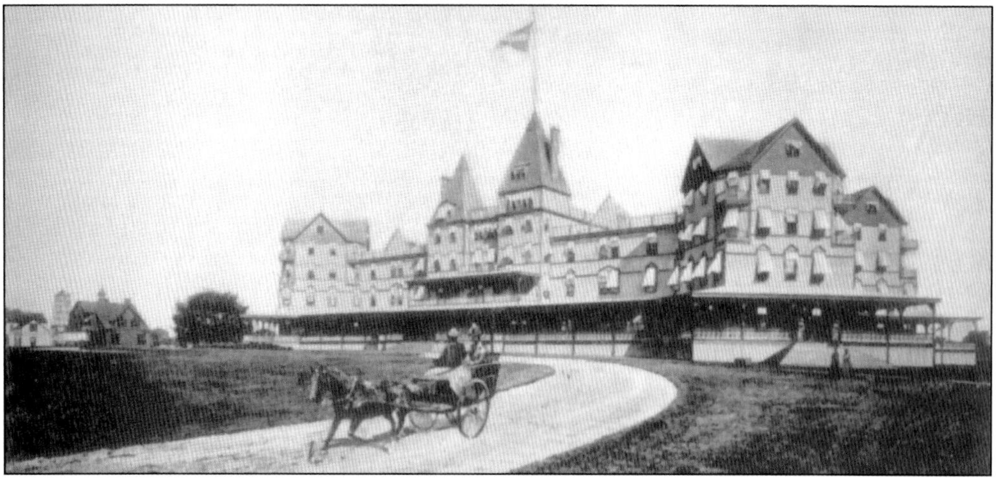

With the growth of an upper middle class, luxury resorts and hotels sprang up across the South Shore of Western Suffolk County. Like for construction labor, demand was high for service jobs such as porters, baggage handlers, waiters, and groundskeepers. Pictured above is Argyle Hotel in Babylon. It had 350 rooms and a demand for cheap labor that employed black people in the surrounding communities and Brooklyn. (Historic Photograph and Postcard Collection of the Town of Babylon, Office of Historic Services)

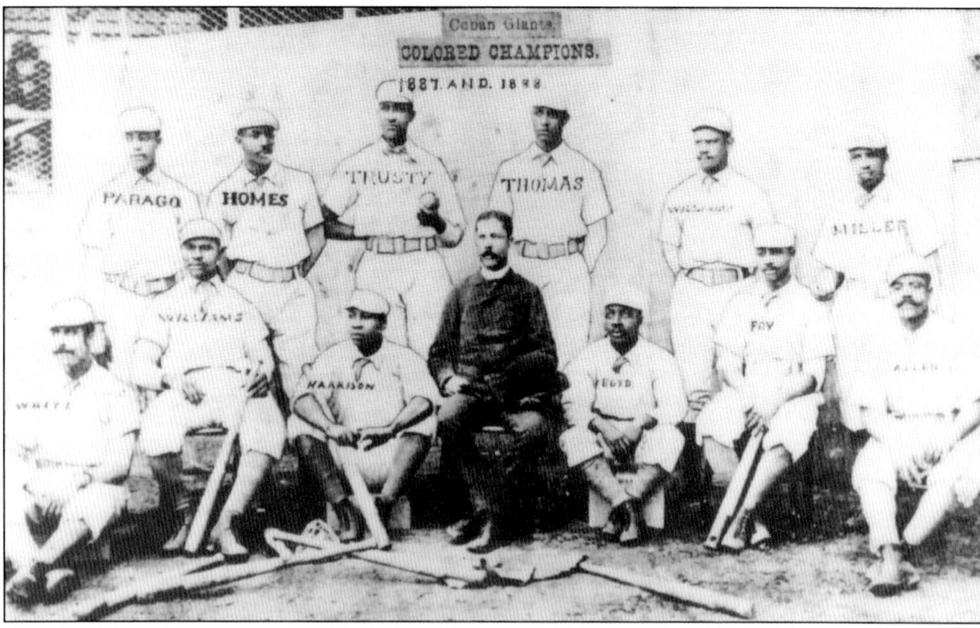

The first black baseball team, the Cuban Giants, formed in 1885. The team was founded and organized by Frank Thompson, head waiter at the Argyle Hotel. The players were all employees at Argyle and were paid wages that ranged from $12 to $18 a week. The team won every game it played against white teams. To prevent racial tensions, manager S.K. Govern advertised them as Latino and told them to mumble when talking so spectators would believe they were Spanish. Pictured from left to right are (first row) Billy Whyte, George Williams, Abe Harrison, Govern, Ben Boyd, Jack Fry, and ? Allen; (second row) George Parago, Ben Holmes, Shep Trusty, Arthur Thomas, Clarence Williams, and Frank Miller. (Historic Photograph and Postcard Collection of the Town of Babylon, Office of Historic Services)

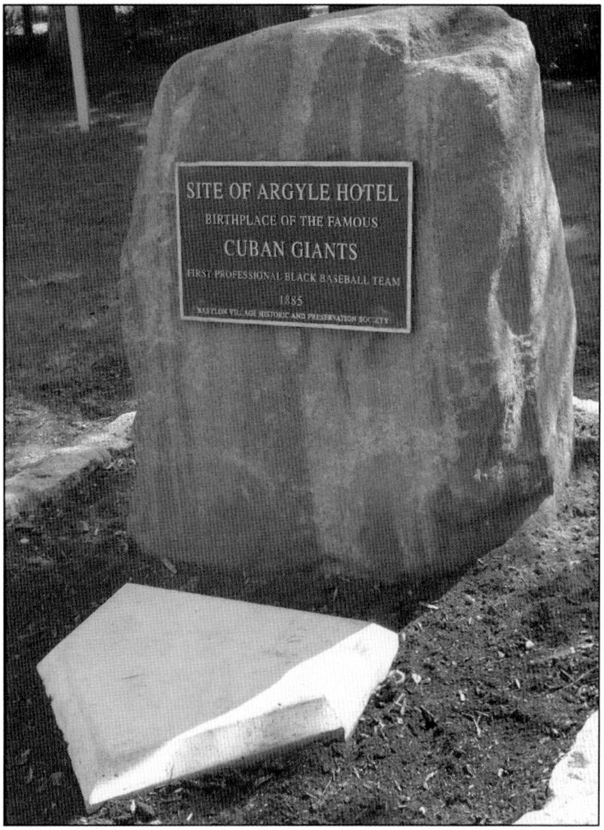

Today, Argyle Hotel is half upscale housing and half Argyle Park. The monument pictured at right reads "Site of Argyle Hotel, Birthplace of the Famous Cuban Giants. First professional Black baseball team 1885." The monument is located on the north side of the park, 100 feet from the current baseball field.

The success of the Cuban Giants inspired black communities across Long Island to form baseball teams. These local black community teams played games at resorts for the guests for extra money. North Amityville's Native American and black community formed the Mohawk team. The Mohawks practiced on a field called "The Big Lot" on Albany Avenue. (Historic Photograph and Postcard Collection of the Town of Babylon, Office of Historic Services)

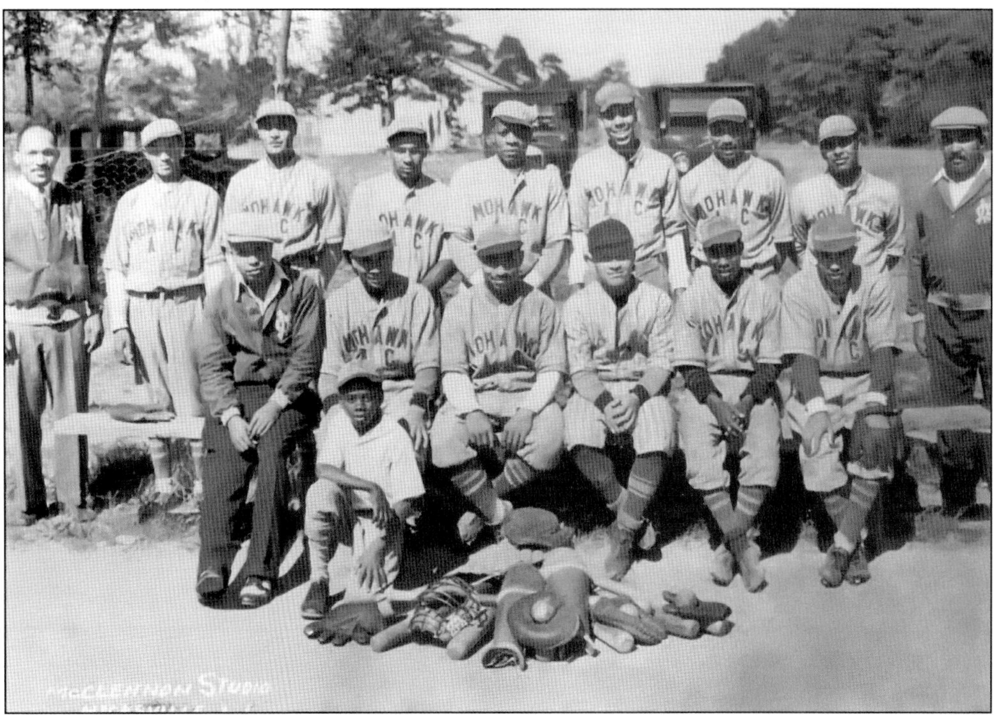

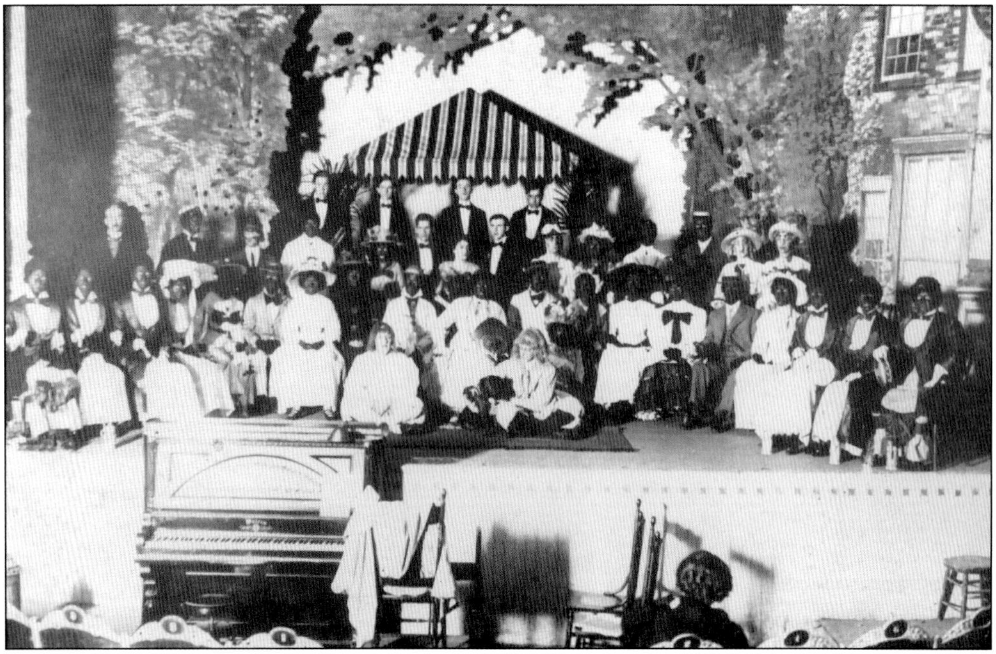

Among South Shore communities such as Bay Shore, minstrel shows were popular local attractions. These shows had their origins in the 1830s within New York City theaters and featured white actors with painted black faces, portraying black people in a stereotype of ignorance or carefree plantation life. These shows reinforced negative stereotypes and dehumanized black people while white audience members watched. Promotion of these stereotypes isolated the black communities from education and business by assuming that blacks are inferior to whites. The plays pictured were in the Carlton Playhouse on Main Street, Bay Shore, in 1917. (Both, Bay Shore Historical Society.)

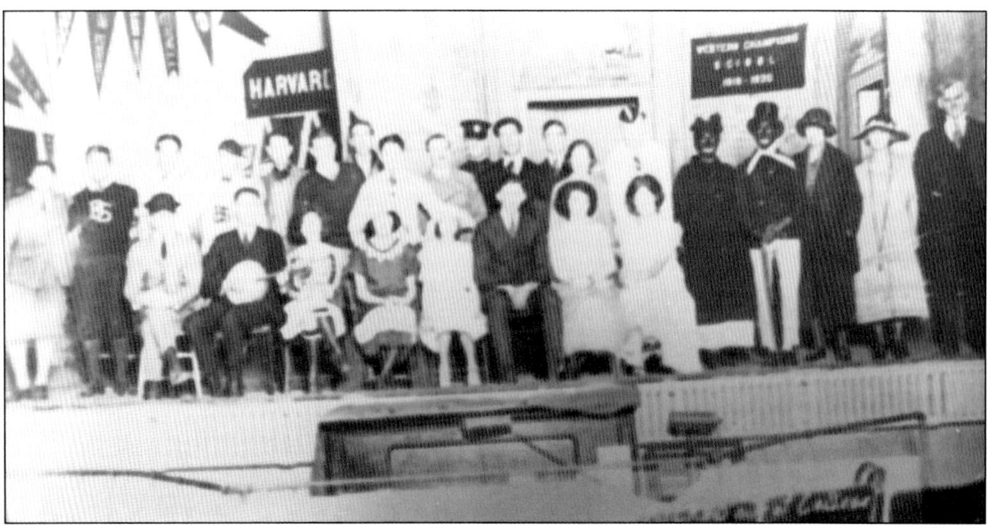

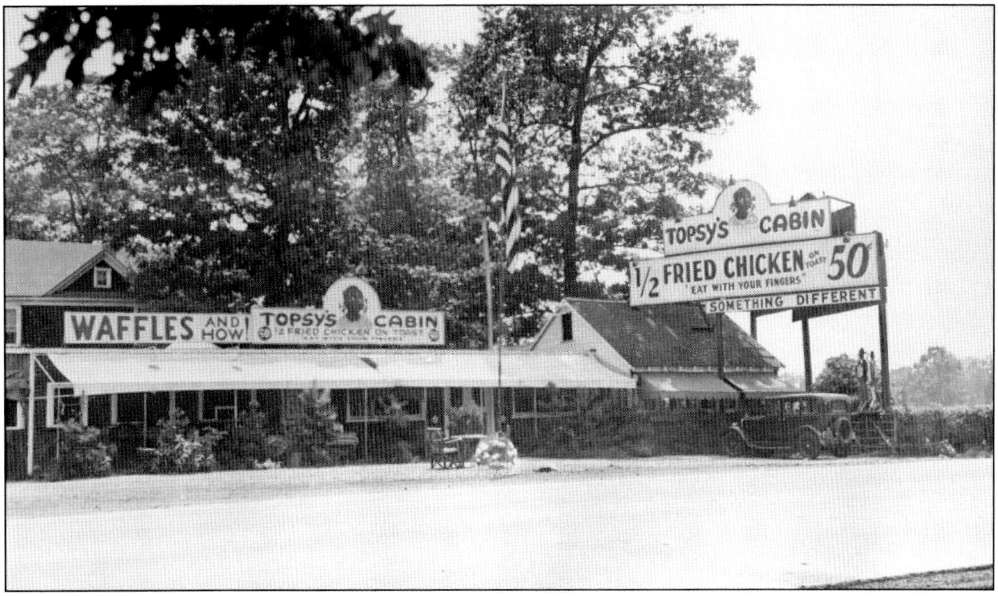

Advertising by local restaurants used racist stereotypical characters such as a pickaninny to promote authentic Southern cooking. Topsy's Cabin, located in Baldwin (and named after a character from the book *Uncle Tom's Cabin*), was owned and operated by a black family. As pictured here, a girl pickaninny was used to promote the business. (Nassau County Photo Archive.)

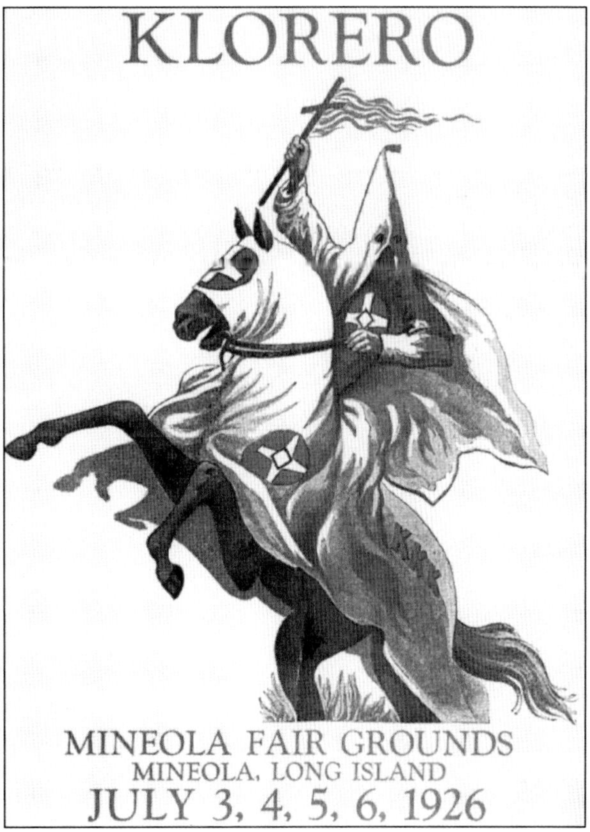

During the 1920s, the Ku Klux Klan became a dominating force on Long Island. The Klan had a strong presence on most of Long Island until the late 1970s. The increased membership of the Klan was in reaction to the growing Catholic, Jewish, and black populations throughout Long Island. The rally in 1923 at Heckscher State Park in East Islip attracted 25,000 men and women. This is an advertisement for the 1926 convention. (Suffolk County Historical Society.)

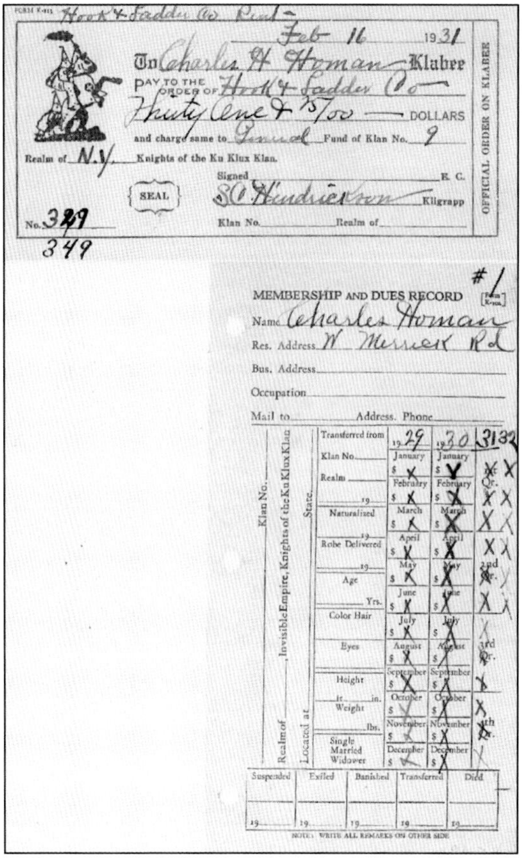

FORM K-113 Hook & Ladder Co. Rent

Feb 16 1931

To Charles H Homan Klabee

Pay to the order of Hook & Ladder Co

Thirty One & 75/100 DOLLARS

and charge same to General Fund of Klan No. 9

Realm of N.Y. Knights of the Ku Klux Klan.

Signed ________ E. C.

SEAL

SC Hendrickson Kligrapp

No. 349

Klan No. ________ Realm of ________

OFFICIAL ORDER ON KLABEE

349

#1

MEMBERSHIP AND DUES RECORD

Name Charles Homan

Res. Address W Merrick Rd

Bus. Address

Occupation

Mail to ________ Address. Phone

Klan No. ________ Invisible Empire, Knights of the Ku Klux Klan

State ________

Realm of ________ Located at ________

Transferred from / Klan No. / Realm / 19 / Naturalized / 19 / Robe Delivered / 19 / Age / Yrs. / Color Hair / Eyes / Height / ft. in. / Weight / lbs. / Single / Married / Widower

1929 / 1930 / 3132

January, February, March, April, May, June, July, August, September, October, November, December

Suspended / Exiled / Banished / Transferred / Died

NOTE: WRITE ALL REMARKS ON OTHER SIDE

Estimated membership of the Klan was one in seven to one in nine Long Island residents. Members of the Klan included Methodist minsters, law enforcement, and elected officials. Members were not secretive about meetings and events. At rallies and parades, members marched in their robes without their faces covered. The Klan organized community vigilante groups to intimidate locals to stay aligned with racist norms. The image at left is a receipt of rental hall from a local fire department. The Klan sponsored department events such as the Labor Day Race, which was a competitive race between local hook and ladder companies. The winning company was awarded the Ku Klux Klan Cup. (Both, Suffolk County Historical Society.)

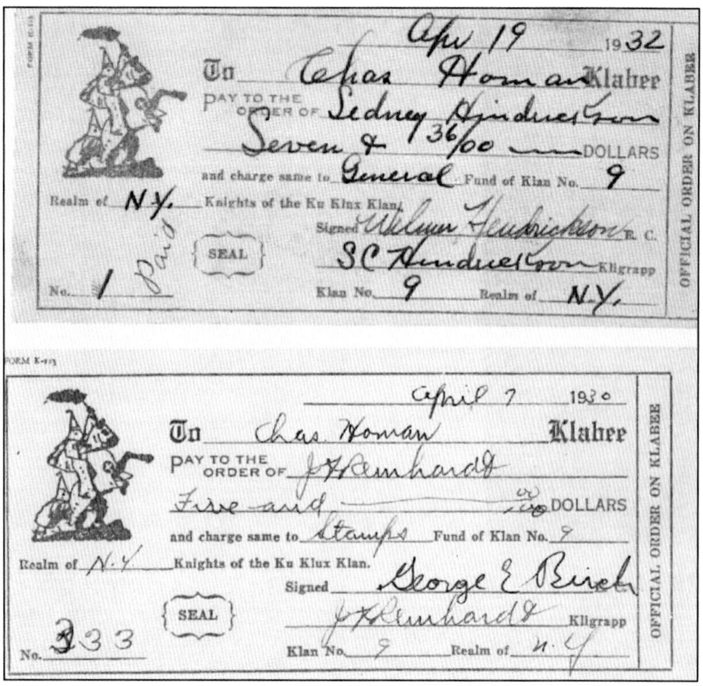

FORM K-113

Apr 19 1932

To Chas Homan Klabee

Pay to the order of Sidney Hendrickson

Seven & 36/100 DOLLARS

and charge same to General Fund of Klan No. 9

Realm of N.Y. Knights of the Ku Klux Klan.

Signed Wilmer Hendrickson E. C.

SEAL

SC Hendrickson Kligrapp

No. 1 Paid

Klan No. 9 Realm of N.Y.

OFFICIAL ORDER ON KLABEE

FORM K-113

April 7 1930

To Chas Homan Klabee

Pay to the order of J Rainhardt

Five and 00/100 DOLLARS

and charge same to Stamps Fund of Klan No. 9

Realm of N.Y. Knights of the Ku Klux Klan.

Signed George E Birch

SEAL

J Rainhardt Kligrapp

No. 333

Klan No. 9 Realm of N.Y.

OFFICIAL ORDER ON KLABEE

Main Office
HEMPSTEAD AVE.
MALVERNE, L.I.
Phone 3331-W Lynbrook

Branch Office
ABREW BUILDING
BAY SHORE, L.I.
Phone 1847 Bay Shore

HOMELAND CORPORATION

A Bond and Mortgage Institution

REAL ESTATE — INSURANCE

DWIGHT C. SQUIRES, Mgr.
Real Estate and Insurance Dept.

Money to Loan on First and Second Mortgages in Nassau and Suffolk Counties

OFFICERS

PAUL W. F. LINDNER	President	Malverne, L. I.
JOHN BOYLE, JR.	Vice-President	Huntington, L. I.
LEO H. K. ANDERSON	2nd Vice-President	Freeport, L. I.
GEORGE H. McDONALD	Secretary and Treasurer	Bay Shore, L. I.
WM. H. HAACK	Assistant Secretary	Babylon, N. Y.
CHAS. W. RIDER	Assistant Secretary	Malverne, L. I.
SIDNEY R. MOLLER	Assistant Treasurer	Hempstead, L. I.

DIRECTORS

ISAAC E. HOUSE	Hempstead, L. I.	(Lumber Dealer, Hempstead, L. I.)
H. WILLARD GRIFFITHS	Hempstead, L. I.	(Lawyer, Griffiths & Gardner, Hempstead, L. I.)
CHAS. A. WERNER	Malverne, L. I.	(New York Manager, Plibrico Jointless Fire Brick Co.)
LEWIS A. HICKS	Valley Stream, L. I.	(Lawyer, President, Village of Valley Stream)
DWIGHT C. SQUIRES	Port Jefferson Station	(Real Estate Broker, President, Long Island Shores, Inc.)
CHAS. T. GORDON	Eastport, L. I.	(President, L. I. Duck Growers' Association)
ARTHUR H. MYERS	Lake Ronkonkoma, L.I.	(Director, Community Trust Co., Sayville, L. I.; President, Radiotel Mfg. Co., Bay Shore, L. I.)

Real estate brokers, mortgage bankers, and insurance companies were the financial backbone to the Klan. These businesses sponsored events and rallies for the Klan. The image above is an advertisement in a Klan pamphlet. The Klan was against integration, and businesses that supported them shared this view. Klan influence in real estate and mortgages enforced residential segregation for decades to come. The culture of racial segregation became ingrained within the layout of residential developments, which makes Long Island one of the most segregated suburbs in America today. (Suffolk County Historical Society.)

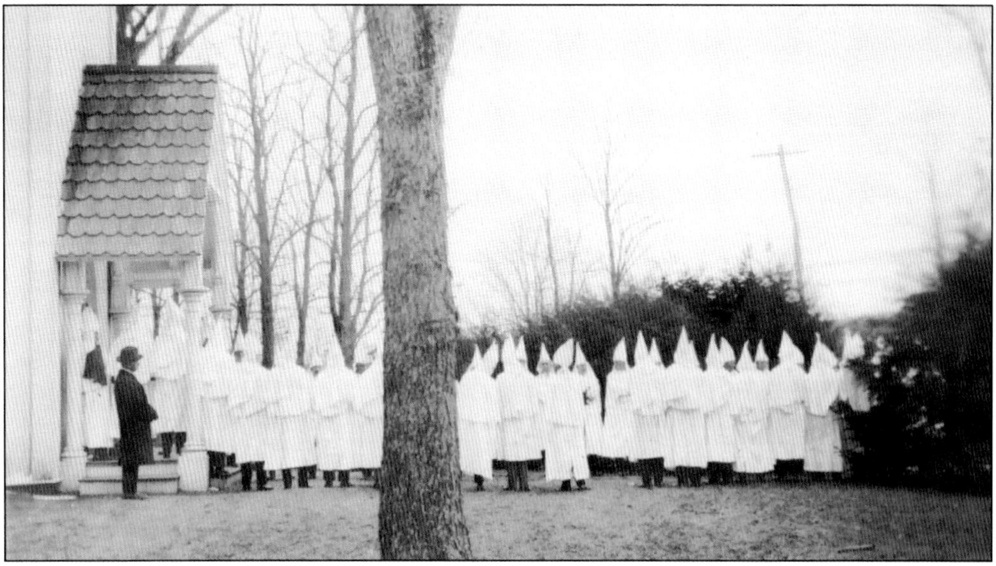

The Long Island Klan was not a secret organization. The Klan marched in community parades with their faces uncovered, held rallies in churchyards during mass, and gave support to local political candidates. The local *County Review* newspaper reported on November 16, 1923, that the "Klan was attending Black churches across the East end of Long Island to explain their principles." In the photograph above is a Klan funeral and burial in Smithtown. Members are pictured attending the ceremony in Klan outfits with their faces exposed. (Both, Smithtown Historical Society Collection.)

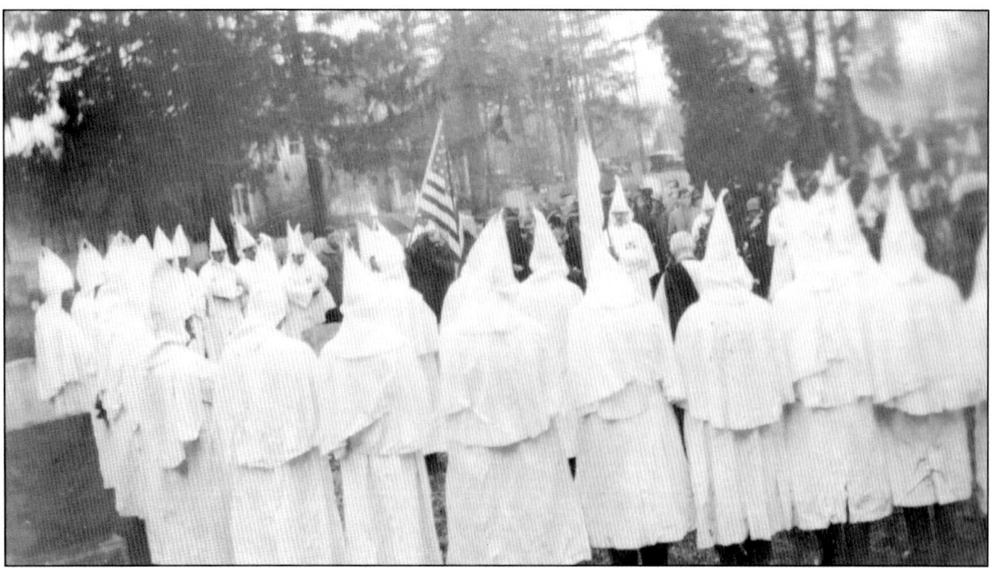

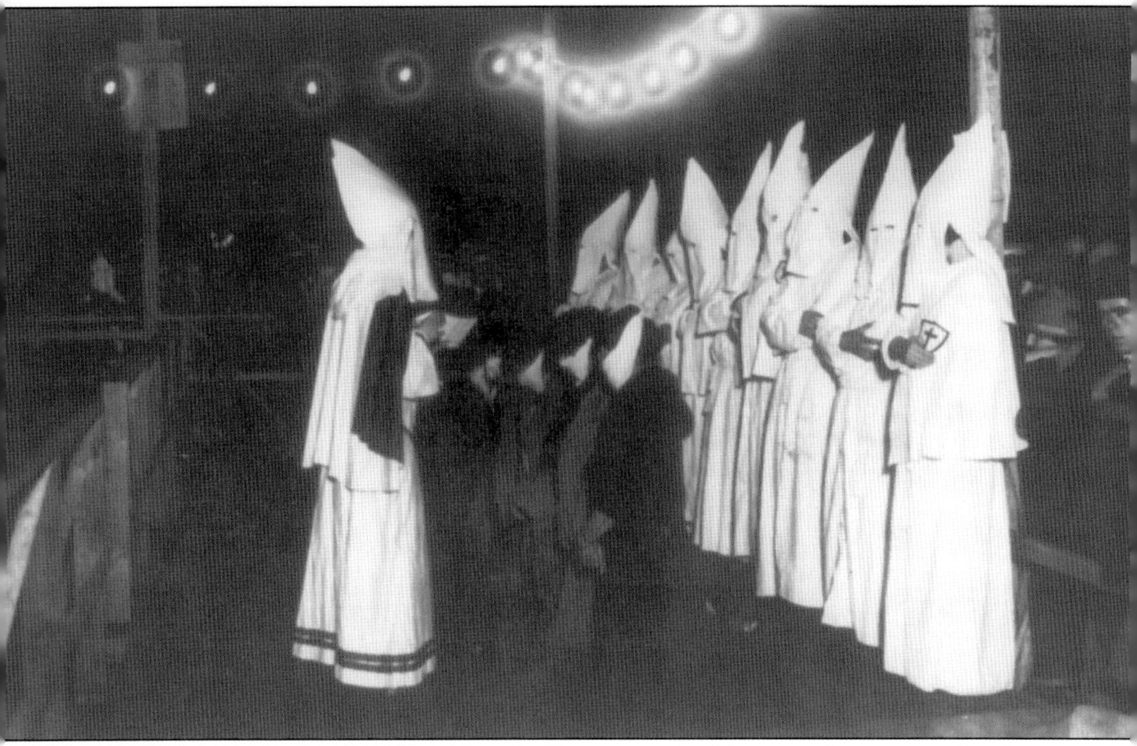

The Klan had open membership for women. In this image, the Klan is inducting new female members during a rally somewhere on Long Island. Klan recruitment happened at local Protestant churches and community parades and events. During these inductions, the Klan had new members promise to promote and protect racial purity. (Library of Congress.)

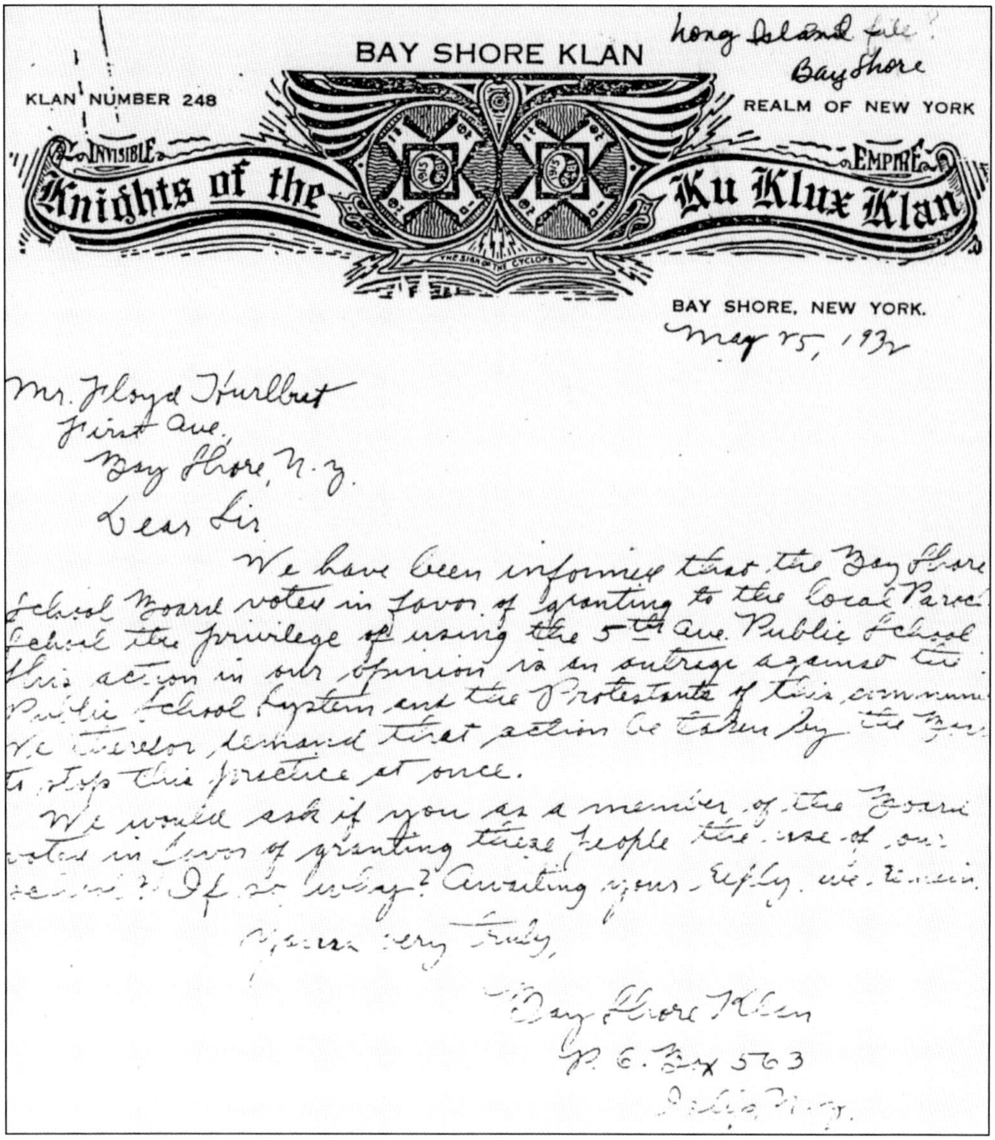

BAY SHORE KLAN

KLAN NUMBER 248

REALM OF NEW YORK

INVISIBLE EMPIRE

Knights of the Ku Klux Klan

THE SIGN OF THE CYCLOPS

Long Island file? Bay Shore

BAY SHORE, NEW YORK.

May 25, 1932

Mr. Floyd Hurlbut
First Ave.
Bay Shore, N. Y.

Dear Sir

We have been informed that the Bay Shore School Board voted in favor of granting to the local Parochial School the privilege of using the 5th Ave. Public School. This action in our opinion is an outrage against the Public School System and the Protestants of this community. We therefore demand that action be taken by the Board to stop this practice at once.

We would ask if you as a member of the Board voted in favor of granting these people the use of our school? If so why? Awaiting your reply, we remain.

Yours very truly,

Bay Shore Klan
P. O. Box 563
[illegible]

The Klan influenced decisions of local school boards. This letter, addressed to Floyd Hurlbut, Bay Shore schools superintendent, demanded an explanation for renting out the Fifth Avenue School to a Catholic organization. The letter goes on to explain how this offends local Protestant groups and says that Hurlbut should reconsider his decision. (Bay Shore Historical Society.)

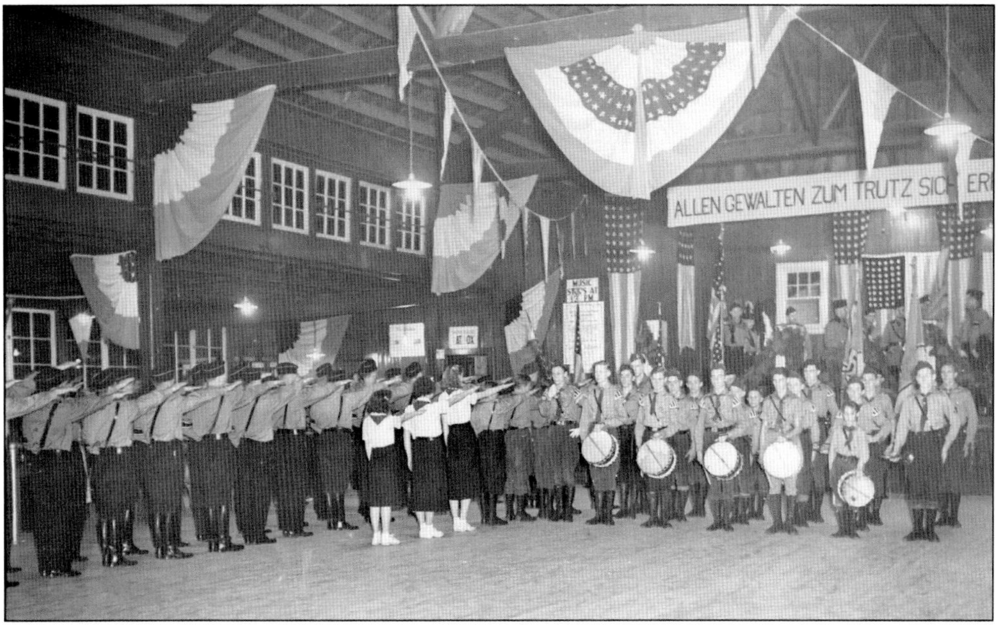

The Klan was not the only hate group spurred by Long Island's changing demographics. Early-20th-century Long Island was home to a large German population. A small fraction of this population formed the American Nazi Party. The home base and fundraising retreat was Camp Siegfried, located in Yaphank, Suffolk County. Pictured are members at an event at Camp Siegfried. While attending Siegfried, members learned anti-Semitism, racial superiority, and other Nazi ideals. Members and visitors to Siegfried were as much as 40,000. While at the camp, attendees were subject to militaristic exercises while studying Nazi science and philosophy. During the 1940s, the camp raised as much as $120,000 for the promotion of Nazi causes throughout Europe. The party fell apart after leader Fritz Kuhn was deported in 1945 to West Germany. (Both, Nassau County Photo Archive.)

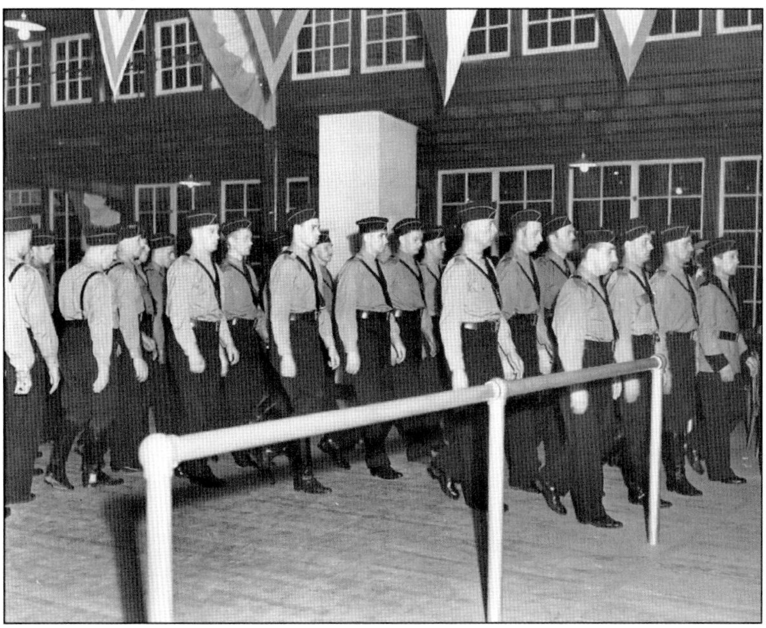

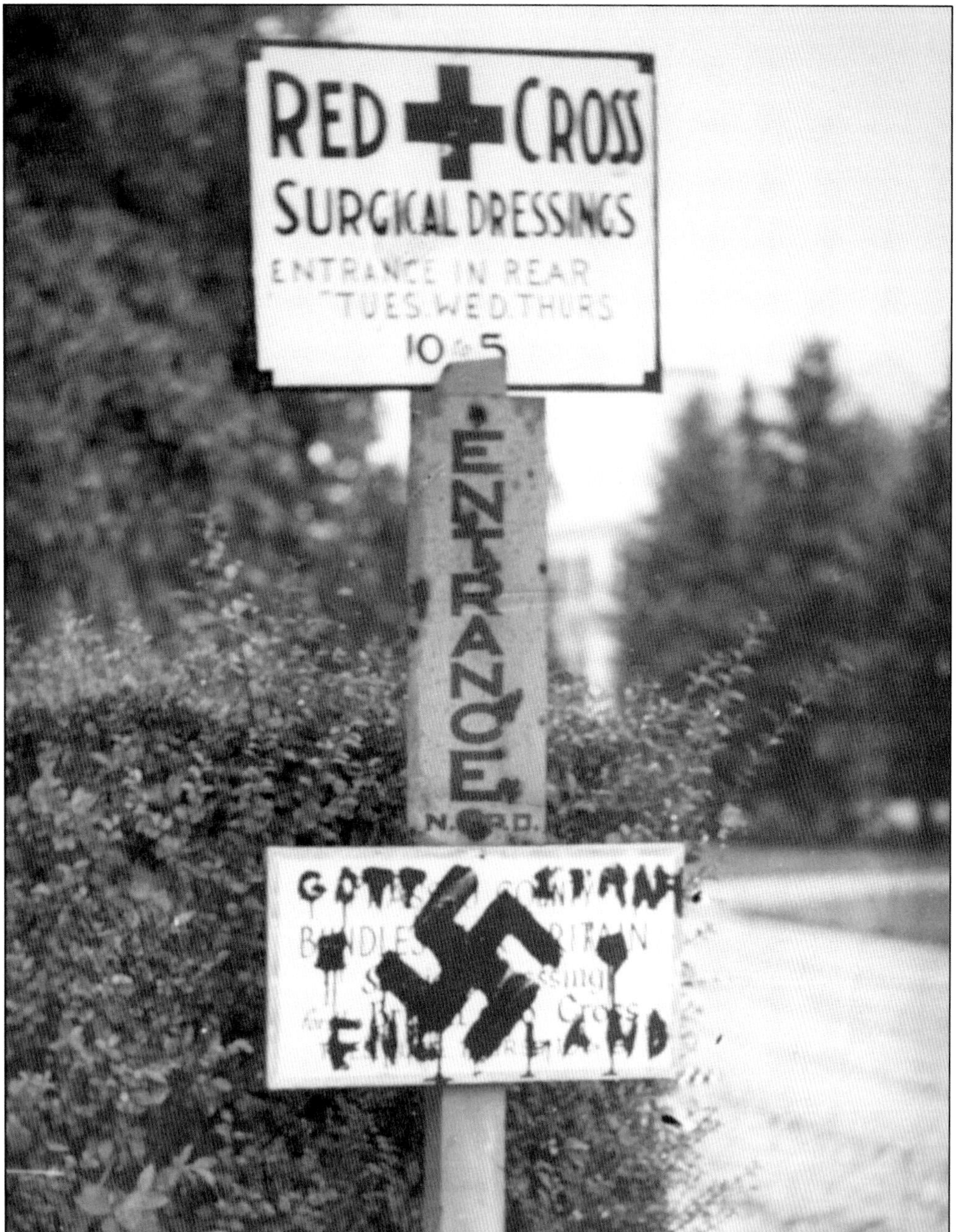

Due to the large memberships of the Ku Klux Klan and American Nazi Party, media did not cover many hate crimes and residential segregation for decades to come. Civil rights protests were rarely on the front pages of local papers, and citizens who came out against racial inequalities in the form of protests were scared of getting vandalism charges. The long-term legacy of both of these groups was that segregation in most aspects of society was the norm. Racial inequality on Long Island became a taboo subject, and it was denied that racism happened in the North. In this 1945 photograph, a swastika is spray-painted on a sign in Hewlett, with the atrocities of the Nazi machine still fresh on every American's mind. (Nassau County Photo Archive.)

Two

Early Fights and Achievements of Integration and Equality

The civil rights movement is rooted in black soldiers coming home from wars. Fighting a war provides soldiers with a sense of ownership of their country and a desire to want better for their children. After the Civil War, black regiments such as New York's 20th had soldiers come home and demand educational equality to their white counterparts. Organizations such as NAACP had their membership swell with black soldiers returning home from World War I. In addition to the increased demand for civil rights correlated with black soldiers coming home from combat, the growing diversity of New York spurred allies to the black rights movement.

Targets of hate groups such as the Ku Klux Klan included not only blacks but Jewish and Catholic people as well. These discriminated groups in many cases formed alliances against the racial caste system through mass demonstration and the rise of a new ideology. Nationwide, political ideologies such as Marxism and socialism were taking root among the poor immigrant and black communities. Marxism and socialism argued that capitalism should be rejected by the masses because it created economic and racial inequality. Socialism had such a strong appeal that labor activist Eugene Debs ran for president as a socialist in 1912. He was defeated, but Debs received a total of 900,000 votes or 6 percent of the presidential vote. The influence of socialism and Marxism among the poor immigrant and working-class communities stunted the growth of the civil rights movement because it became defined by government officials as communist infiltration of American society.

The ideology of equality was fused together with many ideals such as religion. Religious movements formed from preachers demanding equality, through mass demonstrations, and from retreats that modeled just societies through integration. Guiding ideas of equality started a movement that focused on keeping money in the black community to empower and enrich its members. Successful black businessmen took these ideas and reinvested their profits to develop black suburbs. These movements started to slow during World War II and had to be reinvented to achieve success in obtaining equality for the following generation.

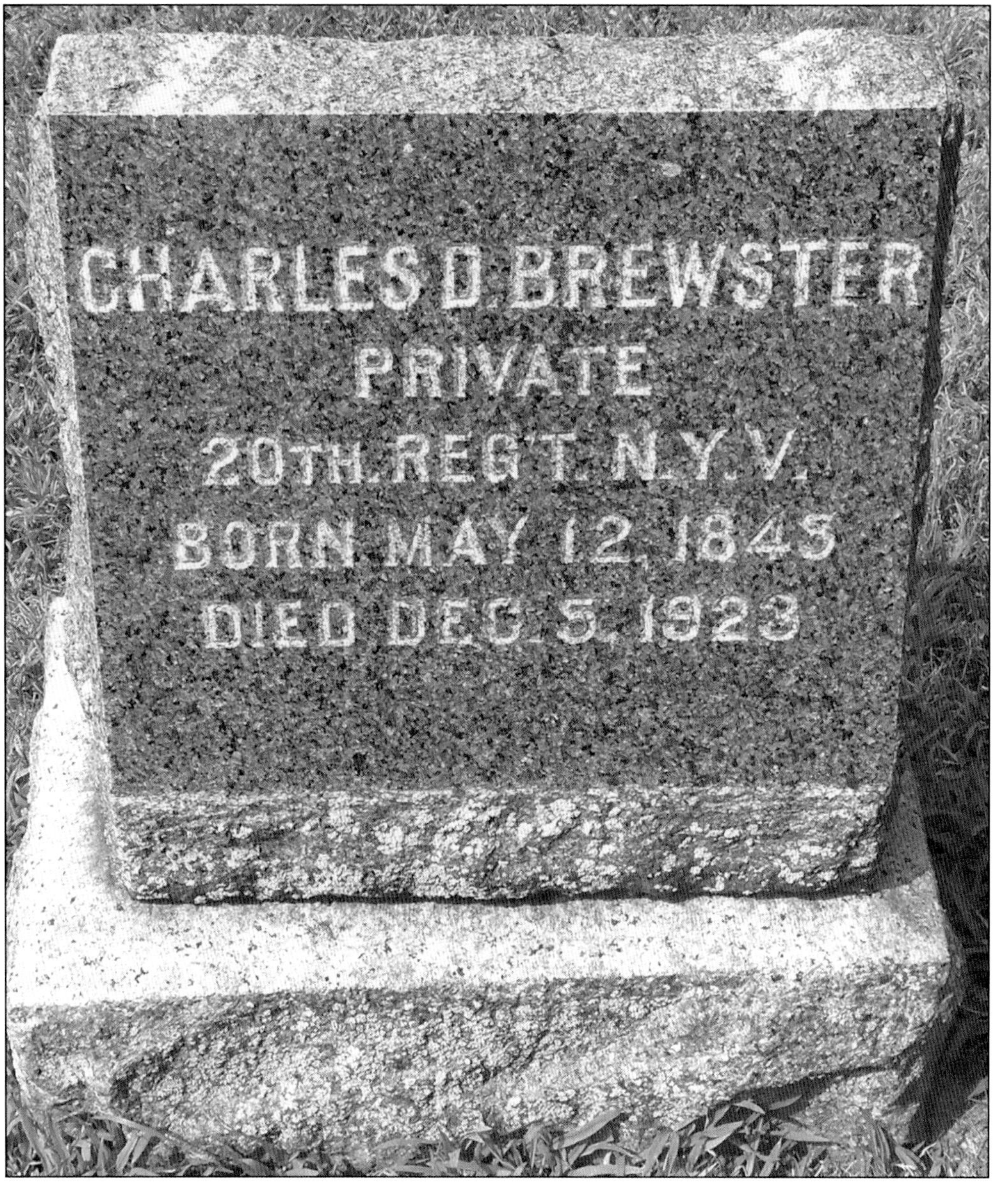

The black and Native American communities of Long Island joined the Union cause during the American Civil War. One of the many colored regiments that were from the Long Island area was the New York 20th Regiment. This and other colored regiments were trained on current-day Rikers Island. Charles Devine Brewster served in this regiment and during his military service was inspired to be part of the early civil rights movement. Brewster would go on to promote school integration throughout New York.

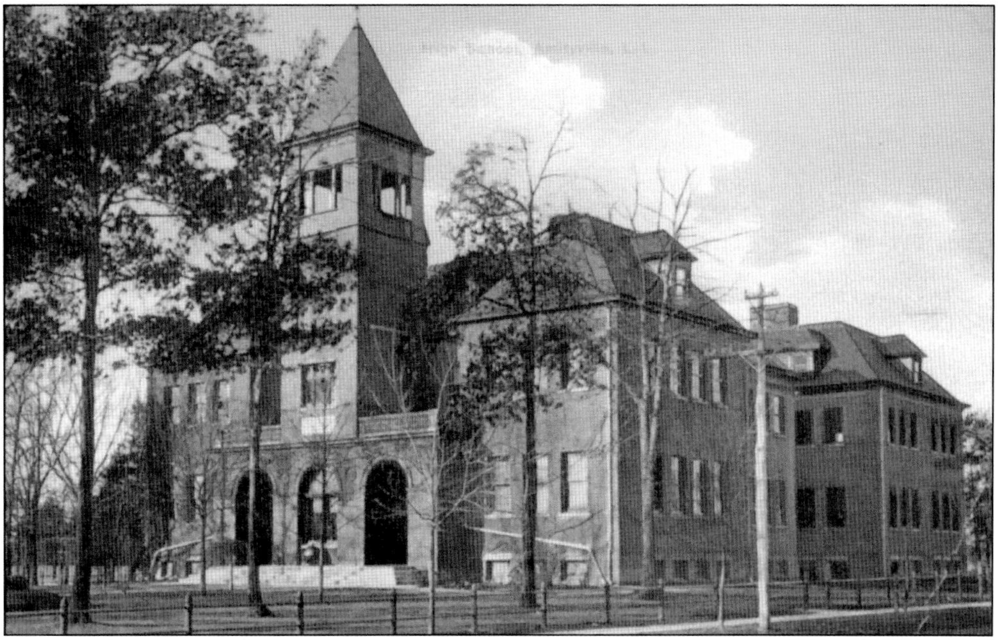

The growing population of Amityville in the 1890s created a demand for a bigger and more modern school. In 1895, a new school was constructed using tax dollars from South Amityville's white population and North Amityville's black and Native American populations. The school pictured above was built only for white students, and black students were barred from attending. Black students within the district were zoned to the colored school located in North Amityville. Charles Devine Brewster put together a petition and started an economic boycott within the black community to have his son and other black children attend the newly built white-only school. Within months of the organized resistance from the black community, the colored school was closed and the black students were allowed to attend the newly built white school. The photograph below shows the school's 1908–1909 class. Diversity remained a struggle for almost a century. In 1900, the school integration battle trickled to urban districts within New York City, which was forced to integrate under Gov. Theodore Roosevelt. (Both, Historic Photograph and Postcard Collection of the Town of Babylon, Office of Historic Services.)

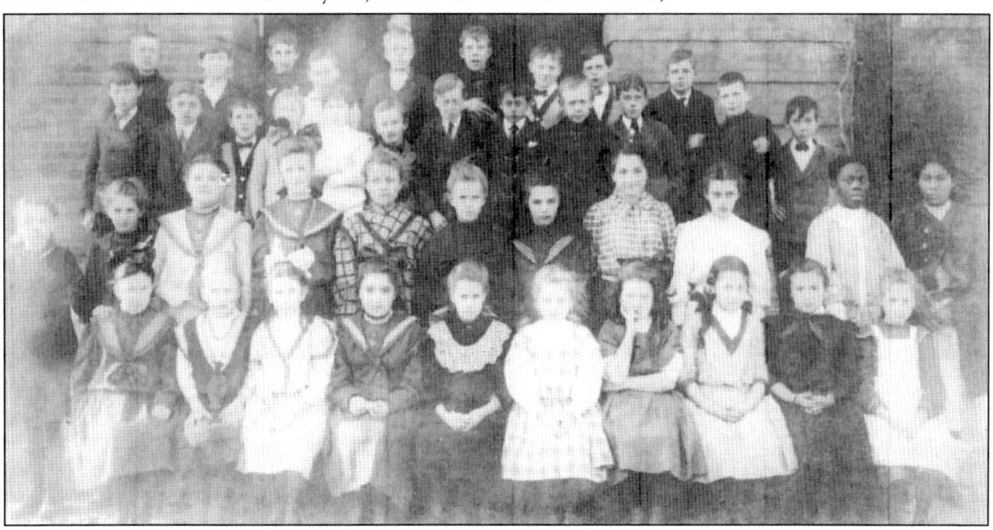

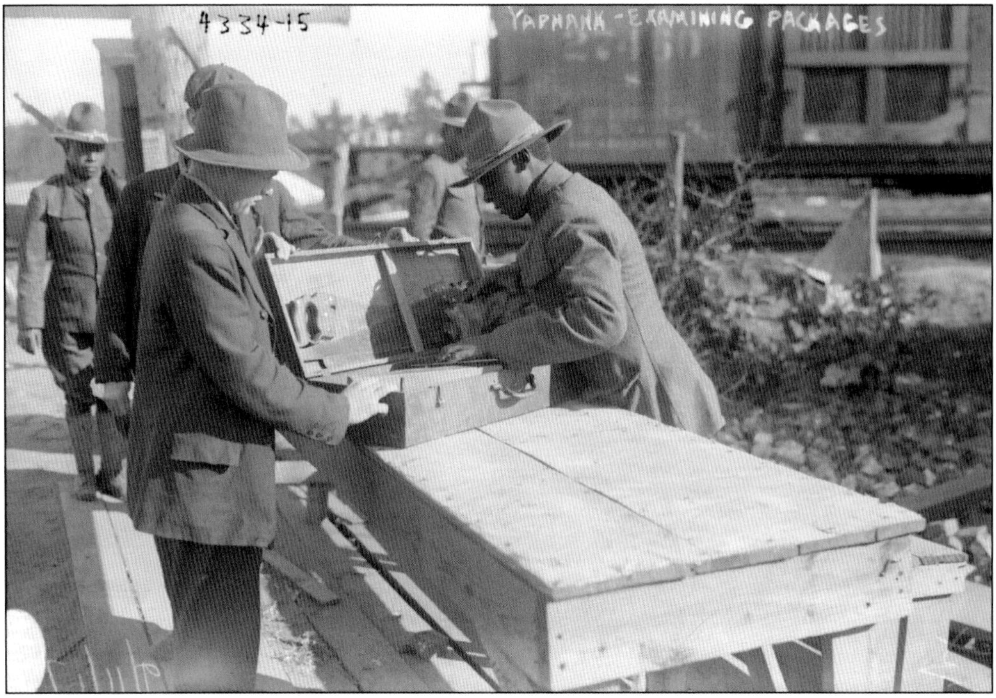

In April 1917, Pres. Woodrow Wilson called on Congress to make the "world safe for democracy." The result was that over 4 million American men served during World War I. Camp Upton in Brookhaven Suffolk County trained 40,000 men. The black 367th Regiment was organized and posted in Camp Upton. The regiment's high command treated the blacks with less respect than whites by issuing orders that required white soldiers not to salute black officers. Despite the lack of respect, the 367th served with distinction in Europe by saving a French unit from the Germans. Pictured here, black soldiers are inspecting incoming draftees. (Both, Library of Congress.)

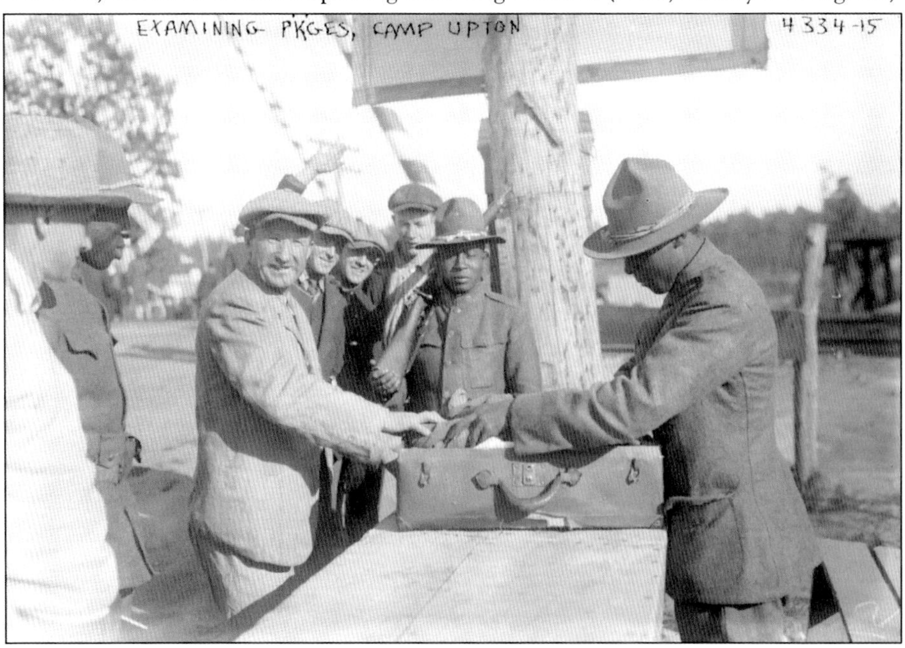

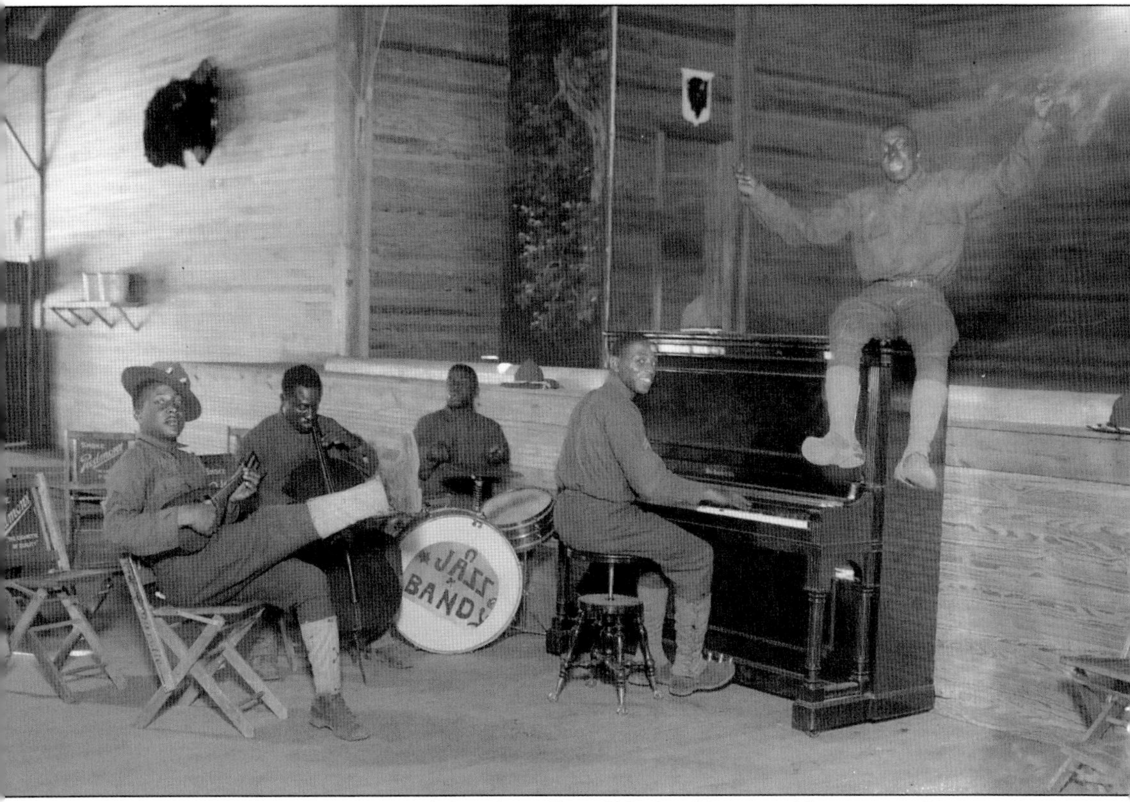

The commanders of Camp Upton feared that the influx of black soldiers would cause racial tensions. These concerns isolated the black regiments from enjoying down time with the white soldiers in town theaters or bars. The black soldiers had to find ways to entertain themselves around the camp. Here, five of the black soldiers formed a jazz band to pass time. (Library of Congress.)

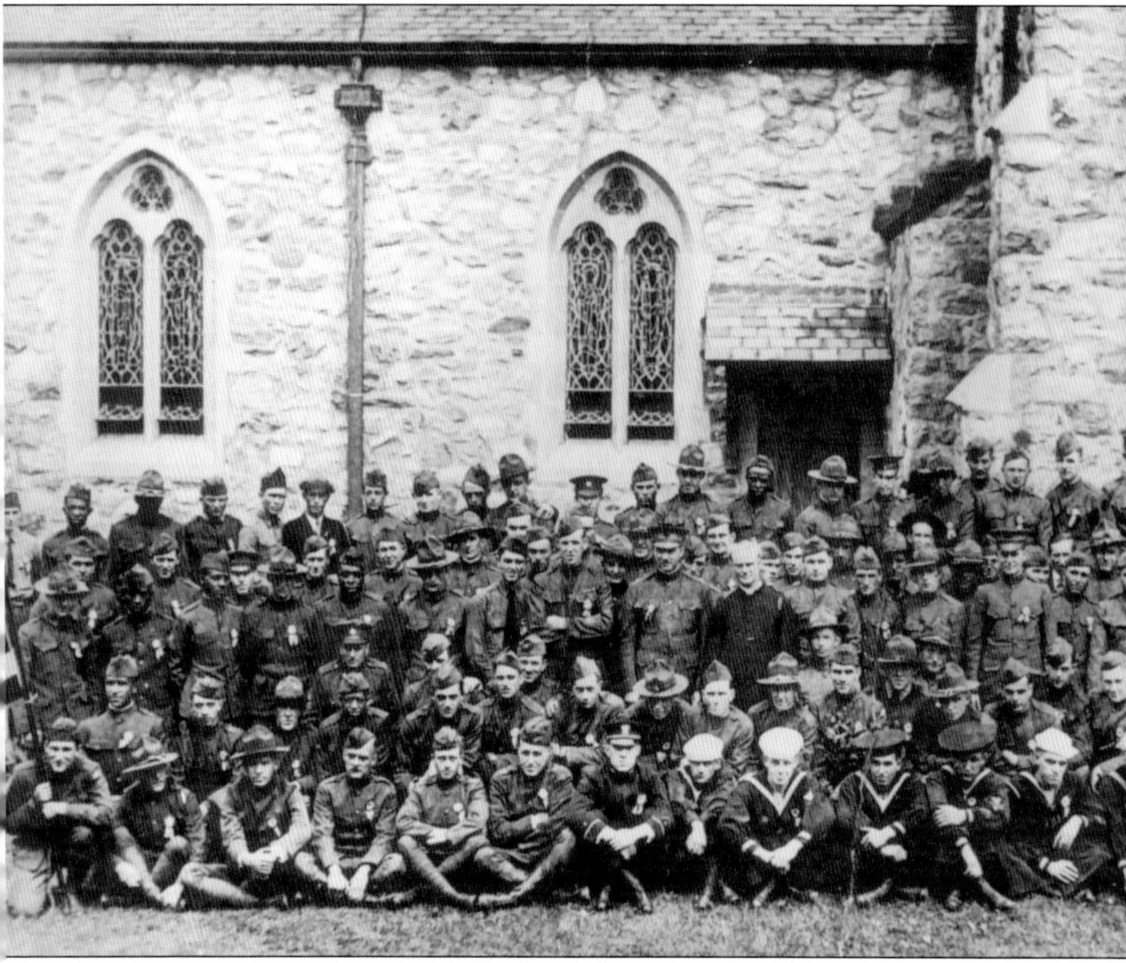

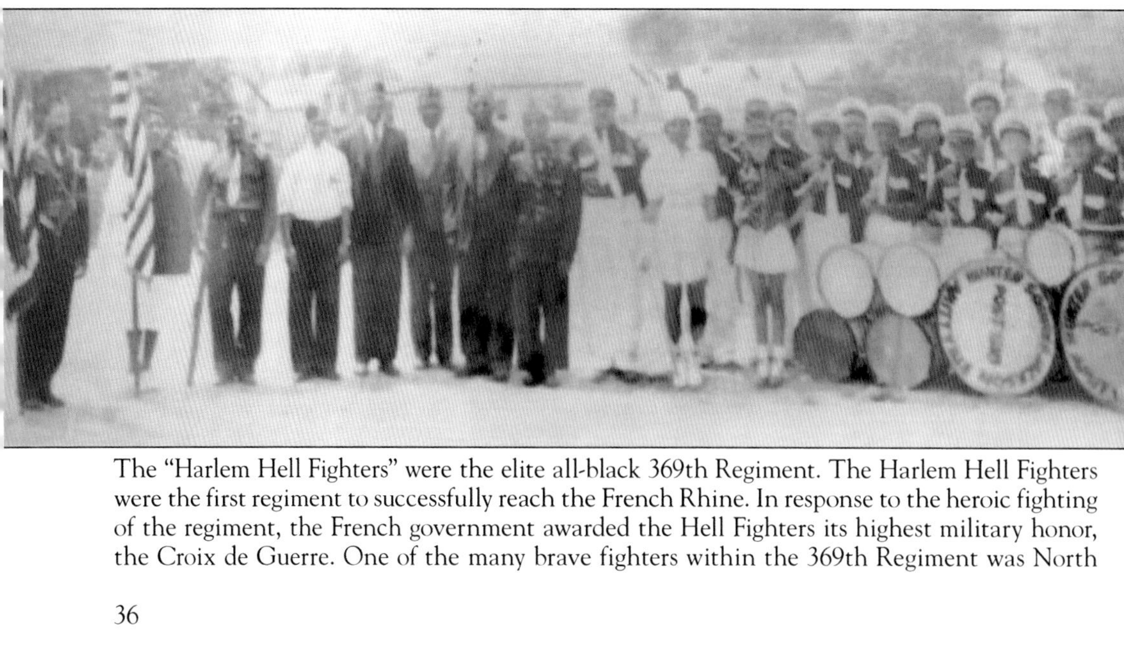

The "Harlem Hell Fighters" were the elite all-black 369th Regiment. The Harlem Hell Fighters were the first regiment to successfully reach the French Rhine. In response to the heroic fighting of the regiment, the French government awarded the Hell Fighters its highest military honor, the Croix de Guerre. One of the many brave fighters within the 369th Regiment was North

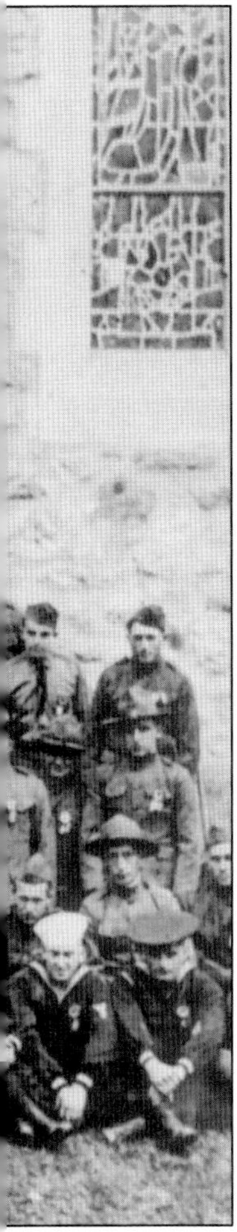

Pictured are Westbury's World War I vets in 1920. Returning black soldiers had faced brutal warfare and wanted the promised American opportunities that were granted to whites. In addition to the returning soldiers, black families from the South migrated north to fill manufacturing jobs. These factors created a demand for equality and fostered the early civil rights movement. (Historical Society of the Westburys Photo Archive.)

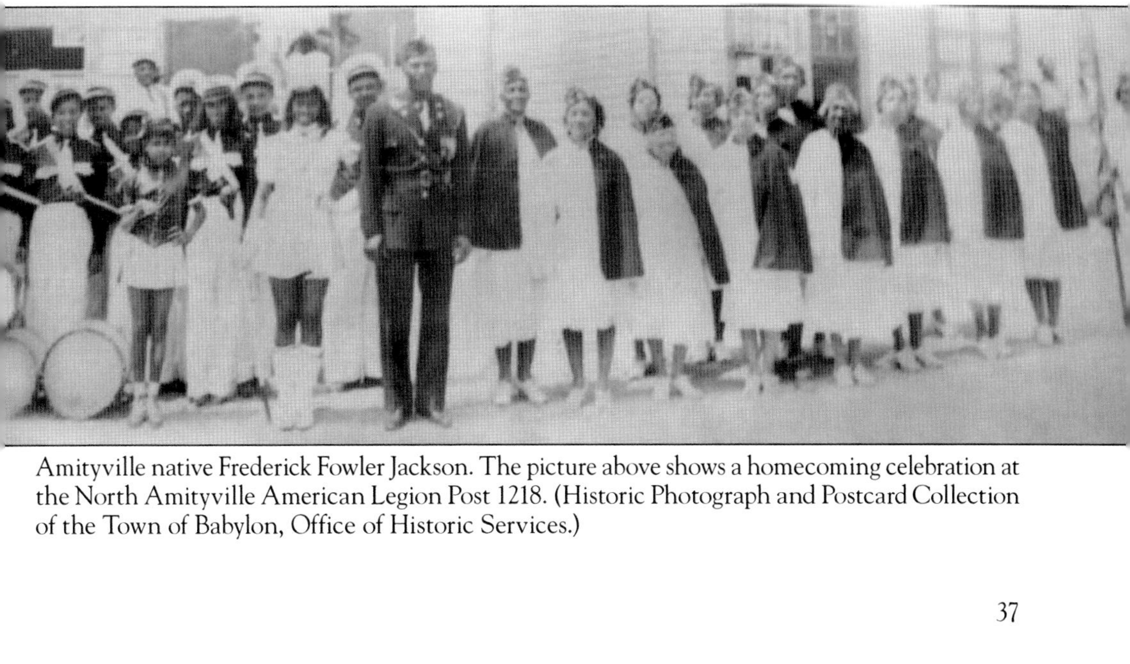

Amityville native Frederick Fowler Jackson. The picture above shows a homecoming celebration at the North Amityville American Legion Post 1218. (Historic Photograph and Postcard Collection of the Town of Babylon, Office of Historic Services.)

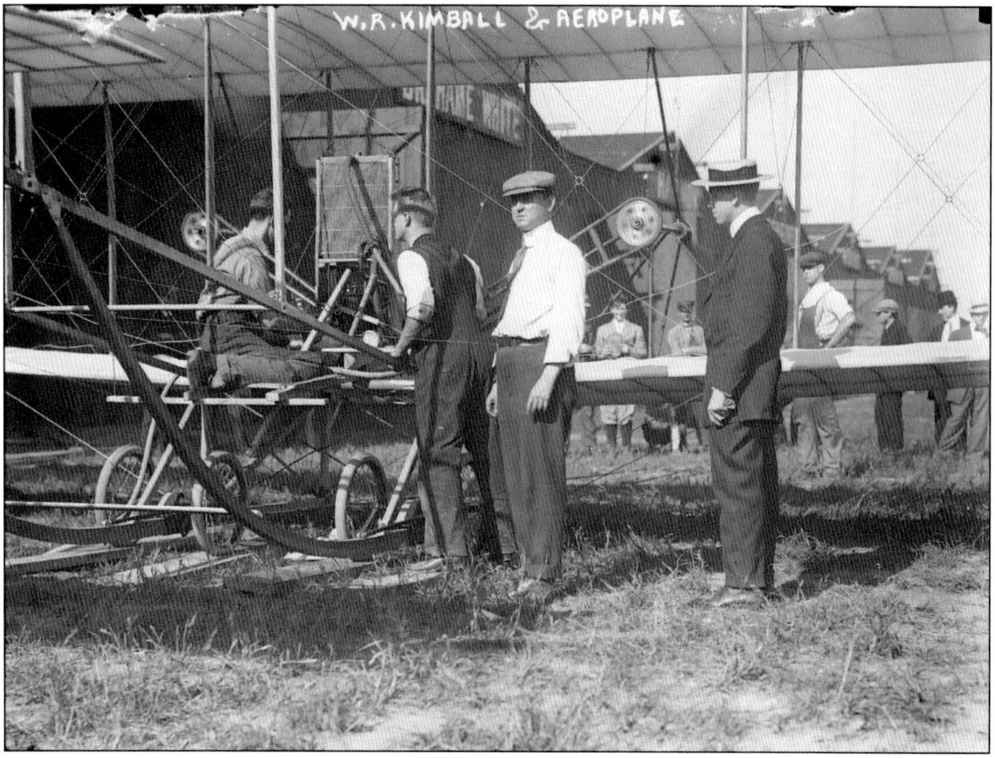

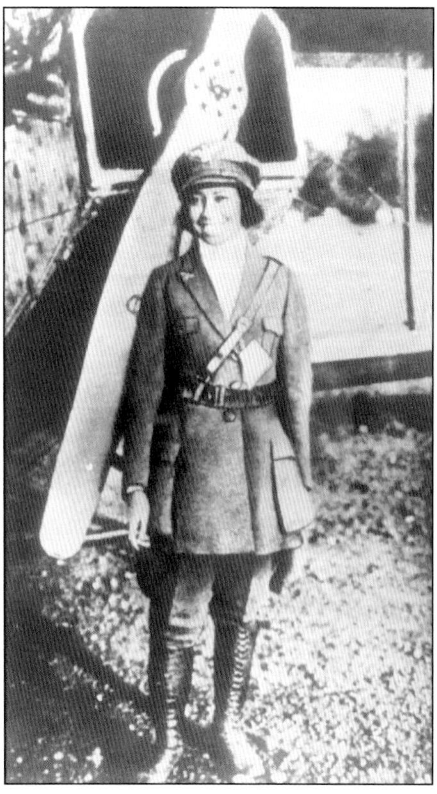

Before and after World War I, Long Island developed a thriving community of aviators that shaped the local economy through airfields and airplane parts manufacturing. This attracted stunt pilots from all over the country to migrate to Curtiss Field in Mineola and Mitchell Field in Garden City. These shows were dominated by white male performers. In the picture above, aviator and inventor Wilbur Kimball is preparing a plane for a show at the 1911 Aerodrome International Aviation Meet in Garden City. (Library of Congress.)

Bessie Coleman stands in front of her Curtiss JN-4D plane. Coleman was the first black female aviator to fly at any air show in Long Island. In September 1922, one thousand black people came out to watch Coleman compete against white pilots at the Curtiss Field, Mineola, air shows. (Nassau County Photo Archive.)

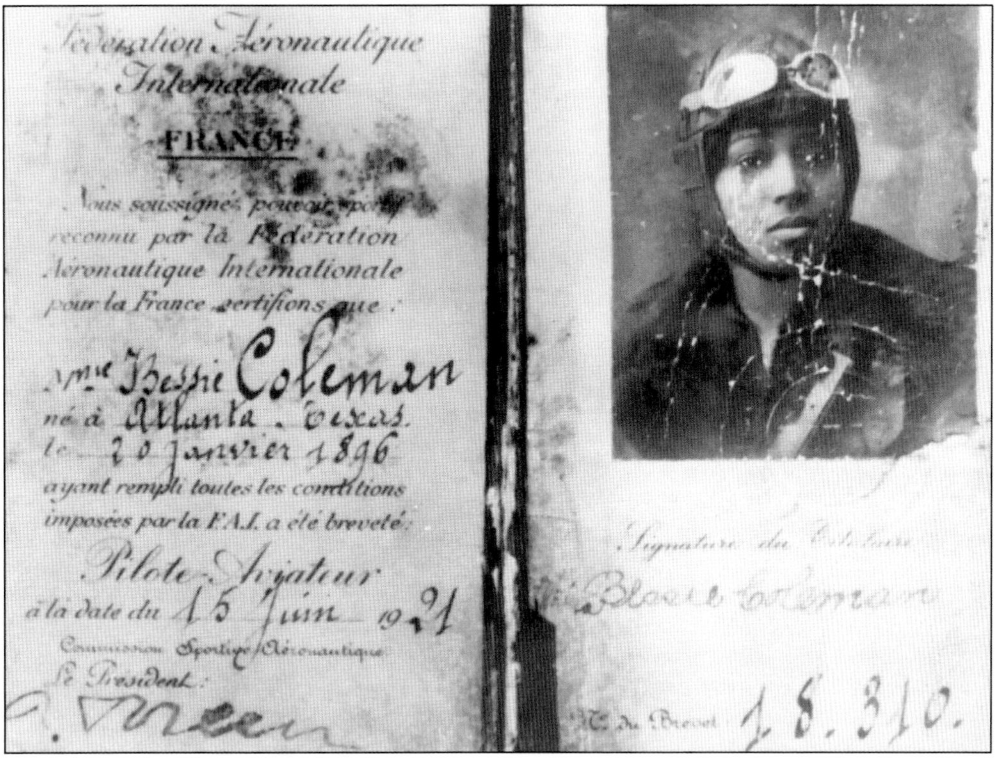

Pictured are Bessie Coleman's pilot license and Coleman in an aviator skull cap. Coleman was not only the first black female to fly in Long Island air shows but also the first licensed black pilot. Coleman was not allowed to attend American aviation training programs because of her gender and race. She was accepted to an aviation program in France, where she earned her international pilot license. On April 30, 1926, Bessie Coleman was killed while practicing for an air show in Florida. Her legacy of determination and daring air show stunts provided black communities inspiration to break racial boundaries. (Both, Nassau County Photo Archive.)

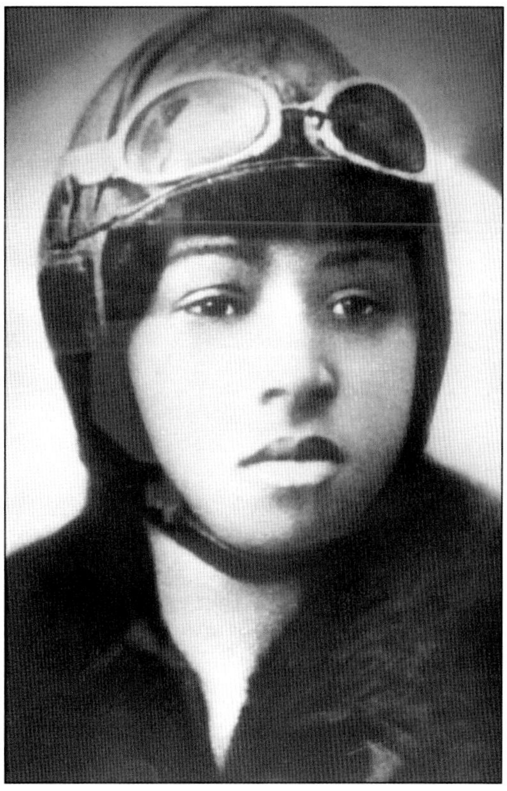

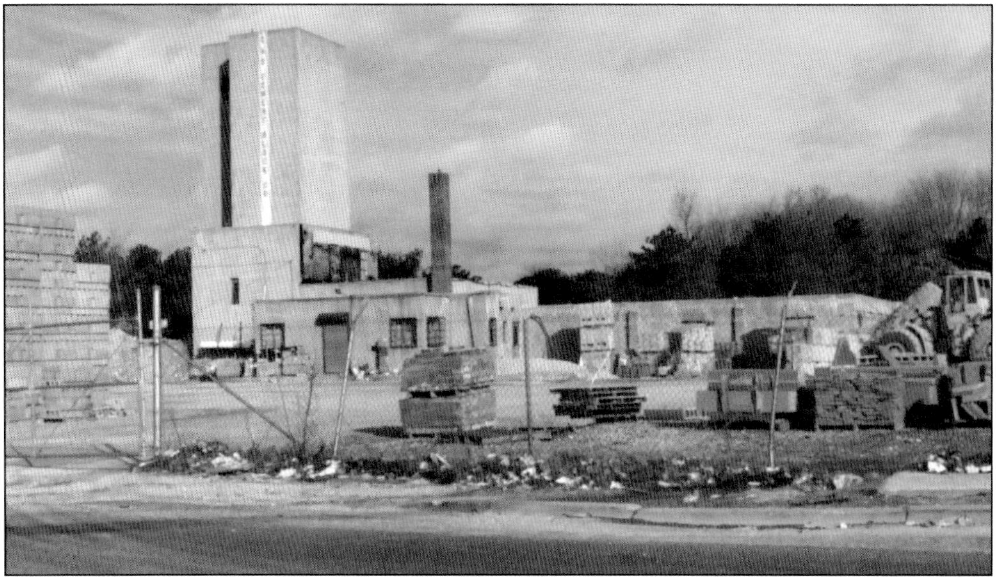

In December 1928, Ignatius Davidson and Mortimer Cumberbach took a $1,900 investment and turned it into thriving $250,000 cement block factory on Straight Path Avenue in Wyandanch. C&D Cement Block was the largest black-owned business in Suffolk County in its time. At its peak, the factory employed just fewer than 50 people and successfully fed all the demand for cinder blocks for the town of Babylon and the surrounding areas. Pictured above is the original factory. (Historic Photograph and Postcard Collection of the Town of Babylon, Office of Historic Services.)

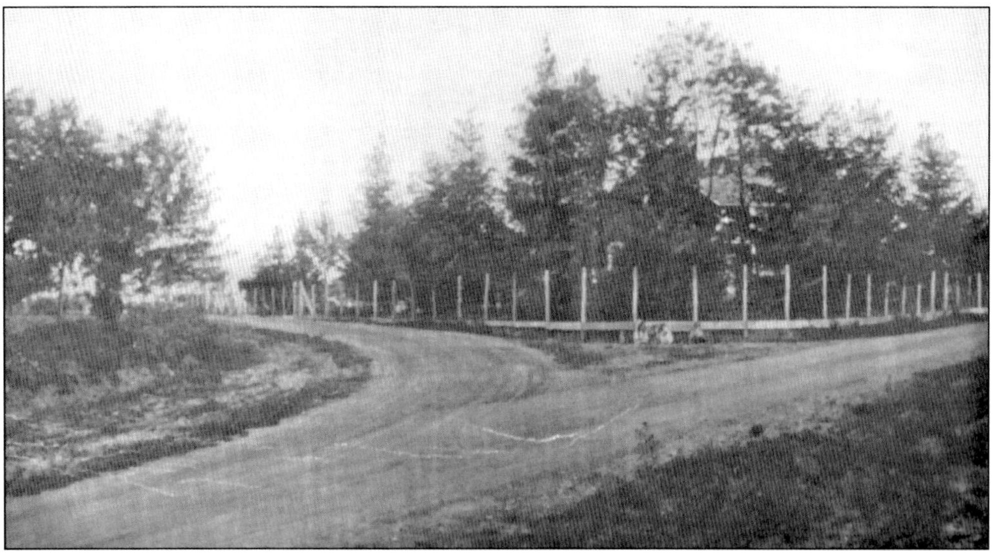

With the success of C&D Cement Block Factory, Davidson and Cumberbach looked to help relieve the bad urban housing conditions and shortages for the black community. In the late 1940s, D&C Realty was formed and purchased 218 lots in Amityville and Wyandanch. On these lots, the realty company built four-room bungalows marketed to black families. In response, local banks froze all loans on the development of these houses, but despite the financial challenges, the house were built and sold to black families. Above is one of the 218 lots in Wyandanch. (Historic Photograph and Postcard Collection of the Town of Babylon, Office of Historic Services)

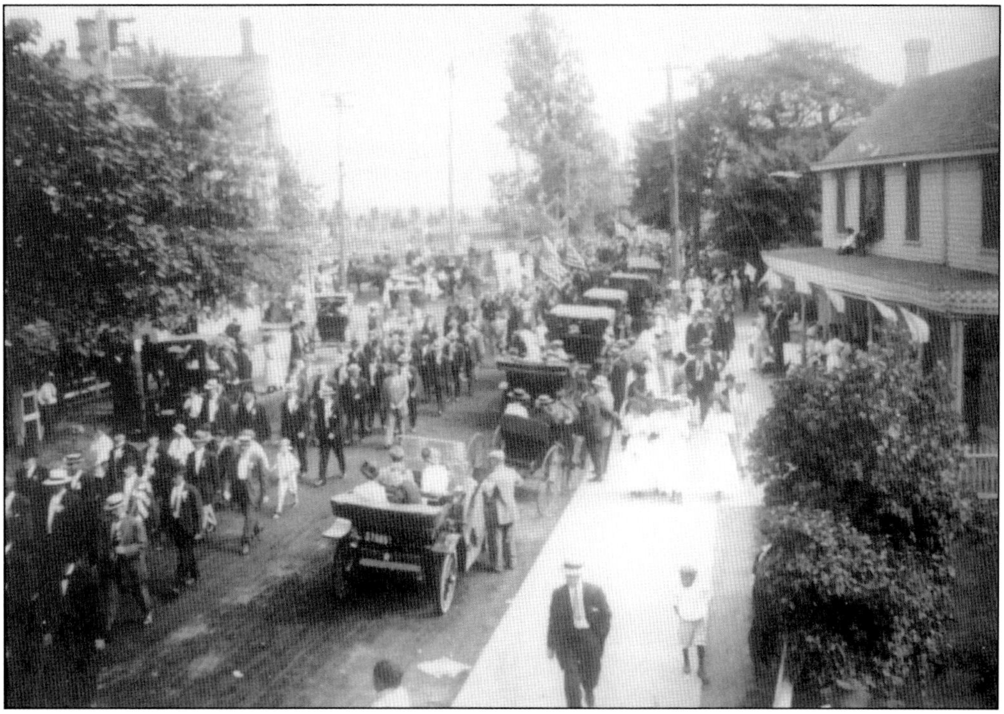

Pictured is a parade of the Society of the Holy Name in Westbury. Originally established in 15th-century Europe, this organization's goal in America was to unite Catholics. During the 1920s, the Ku Klux Klan targeted not only blacks and Jews but also anyone who was Catholic. The Society of the Holy Name demonstrated in heavy populated Klan areas to show off Catholic unity and strength. (Historical Society of the Westburys Photo Archive.)

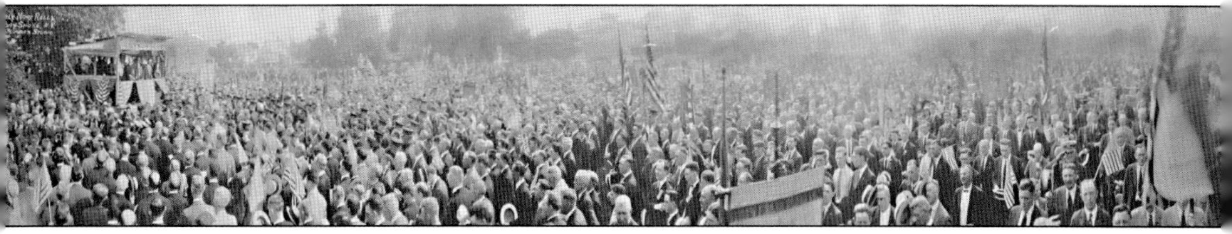

This is the June 25, 1923, rally of the Society of the Holy Name in Bay Shore. This rally was organized by Father Donovan and had an attendance of more than 40,000 people. The main objectives were to fight intolerance among local groups such as the Klan and to confront growing atheism. Keynote speakers at the meeting included Dr. John Coyle from the Knights of Columbus, who demanded local political officials and fellow Catholics unify against the local Klan. (Bay Shore Historical Society.)

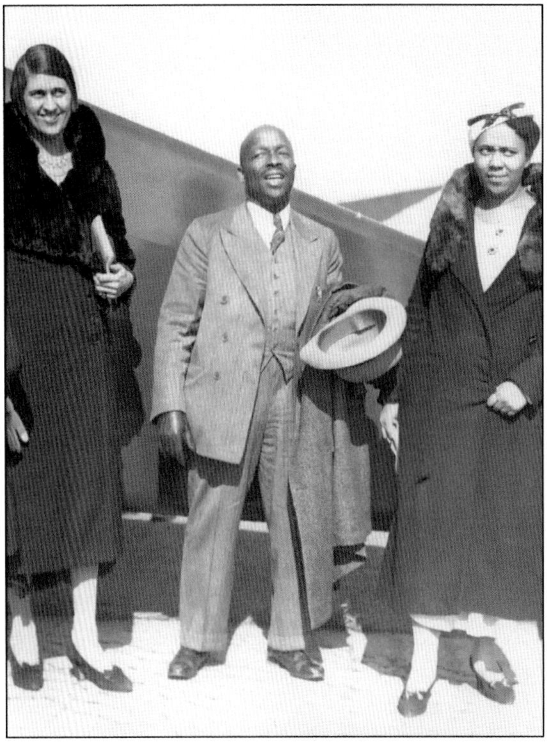

Father Divine, born George Baker, formed a religious movement that combined social issues of racial integration, Catholicism, and Pentecostalism into what was called the Peace Mission. Under Divine's leadership, the mission opened and operated several churches and soup kitchens across the northeast that provided food to the hungry. To fund day-to-day operations of its food banks and churches, the mission diversified its wealth in small businesses that exceeded more than $15 million in savings during the Depression. The business model for these companies was that employees must earn a livable wage. The image at left shows Mother Divine on the left, Father Divine in the center, and Faithful Mary on the right. Below, a crowd greets Lawyer John Faithful on the right, Father Divine, Faithful Mary, and Mother Divine (Edna Rose Richings). (Both, Nassau County Photo Archive.)

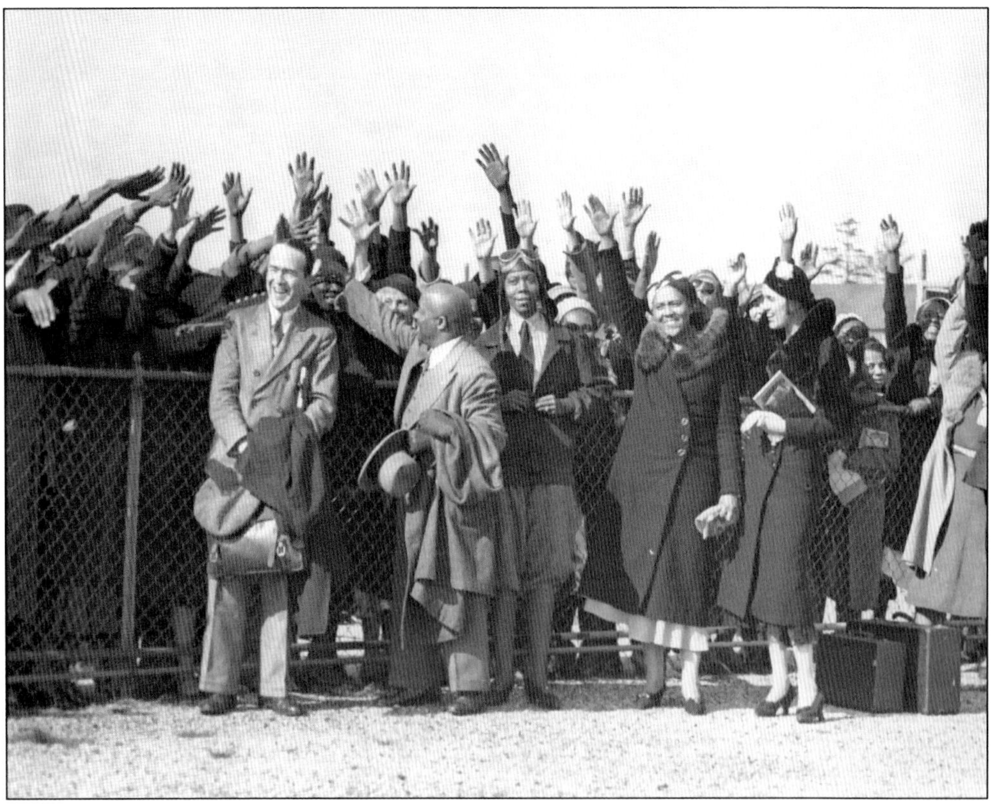

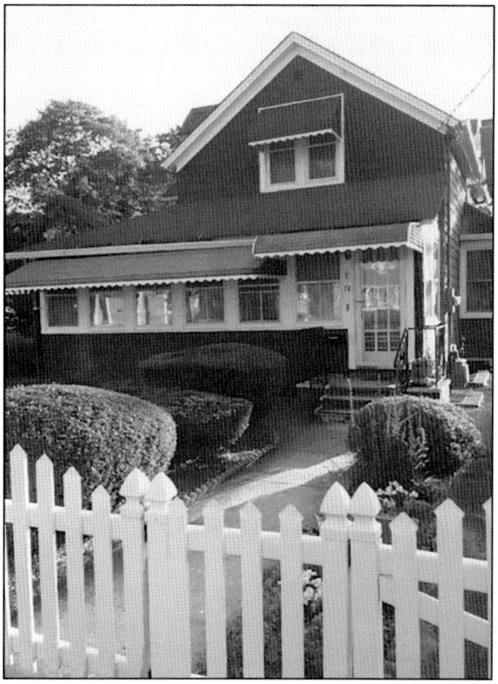

One of the many missions Father Divine established was located on 72 Macon Street in Sayville. In the 1920s, Sayville had a large Ku Klux Klan and German American population. In order for Divine to buy this house, white congregation members were sent to the community to make cash offers. By 1931, residents of the Sayville community got upset with the traffic of his congregation coming and going and that white women were staying in a house with black men. Local law enforcement arrested Father Divine for disturbing the peace. After sentencing Father Divine to a year in jail, the judge suffered a heart attack and died. Following the death, Divine's popularity grew, and his conviction was overturned.

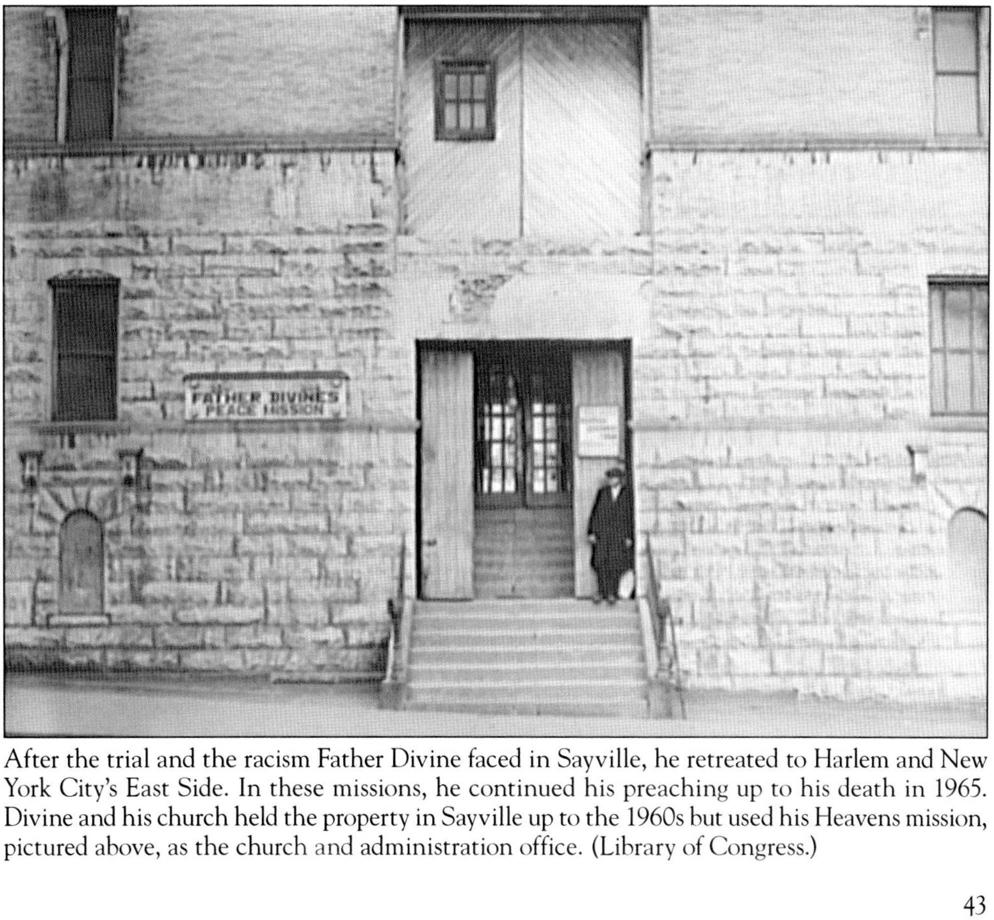

After the trial and the racism Father Divine faced in Sayville, he retreated to Harlem and New York City's East Side. In these missions, he continued his preaching up to his death in 1965. Divine and his church held the property in Sayville up to the 1960s but used his Heavens mission, pictured above, as the church and administration office. (Library of Congress.)

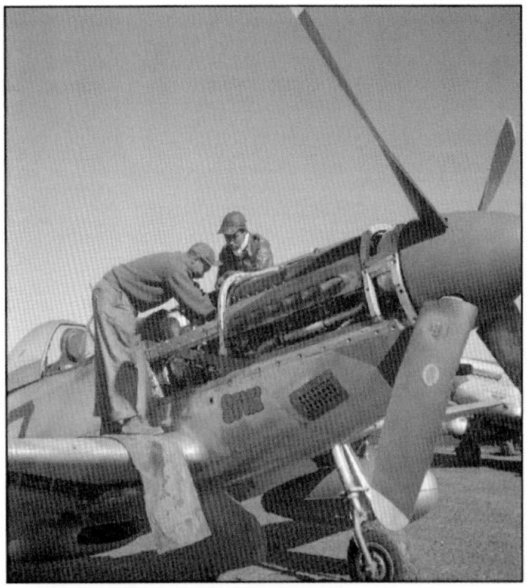

At the dawn of World War II, black Americans supported the cause to end tyranny. The 332nd Fighter Group and 477th Bombardment Group became known as the legendary Tuskegee Airmen. These airmen became the first black aviators in the US armed forces. As in the Civil War and World War I, military units were racially segregated. The airmen were awarded one Silver Star, 96 Flying Crosses, 14 Bronze Stars, 744 Air Medals, and 8 Purple Hearts. Eight of the airmen were from Long Island. George Arnold Lynch (below, standing in the back row, second from left), from Valley Stream, is among the men awaiting orders. Roscoe C. Brown (on the right side in the picture at left) had a home in Sag Harbor. (Both, Library of Congress)

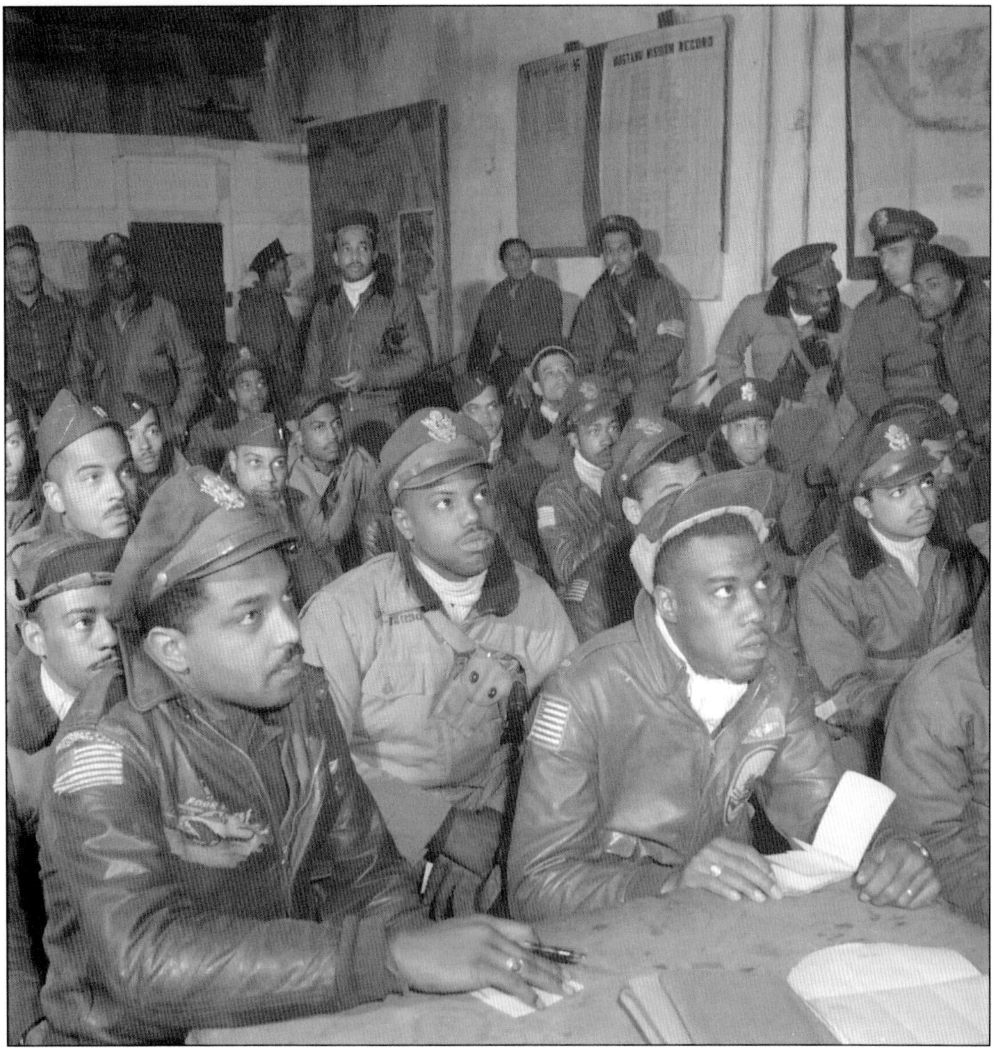

Three

Development of Levittown and Post–World War II Long Island

After World War II, the returning soldiers and their benefits guaranteed in the Servicemen's Readjustment Act (GI Bill) created a demand for low-cost housing. Long Island was an ideal location for the new housing due to its distance from New York City and surplus land left vacant after golden nematodes and the Colorado potato beetle devastated potato harvests. Prior to World War II, construction of the Southern State and Northern State Parkways connected Nassau and Suffolk Counties to the city by car instead of public transportation. Developers such as Levitt & Sons, Thomas Romano, and William Zeckendorf utilized the existing parkways to design suburbs and commerce around accessibility by car. With housing shaping the local economy, air defense plants such as Grumman, Republic, and Sperry expanded manufacturing plants in Lake Success, Farmingdale, Bethpage, East Islip, and Calverton to harvest the potential labor pool.

These boom years on Long Island were not accessible to everyone but were mainly designed for the white population. Developers such as Levitt & Sons barred black families from renting their homes and steered black families from buying their homes. Allies of Levitt & Sons included local banks, which refused to provide mortgages to blacks seeking houses in white areas. Urban planner Robert Moses was vocal in his opposition to racial integration, and it is debated whether he designed his projects to reflect his views. These newly designed suburbs institutionalized segregation and a racial caste system for blacks on Long Island.

The white robes of the Ku Klux Klan in the 1920s were replaced in the early 1950s by the suits of developers who used arguments of economics instead of racial supremacy to justify segregation. With new jobs in aerospace manufacturing, health care, and public works projects, more African Americans joined the middle class and wanted the same housing opportunities. They combated racial discrimination in housing and schools as the civil rights movement evolved its goals of political and economic equality.

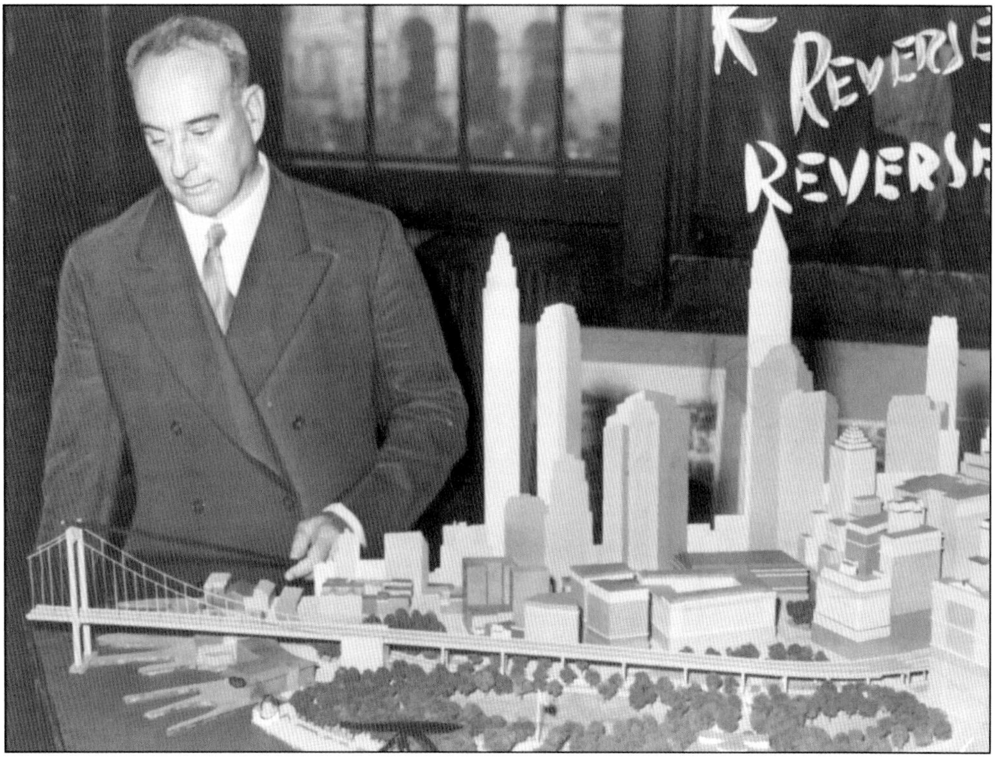

Robert Moses was known for designing over 116 projects, including 52 parkways within the New York metropolitan area. Well-known suburban and urban parks include Jones Beach, Heckscher State Park, Sunken Meadow Park, and Shea Stadium. These projects totaled $125 billion in today's money. All of these projects were created around the automobile, which made Long Island a commuter suburb. These parkways and parks laid the groundwork for much suburban development. (Library of Congress.)

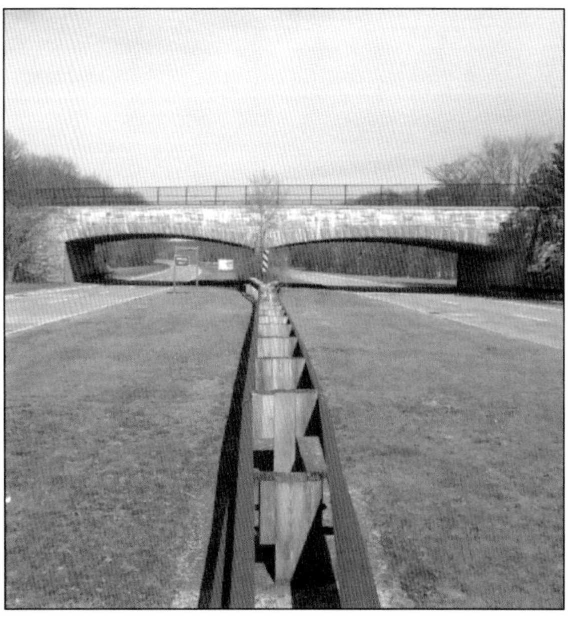

By the mid-1930s, construction of Robert Moses's Southern State Parkway, Northern State Parkway, and Meadowbrook Parkway were nearly complete. These parkways allowed better accessibility to middle-class people who owned cars within the city. It is debated today whether Moses designed the bridges lower to prevent city buses, which were used widely among minority groups, from using the parkways.

Robert Moses's design of parks was geared towards white populations. Moses limited community park projects to white areas. Employment within his parks, such as Jones Beach, struggled with integration within the workforce. Signs like this hung in his parks such as Jones Beach. (Library of Congress.)

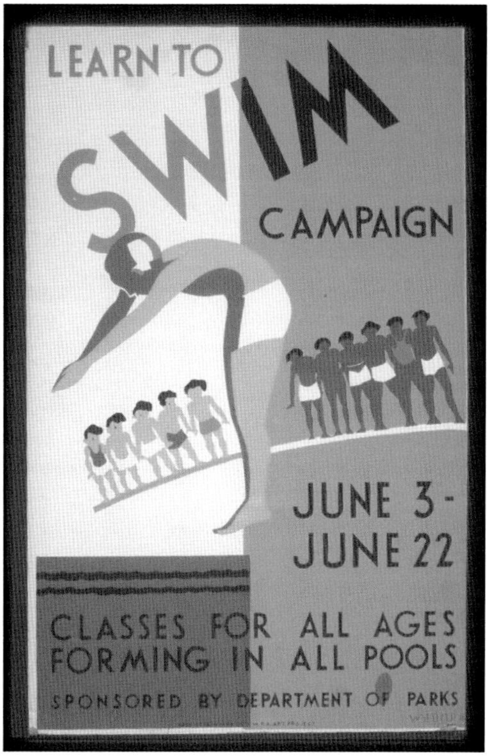

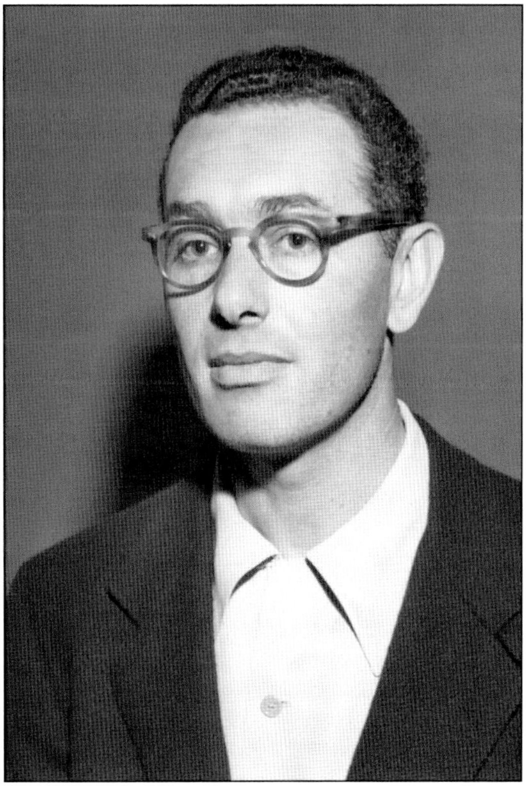

Alfred Levitt (pictured) and William Levitt were the developers of Levittown. Alfred Levitt applied the assembly-line model to home construction by shipping prefabricated sections of the home to the site and having workers assemble them. This method set a record of building 36 houses a day. His large-scale developments included a Levittown in Nassau County and one in Pennsylvania. (Nassau County Photo Archive.)

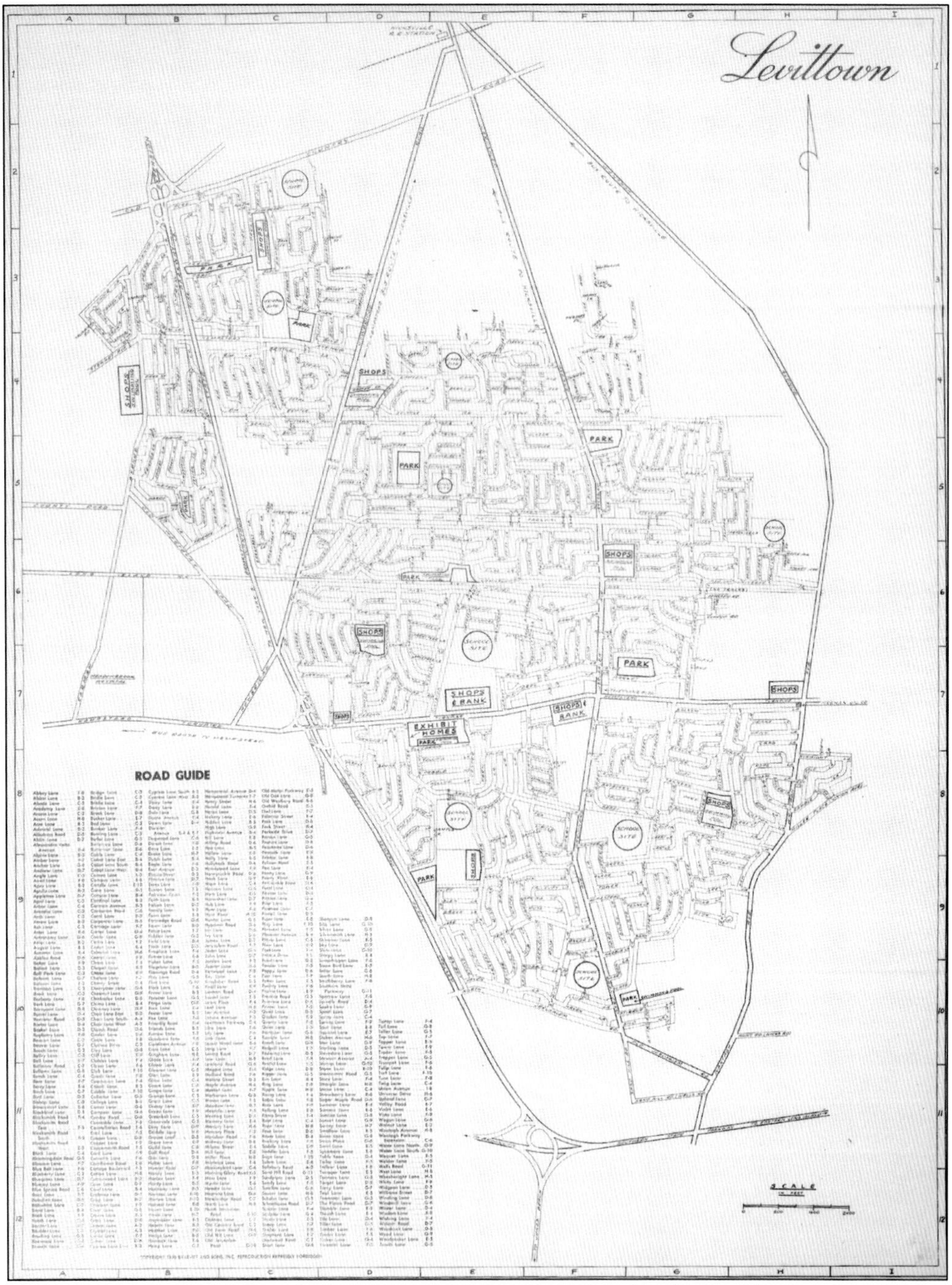

Levittown communities were built around public pools, park, schools, churches, and small-scale strip malls, with access to major highways. Roads were constructed curved for the dual purpose of enforcing a slower speed limit and maximizing the number of houses constructed on a block. The design was based on a family-friendly community for the average suburban family.

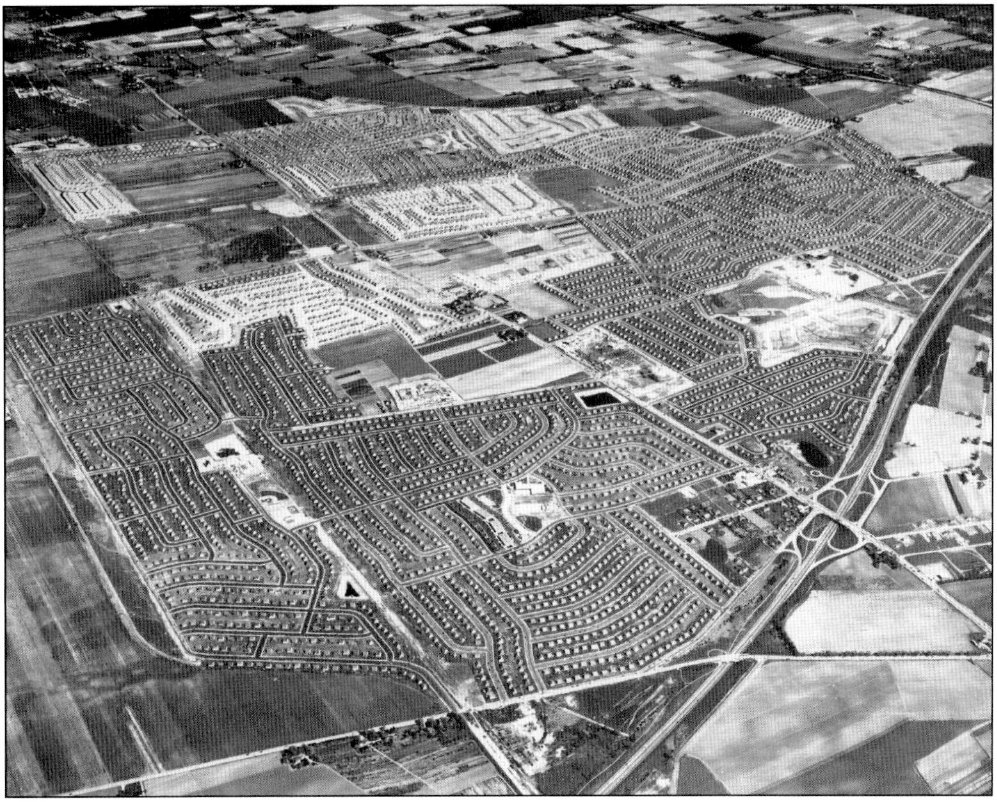

Levitt & Sons purchased 1,200 acres of land on the Island Trees farm and estates for an estimated $300 an acre from the Merillon Corporation, which was originally owned by Alexander Turner Stewart, developer of Garden City. The surrounding land used to be potato farms but was quarantined because of a golden nematode outbreak, which devastated potato crops. By 1951, developers had constructed 17,447 homes on this land and the surrounding property, which made up parts of the towns of Levittown, Wantagh, Hicksville, and Westbury. This aerial view shows the construction and completed development on the Island Tree plots. (Both, Nassau County Photo Archive.)

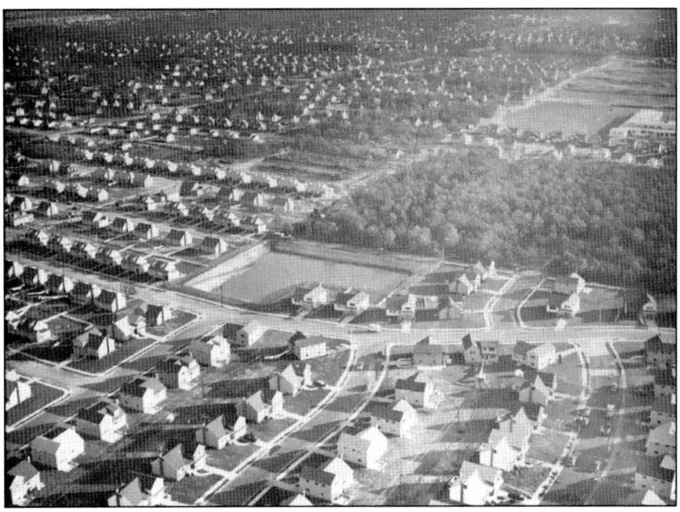

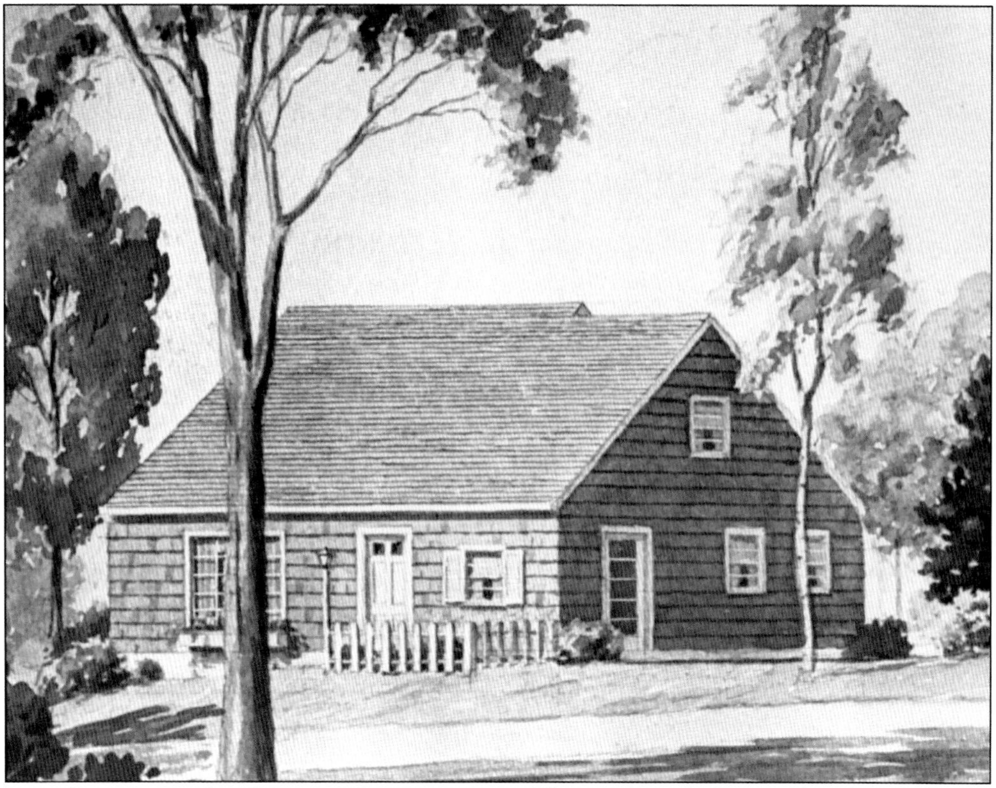

Levitt houses started at 800 square feet on concrete slabs in a Cape Cod or ranch style. The homes included built-in televisions, washers and dryers, built-in kitchen appliances, and an optional car port. The homes came in five colors but were mostly identical to all the other homes in the development. Each home had a small back yard for hosting children's play dates or barbecues. These homes were ideal for people who worked in the city due to being just 25 miles from Manhattan and 10 miles from the Queens-Nassau border. Surrounding towns, such as Bethpage and Hicksville, provided train service to and from Manhattan. (Both, Nassau County Photo Archive.)

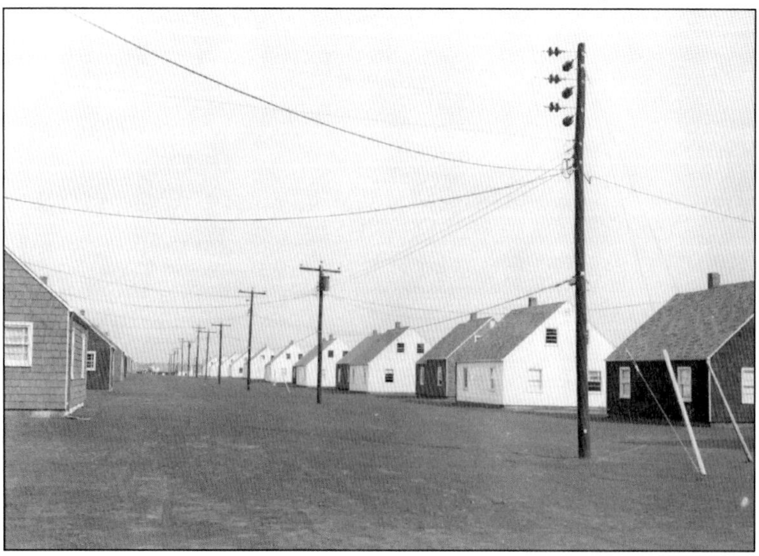

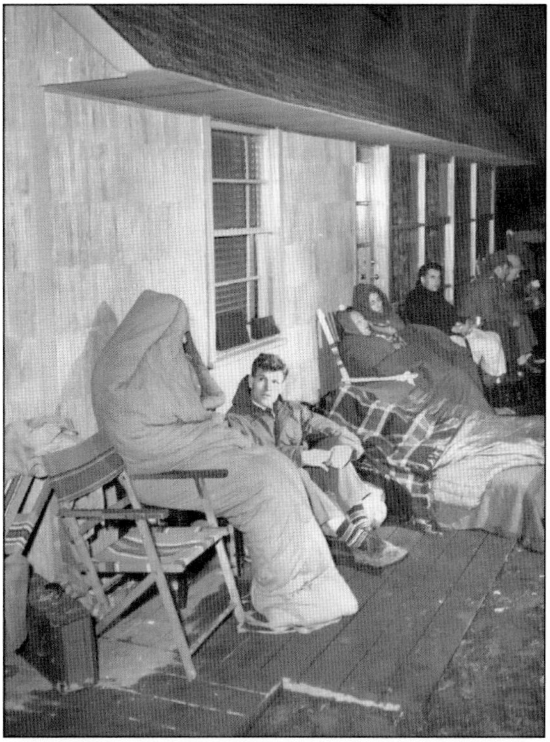

With all the soldiers coming home, America was facing a housing shortage. The Levitt house was the answer to this demand. A two-bedroom house in the community in 1947 retailed for $6,900. Due to increased demand, the price was raised to $7,990. William Levitt credited his success to selling many houses for the lowest price. In these photographs, people are camping out to secure one of the many 800-square-foot houses. For veterans buying a Levitt house, no down payment was required, which increased demand. (Both, Nassau County Photo Archive.)

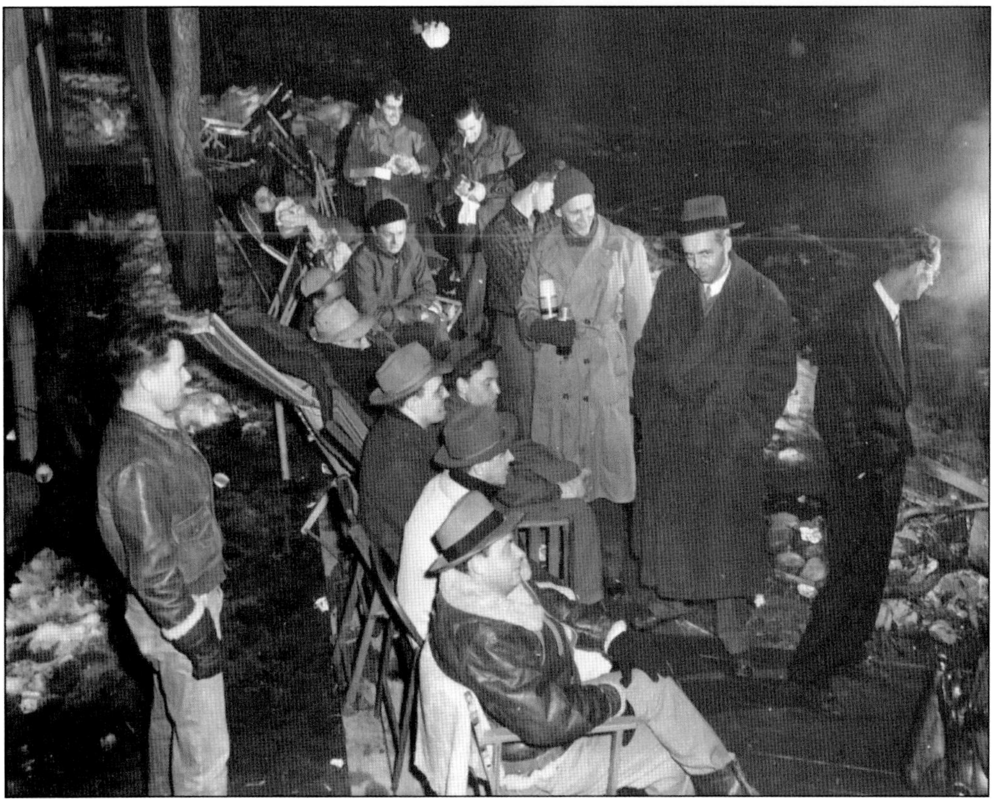

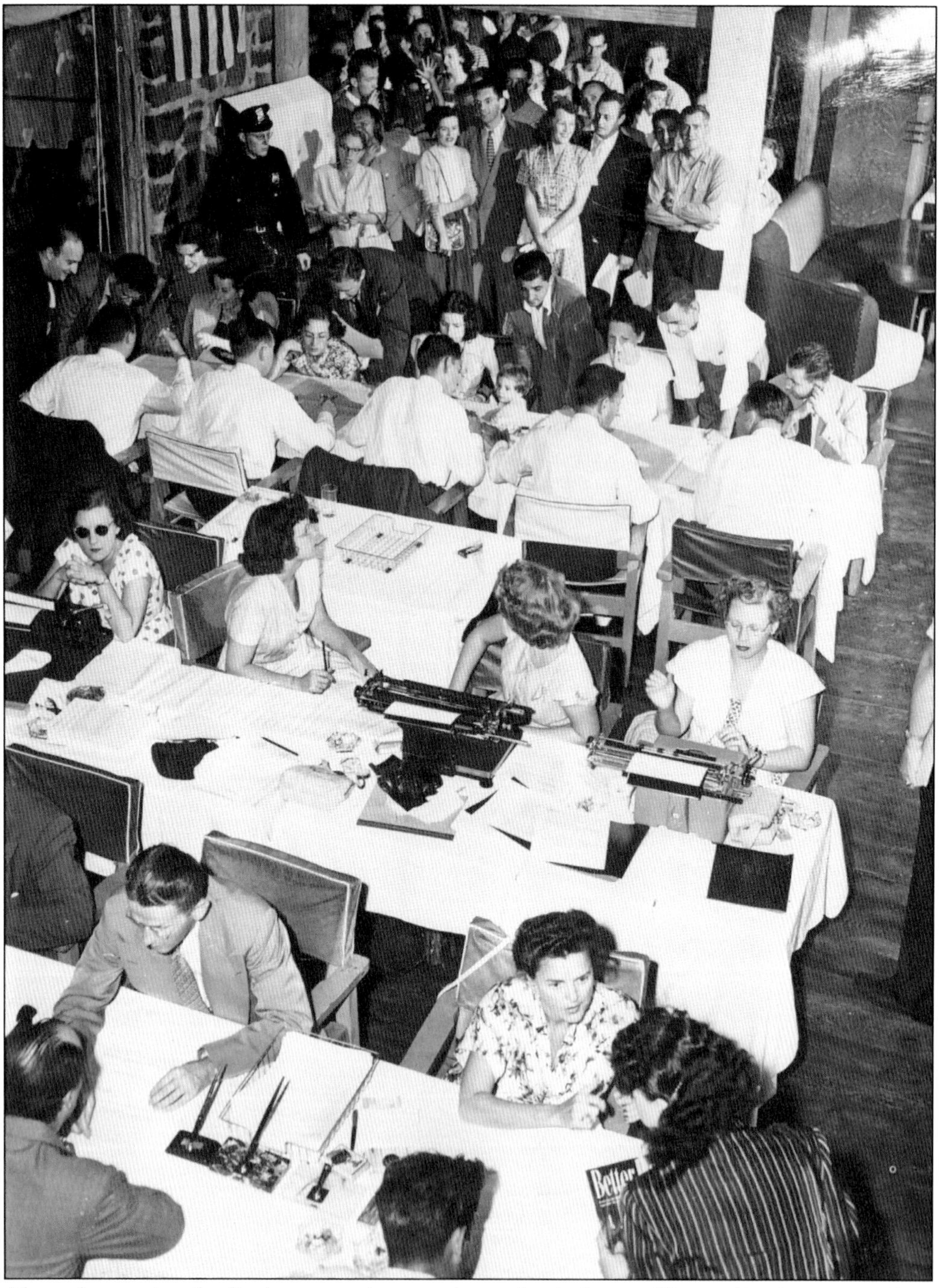

Above, buyers sign the final paperwork to purchase a Levitt house. The application process for a Levitt house was easy. The houses were sold or rented with the option to buy. The sales department racially screened all prospective buyers before final paperwork was done. One black prospective buyer and returning soldier, Eugene Burnett, was told by the salesman that "the owners of the development have not as yet decided whether they're going to sell these homes to Negroes." (Nassau County Photo Archive.)

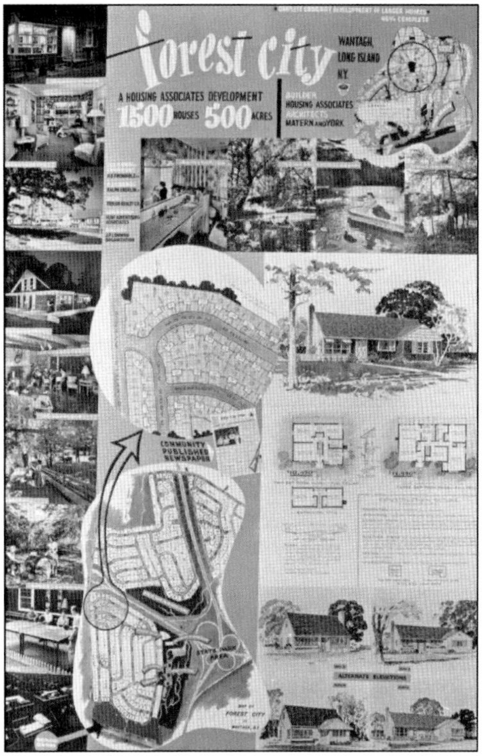

Levitt & Sons Development Company built a total of 17,447 homes in Wantagh, Westbury, Hicksville, and Levittown. The Levitt model of assembly-line houses, cheap mortgages, and racial steering was used as a blueprint in other developments throughout Long Island. Nassau County's population increased from 672,765 in 1950 to 1,300,171 in 1960. Pictured here are examples of towns and developments that had their populations soar. Forrest City development was located in Wantagh and included 500 acres with 1,500 homes. The village of Sea Cliff overnight went from a city getaway to blocks of suburban homes. (Right, Nassau County Photo Archive; below, Library of Congress.)

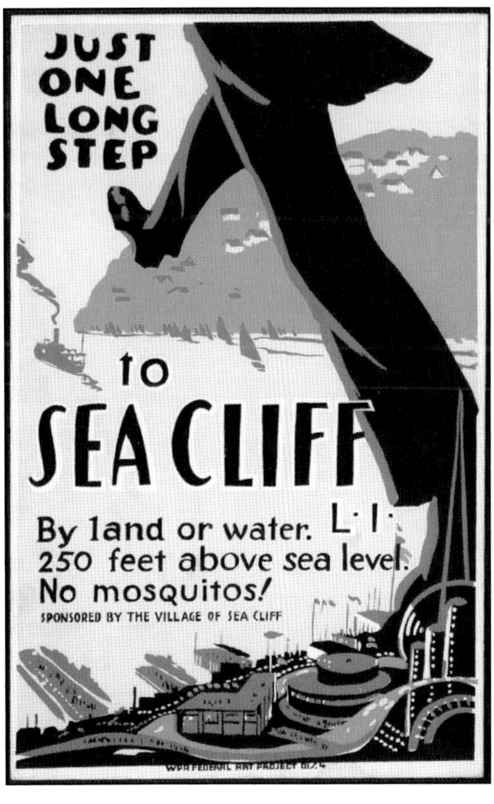

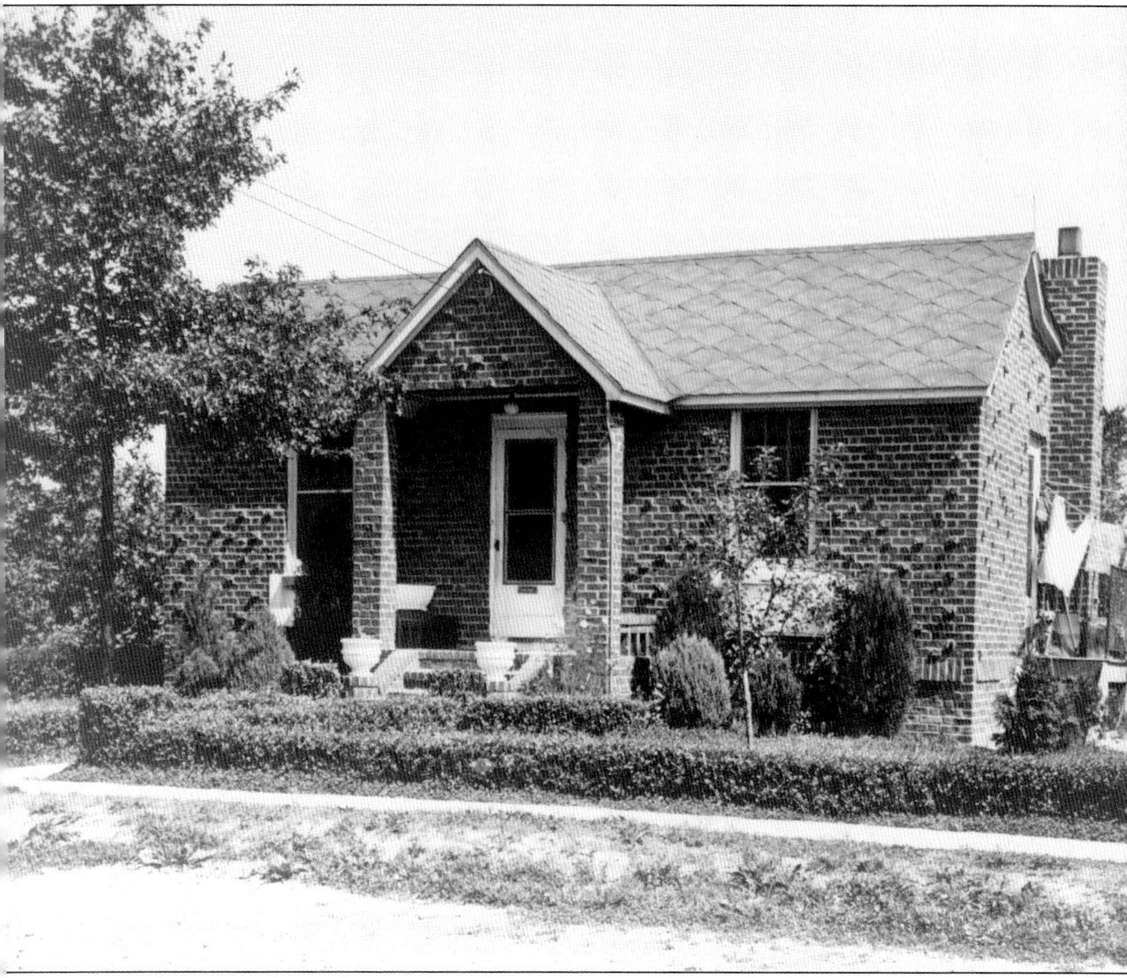

With the population boom in Nassau, neighboring Suffolk County started to have aggressive population growth. The Suffolk County population increased from 276,129 in 1950 to 666,784 in 1960. The township within Suffolk that experienced the fastest and highest growth was Babylon. The population of Babylon went from 45,556 in 1950 to 142,309 in 1960. Homes built within this town were similar to Levitt Cape Cods, and developers adopted the same practices in marketing them. Above is a typical Cape Cod found within the Babylon developments. (Library of Congress.)

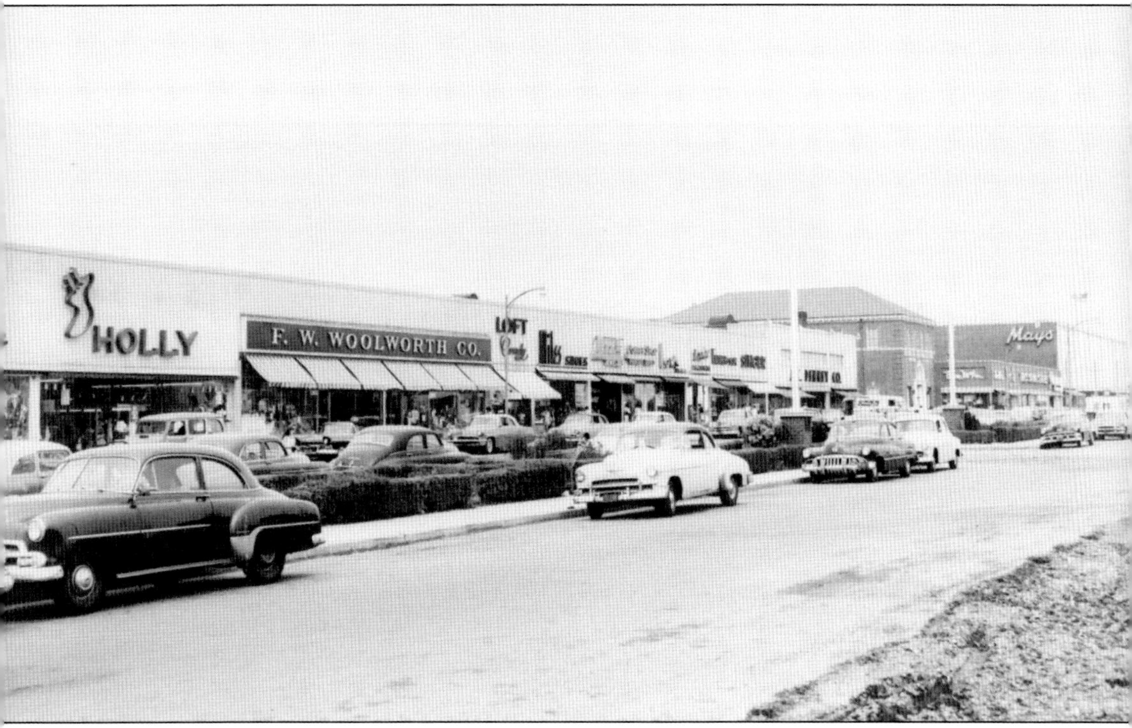

The development of Levittown incorporated several strip malls. These strip malls brought with them retail jobs and tax revenue for the local town. Retail and commercial tax comprised 40 percent of the school tax revenue. Revenue from commercial taxes determined the quality of education students would receive within the community. Black communities such as Roosevelt were deprived of this revenue. The commercial district of Roosevelt became blighted due to white flight of businesses to the surrounding white towns. Above is a strip mall incorporated within the Levittown development. (Library of Congress.)

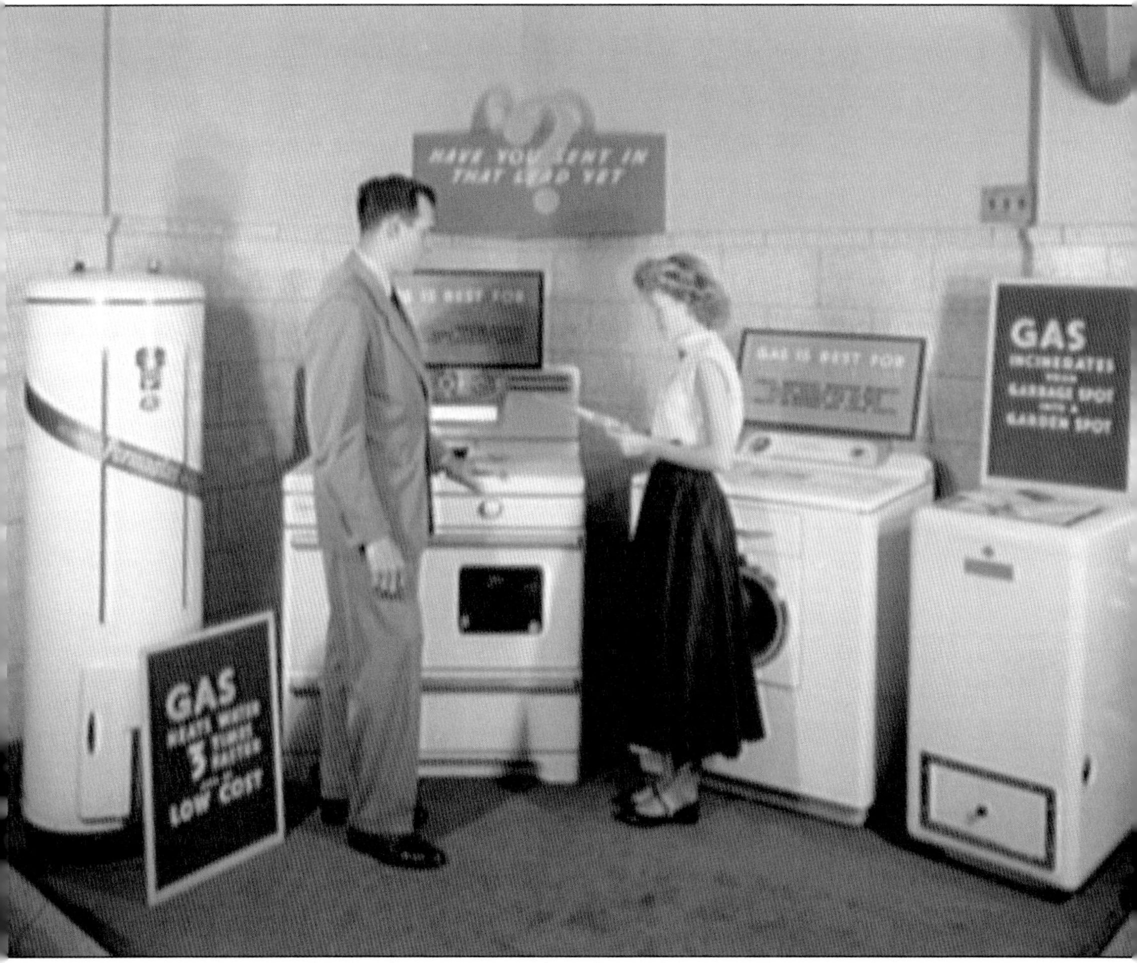

Levittown and similar developments brought a demand for public utility and county infrastructure. The resulting jobs provided great pay, retirement pensions, and family package health insurance. Long Island Light and Power Company (LILCO) absorbed local power companies and provided electricity to 2.7 million people. LILCO had several complaints of racially based hiring practices and two high-profile lawsuits alleging age and race discrimination. Pictured above is LILCO's Mineola showroom. (Library of Congress.)

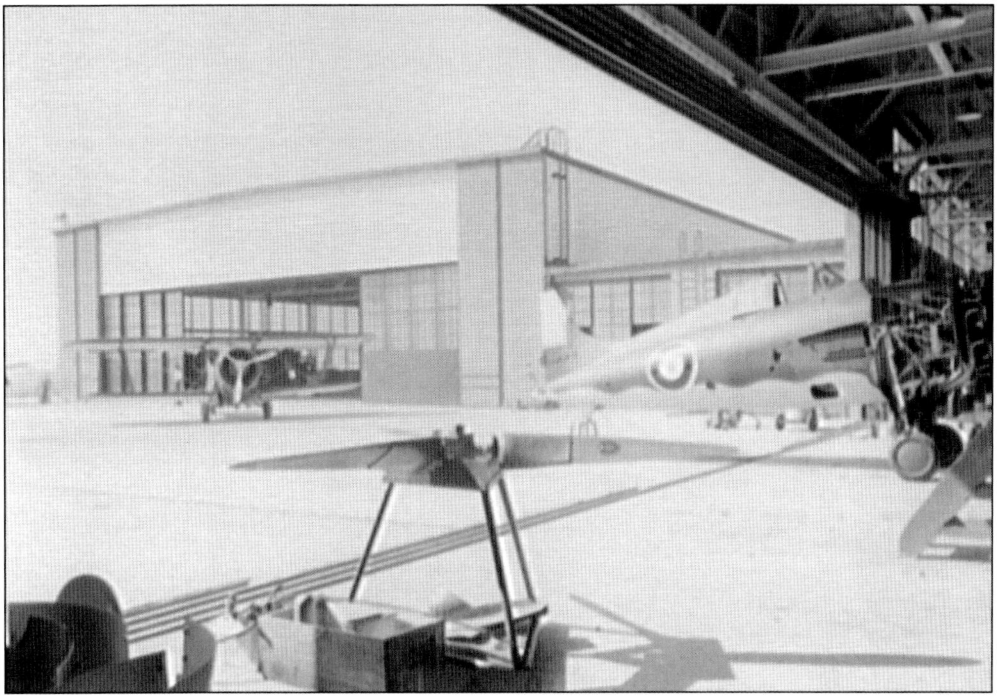

Military defense and aerospace manufacturing industries employed as many as 80,000 people across Long Island. During World War II, these companies, such as Grumman, broke racial and gender barriers by hiring minorities and women to manufacture military planes. These jobs included manufacturing military planes such as the F6F Hellcat, TBF Avenger, and F-14 Tomcat, as well as the Apollo Lunar Module. Civilian products included Grumman canoes, aluminum trucks for the US Postal Service and UPS, and fire trucks. At its peak, Grumman employed 23,000 people in plants in Bethpage, Calverton, and East Islip. Pictured above is Grumman's Bethpage plant, with Avengers (outside the hangar) and US-2Cs (in the hangar) under construction. In the 1950s and 1960s, the number of blacks employed by the defense industry was down to five percent. (Both, Library of Congress.)

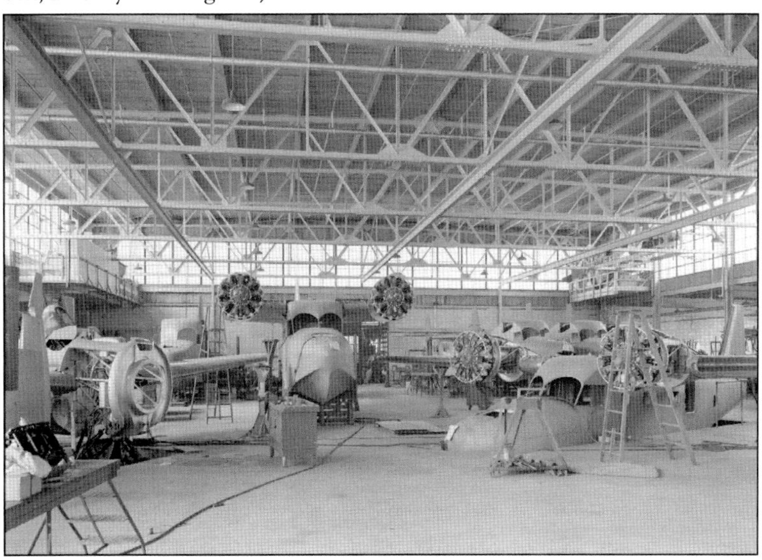

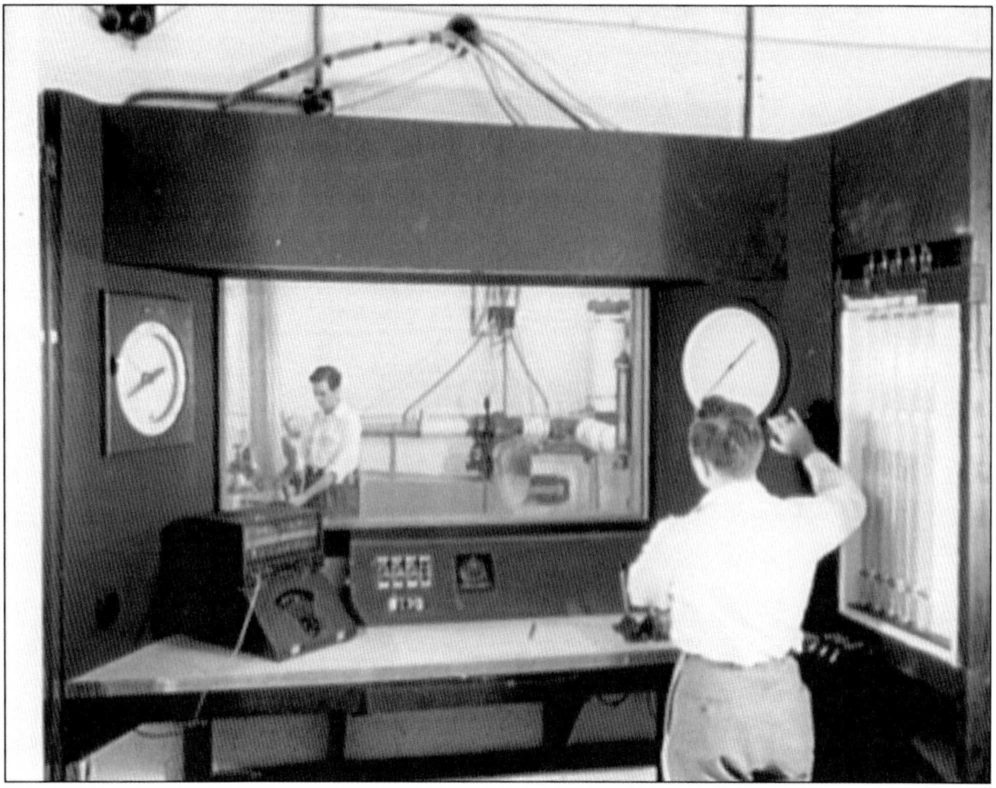

Fairchild Aircraft Company had offices in Farmingdale, Jamaica, and Bay Shore. Residential developments were built around the Bay Shore, Syosset, and Farmingdale offices. Just like other defense companies, during World War II, Fairchild Aircraft broke racial and gender barriers by hiring minorities and women to manufacture military planes. Military aircraft manufactured at these sites included the AC-119G Shadow and C-123 Provider cargo plane. The plants also made AUM-2 Petrel missiles and XSM-73 Goose missiles. Civilian manufacturing included the Dornier 728 commuter jet and photography and X-ray equipment. The Bay Shore and Syosset offices built aerial cameras, X-ray equipment, and radio compasses. Above are the Bay Shore offices of Fairchild Aircraft Company. (Both, Library of Congress.)

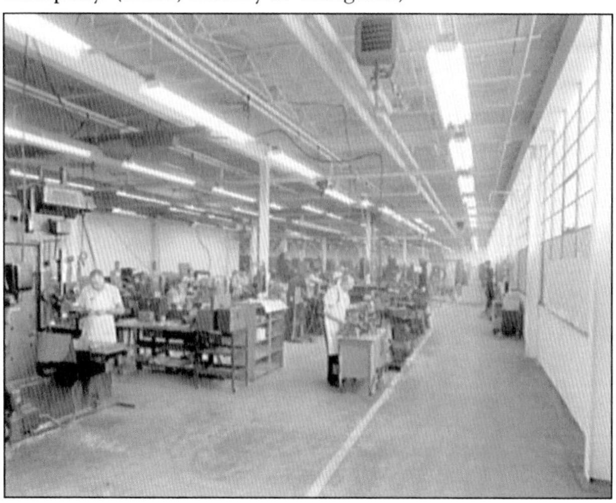

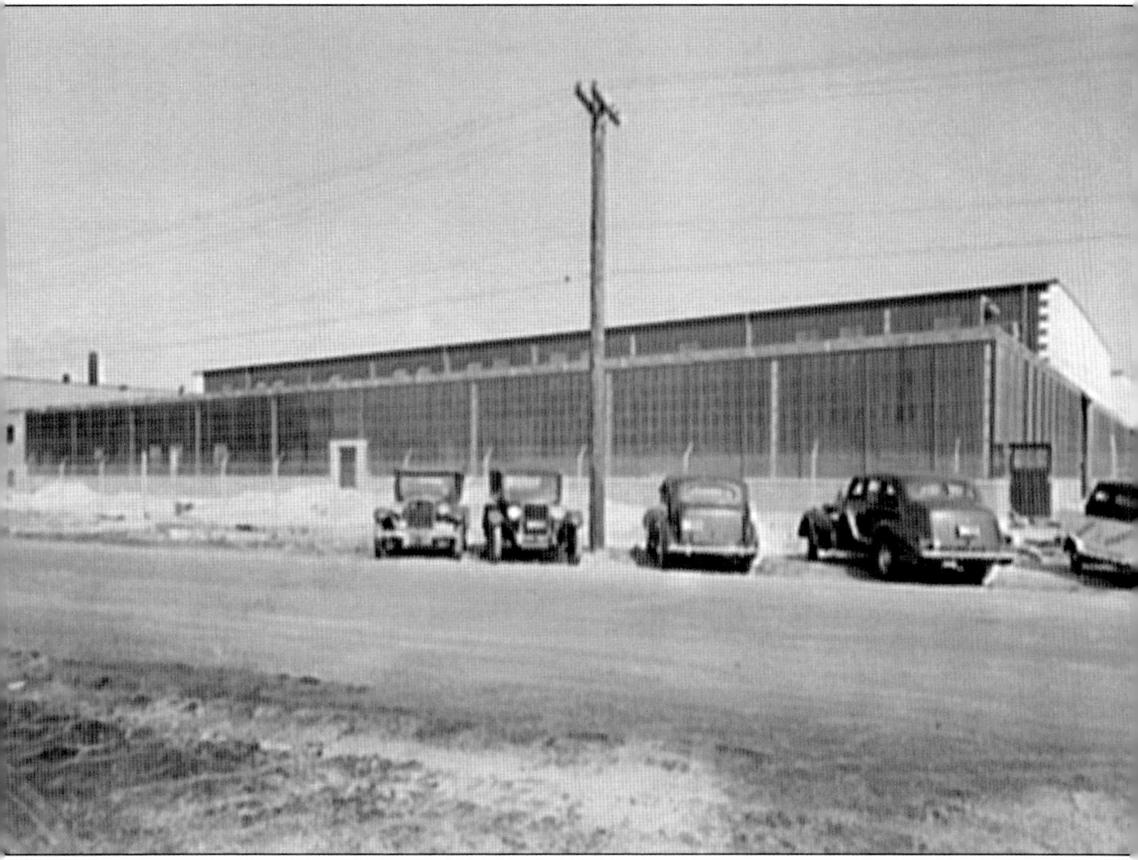

Republic Aviation, Sherman Fairchild, and Liberty Aircraft were located in Farmingdale. These manufacturers are known for producing the Thunderbolt during World War II. The racially integrated development of Ronek Park in Amityville was built around the site for its abundant jobs. Jobs within Republic were in manufacturing, engineering, or in the airport itself. Above is the former Liberty Aircraft Company in Farmingdale. (Library of Congress.)

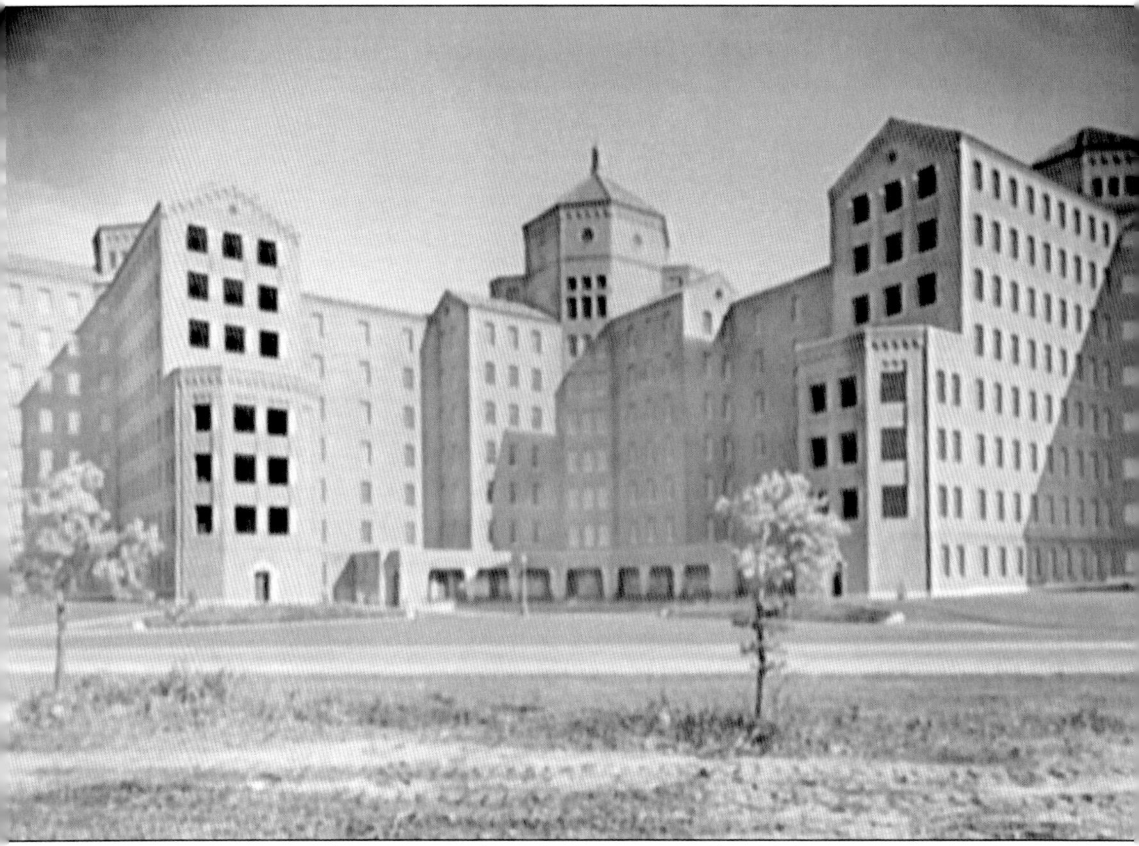

Pilgrim State Hospital in Brentwood was the largest mental health facility of its time. The hospital employed as many as 4,000 people during its peak population of just under 14,000 patients. Jobs within the hospital included railroad track repair within the grounds, and utility jobs within the hospital power stations. The housing developments of Deer Park and Brentwood were built and marketed to workers. (Library of Congress.)

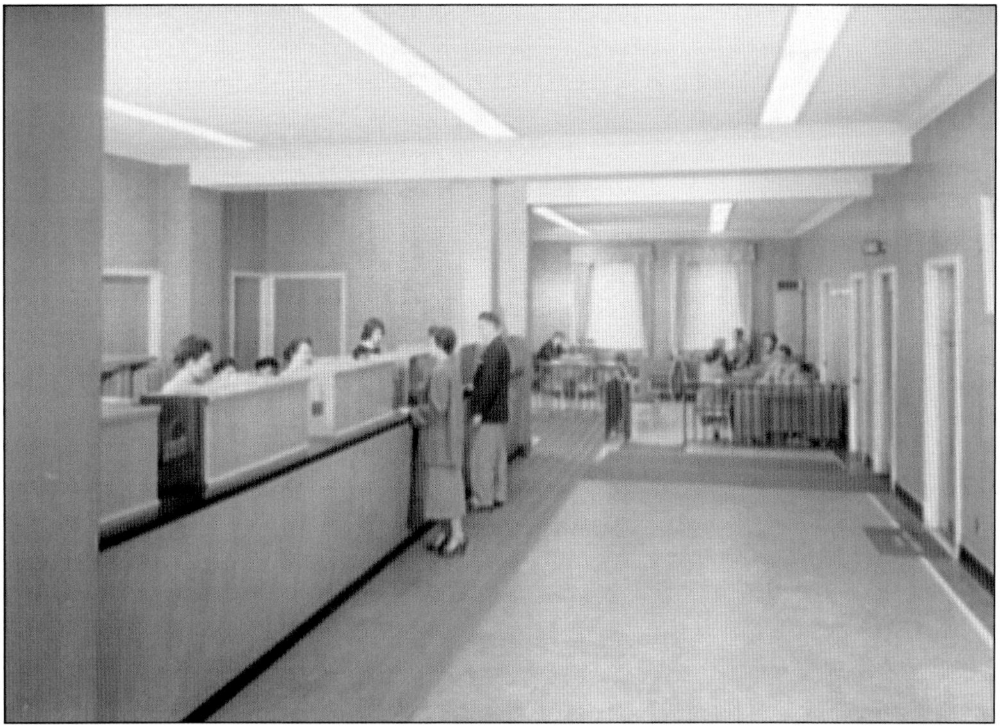

The Federal Housing Administration (FHA) played a dominate role in segregating Long Island through its lending processes. The FHA's practice of redlining limited financing to some neighborhoods based on racial makeup. The FHA argued that this process was necessary to secure raising values on its investments. Other race-based lending practices included having local banks collectively freeze funds on certain areas and developments. One example of frozen funds of a construction project was the Amityville Lawns development. This development was organized by the black-owned C&D Cement Company. The development had a goal of constructing 211 to 294 houses and marketing them as an integrated community. Pictured here are the lobby and loan processing department of the National Bank of Hicksville. This bank and many others across Long Island struggled with ethical lending practices and employment integration. (Both, Library of Congress.)

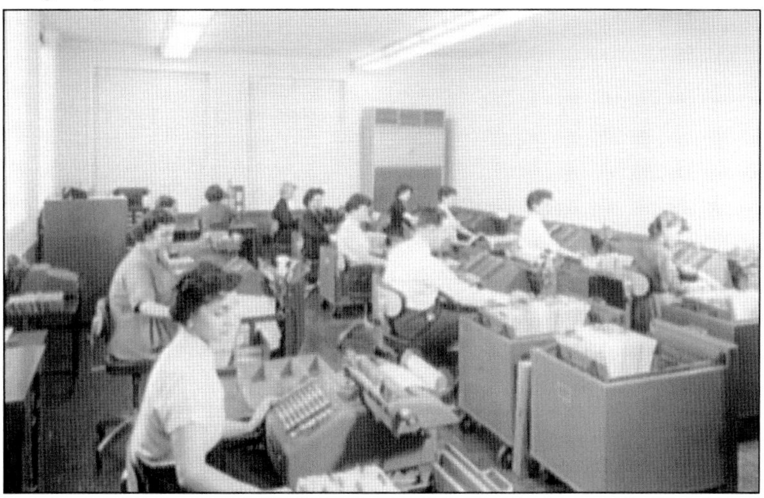

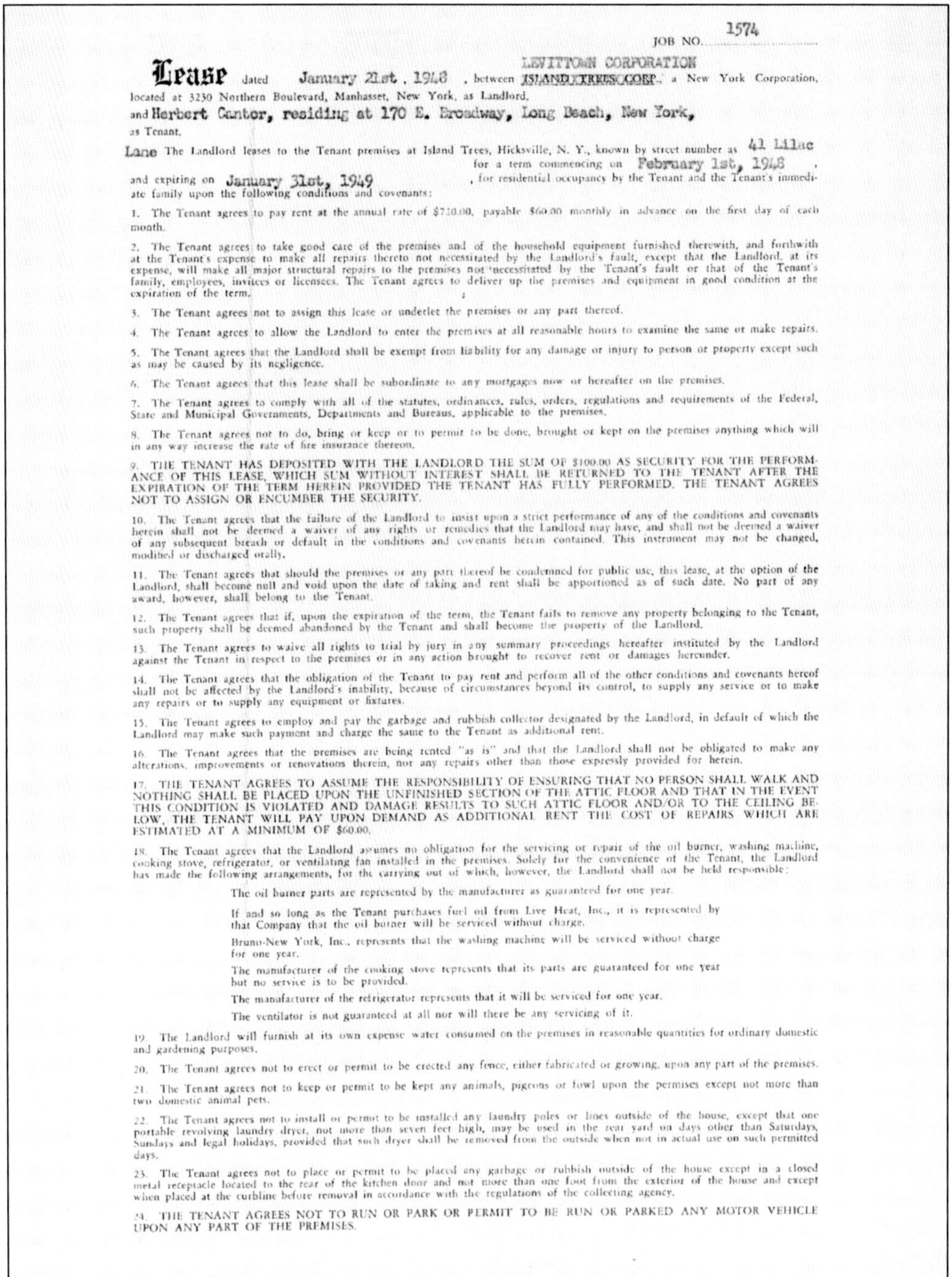

JOB NO. 1574

Lease dated January 21st, 1948, between ~~ISLAND TREES CORP.~~ LEVITTOWN CORPORATION, a New York Corporation, located at 3230 Northern Boulevard, Manhasset, New York, as Landlord, and Herbert Cantor, residing at 170 E. Broadway, Long Beach, New York, as Tenant.

The Landlord leases to the Tenant premises at Island Trees, Hicksville, N. Y., known by street number as 41 Lilac Lane for a term commencing on February 1st, 1948, and expiring on January 31st, 1949, for residential occupancy by the Tenant and the Tenant's immediate family upon the following conditions and covenants:

1. The Tenant agrees to pay rent at the annual rate of $720.00, payable $60.00 monthly in advance on the first day of each month.

2. The Tenant agrees to take good care of the premises and of the household equipment furnished therewith, and forthwith at the Tenant's expense to make all repairs thereto not necessitated by the Landlord's fault, except that the Landlord, at its expense, will make all major structural repairs to the premises not necessitated by the Tenant's fault or that of the Tenant's family, employees, invitees or licensees. The Tenant agrees to deliver up the premises and equipment in good condition at the expiration of the term.

3. The Tenant agrees not to assign this lease or underlet the premises or any part thereof.

4. The Tenant agrees to allow the Landlord to enter the premises at all reasonable hours to examine the same or make repairs.

5. The Tenant agrees that the Landlord shall be exempt from liability for any damage or injury to person or property except such as may be caused by its negligence.

6. The Tenant agrees that this lease shall be subordinate to any mortgages now or hereafter on the premises.

7. The Tenant agrees to comply with all of the statutes, ordinances, rules, orders, regulations and requirements of the Federal, State and Municipal Governments, Departments and Bureaus, applicable to the premises.

8. The Tenant agrees not to do, bring or keep or to permit to be done, brought or kept on the premises anything which will in any way increase the rate of fire insurance thereon.

9. THE TENANT HAS DEPOSITED WITH THE LANDLORD THE SUM OF $100.00 AS SECURITY FOR THE PERFORMANCE OF THIS LEASE, WHICH SUM WITHOUT INTEREST SHALL BE RETURNED TO THE TENANT AFTER THE EXPIRATION OF THE TERM HEREIN PROVIDED THE TENANT HAS FULLY PERFORMED. THE TENANT AGREES NOT TO ASSIGN OR ENCUMBER THE SECURITY.

10. The Tenant agrees that the failure of the Landlord to insist upon a strict performance of any of the conditions and covenants herein shall not be deemed a waiver of any rights or remedies that the Landlord may have, and shall not be deemed a waiver of any subsequent breach or default in the conditions and covenants herein contained. This instrument may not be changed, modified or discharged orally.

11. The Tenant agrees that should the premises or any part thereof be condemned for public use, this lease, at the option of the Landlord, shall become null and void upon the date of taking and rent shall be apportioned as of such date. No part of any award, however, shall belong to the Tenant.

12. The Tenant agrees that if, upon the expiration of the term, the Tenant fails to remove any property belonging to the Tenant, such property shall be deemed abandoned by the Tenant and shall become the property of the Landlord.

13. The Tenant agrees to waive all rights to trial by jury in any summary proceedings hereafter instituted by the Landlord against the Tenant in respect to the premises or in any action brought to recover rent or damages hereunder.

14. The Tenant agrees that the obligation of the Tenant to pay rent and perform all of the other conditions and covenants hereof shall not be affected by the Landlord's inability, because of circumstances beyond its control, to supply any service or to make any repairs or to supply any equipment or fixtures.

15. The Tenant agrees to employ and pay the garbage and rubbish collector designated by the Landlord, in default of which the Landlord may make such payment and charge the same to the Tenant as additional rent.

16. The Tenant agrees that the premises are being rented "as is" and that the Landlord shall not be obligated to make any alterations, improvements or renovations therein, nor any repairs other than those expressly provided for herein.

17. THE TENANT AGREES TO ASSUME THE RESPONSIBILITY OF ENSURING THAT NO PERSON SHALL WALK AND NOTHING SHALL BE PLACED UPON THE UNFINISHED SECTION OF THE ATTIC FLOOR AND THAT IN THE EVENT THIS CONDITION IS VIOLATED AND DAMAGE RESULTS TO SUCH ATTIC FLOOR AND/OR TO THE CEILING BELOW, THE TENANT WILL PAY UPON DEMAND AS ADDITIONAL RENT THE COST OF REPAIRS WHICH ARE ESTIMATED AT A MINIMUM OF $60.00.

18. The Tenant agrees that the Landlord assumes no obligation for the servicing or repair of the oil burner, washing machine, cooking stove, refrigerator, or ventilating fan installed in the premises. Solely for the convenience of the Tenant, the Landlord has made the following arrangements, for the carrying out of which, however, the Landlord shall not be held responsible:

The oil burner parts are represented by the manufacturer as guaranteed for one year.

If and so long as the Tenant purchases fuel oil from Live Heat, Inc., it is represented by that Company that the oil burner will be serviced without charge.

Bruno-New York, Inc., represents that the washing machine will be serviced without charge for one year.

The manufacturer of the cooking stove represents that its parts are guaranteed for one year but no service is to be provided.

The manufacturer of the refrigerator represents that it will be serviced for one year.

The ventilator is not guaranteed at all nor will there be any servicing of it.

19. The Landlord will furnish at its own expense water consumed on the premises in reasonable quantities for ordinary domestic and gardening purposes.

20. The Tenant agrees not to erect or permit to be erected any fence, either fabricated or growing, upon any part of the premises.

21. The Tenant agrees not to keep or permit to be kept any animals, pigeons or fowl upon the permises except not more than two domestic animal pets.

22. The Tenant agrees not to install or permit to be installed any laundry poles or lines outside of the house, except that one portable revolving laundry dryer, not more than seven feet high, may be used in the rear yard on days other than Saturdays, Sundays and legal holidays, provided that such dryer shall be removed from the outside when not in actual use on such permitted days.

23. The Tenant agrees not to place or permit to be placed any garbage or rubbish outside of the house except in a closed metal receptacle located to the rear of the kitchen door and not more than one foot from the exterior of the house and except when placed at the curbline before removal in accordance with the regulations of the collecting agency.

24. THE TENANT AGREES NOT TO RUN OR PARK OR PERMIT TO BE RUN OR PARKED ANY MOTOR VEHICLE UPON ANY PART OF THE PREMISES.

LEVITTOWN HISTORY COLLECTION

Entering the middle class came with the privileges of safe areas to raise a family, good-quality public schools, and a house that would increase in value to create generational wealth. Levittown embodied this dream only for white American families. Levittown's rent with the option to buy was the main pathway to home ownership for thousands of people. As seen above, clause 26 states, "The tenant agrees not to permit the premises to be used or occupied by any person other than

25. THE TENANT AGREES TO CUT OR CAUSE TO BE CUT THE LAWN AND REMOVE OR CAUSE TO BE REMOVED TALL GROWING WEEDS AT LEAST ONCE A WEEK BETWEEN APRIL FIFTEENTH AND NOVEMBER FIFTEENTH IN EACH YEAR. UPON THE TENANT'S FAILURE THE LANDLORD MAY DO SO AND CHARGE THE COST THEREOF TO THE TENANT AS ADDITIONAL RENT.

26. THE TENANT AGREES NOT TO PERMIT THE PREMISES TO BE USED OR OCCUPIED BY ANY PERSON OTHER THAN MEMBERS OF THE CAUCASIAN RACE BUT THE EMPLOYMENT AND MAINTENANCE OF OTHER THAN CAUCASIAN DOMESTIC SERVANTS SHALL BE PERMITTED.

27. The Tenant agrees not to place or permit to be placed upon the premises any sign whatsoever except a family or professional name or address plate whose size, style and location are first approved in writing by the Landlord.

28. The Tenant agrees not to use or permit the premises to be used for any purpose other than as a private dwelling for one family or as a professional office of a physician or dentist resident therein.

29. The Tenant agrees not to erect or permit to be erected on the premises any building or structure, or to make or permit to be made any alterations or additions to the premises, or paint or permit to be painted the exterior of the house other than in the original color, unless appropriate plans, specifications and/or colors are first approved in writing by the landlord.

30. The Tenant agrees not to do or permit to be done on the premises anything of a disreputable nature, or constituting a nuisance, or tending to impair the condition or appearance of the premises, or tending to interfere unreasonably with the use and enjoyment of other premises by other Tenants.

31. The Tenant agrees that, if default be made in the performance of any of the conditions or covenants herein, or if the premises shall become vacant or if the Tenant shall file a petition in bankruptcy or be adjudicated a bankrupt or make an assignment for the benefit of creditors, the Landlord may (A) re-enter the premises by force, summary proceedings or otherwise, and remove all persons therefrom, without being liable to prosecution therefor, and the Tenant hereby expressly waives the service of any notice in writing of intention to re-enter, or (B) the Landlord may terminate this lease on giving to the Tenant 5 days' notice in writing of its intention so to do, and this lease shall expire on the date fixed for the expiration hereof. Such notice may be given by mail to the Tenant addressed to the premises. The Tenant agrees, in either event, to pay at the same times as the rent is payable hereunder a sum equivalent to such rent; and the Landlord may rent the premises on behalf of the Tenant, (for a period of time beyond the original expiration date of this lease, if it so elects), without releasing the Tenant from any liability, applying any moneys collected, first to the expense of resuming or obtaining possession, second to the restoration of the premises to a rentable condition, and then to the payment of the rent and all other charges due and to become due to the Landlord, any surplus to be paid to the Tenant who shall remain liable for any deficiency.

32. The Landlord agrees that the Tenant on performing the conditions and covenants aforesaid shall and may peacefully and quietly have, hold and enjoy the premises for the term aforesaid.

33. It is mutually agreed that the conditions and covenants contained in this lease shall be binding upon the parties hereto and upon their respective successors, heirs, executors, administrators and assigns.

IN WITNESS WHEREOF, the Landlord has caused these presents to be signed by its proper corporate officer and caused its proper corporate seal to be hereto affixed and the Tenant has hereunto set his hand and seal.

LEVITTOWN CORPORATION
XXXXXXXXXXXXXXXX.

By: .... Authorized Officer

.... L. S.

NO NOTICES WILL BE MAILED. RENT IS DUE AND PAYABLE ON THE FIRST OF EACH MONTH AT THE OFFICE IN THE ISLAND TREES COMMUNITY.

members of the Caucasian race but the employment and maintenance of other than Caucasian domestic servants shall be permitted." One of many people evicted from Levittown because of this racist clause was William Cotter in 1953. The clause was removed years later due to pressure from local grassroots groups petitioning the FHA to withdraw mortgage insurance for all Levitt developments. (Both, Levittown Library historical archives.)

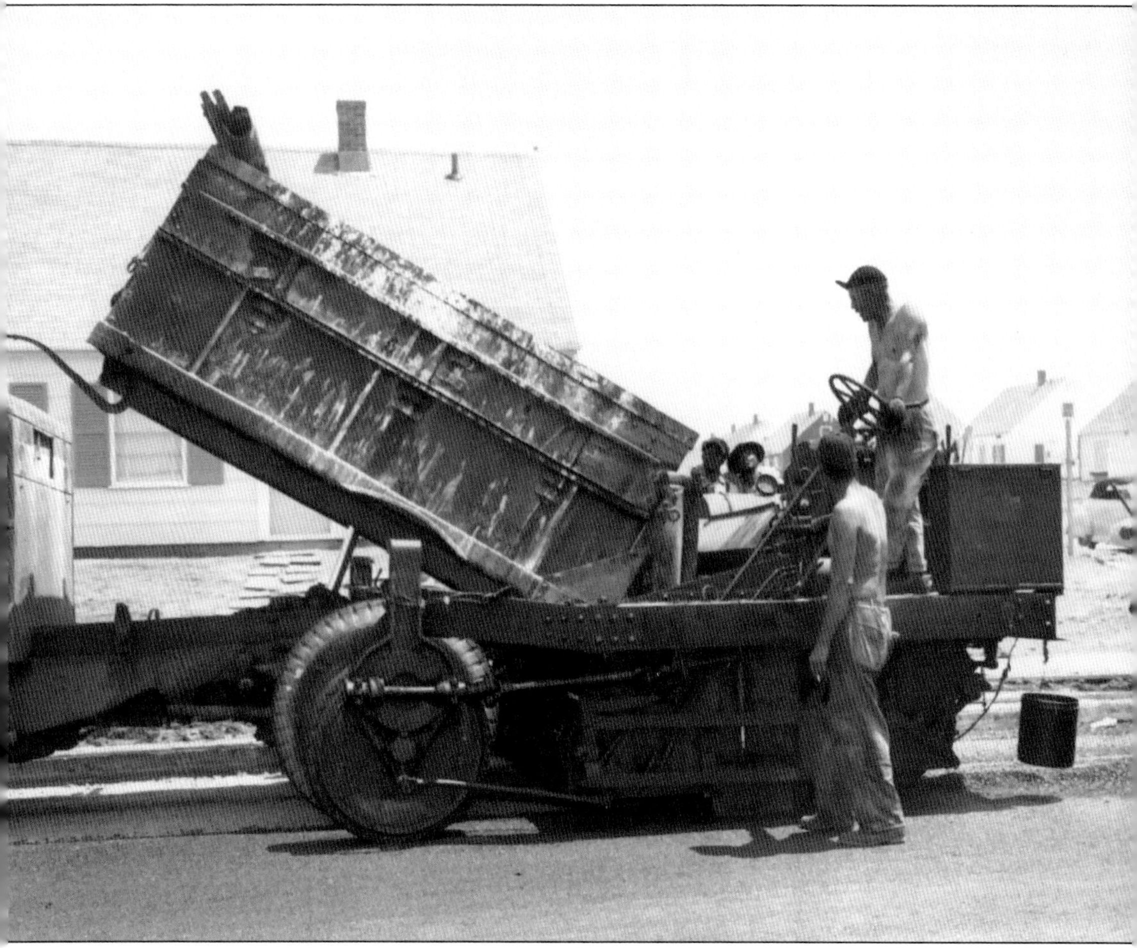

Racial residential restrictions in Levittown were not extended in the construction of the houses and public works. The boom in construction resulted in employment for many African Americans. The picture above shows African Americans constructing roads for Levittown. Despite the African Americans' tireless labor constructing the developments, they would be restricted from owning or renting a home in the town. (Hofstra University Library Special Collections.)

Four

Battlegrounds for Integration

Just as with World War I, World War II had returning black troops demanding equality. An estimated 1.2 million blacks served during World War II guided by the idea that they were ending tyranny. Upon returning home, blacks found the same conditions they endured prior to World War II. Fighting tyranny abroad did not extend to ending racial oppression at home. Developments such as Levittown extended the ideal American dream to returning white soldiers but barred blacks. Mortgage lending, schools, and anything that would have been a pathway to the middle class was stunted for blacks. Local media ignored these inequalities unless there were mass demonstrations. To obtain equality, blacks had to unify and organize against institutionalized racism.

Groups such as the Congress of Racial Equality (CORE), Committee to End Discrimination, local church groups, and labor unions such as Local 259 collaborated with the NAACP to further opportunities for blacks. These groups built their membership and momentum through shared guiding ideas and strong leadership. Local civil rights leaders such as Lincoln Lynch developed decision-making, communication, and organization skills in the military during World War II. Blacks following these groups had their frustration heightened by financially making it to the middle class through aerial and defense plant jobs but not being able to have middle-class privileges for their families. Generational wealth could not be accumulated due to aggressive lending practices that did not allow families to obtain mortgages in areas with growing value. Schools in minority areas were left underfunded due to white schools cutting out business districts for tax revenue for schools.

Tactics used by CORE and the NAACP were mass demonstrations, civil disobedience, and boycotts to attracted the media. These demonstrations not only focused on Nassau and Suffolk Counties but were exported to suburban parts of Queens. Businesses such as Vigilant Real Estate, Levitt & Sons Real Estate Company, LILCO, and Woolworth were targets of these boycotts and demonstrations. Through media and community pressure, Levitt & Sons and Woolworth changed their racial policies. Counter demonstrations against CORE and the NAACP included local racist groups that would burn crosses, wave Confederate flags while shouting racial slurs, and threaten harm to families of the activists. Initial results were the demonstrators being arrested and lawyers working for the NAACP getting them out of jail the following day.

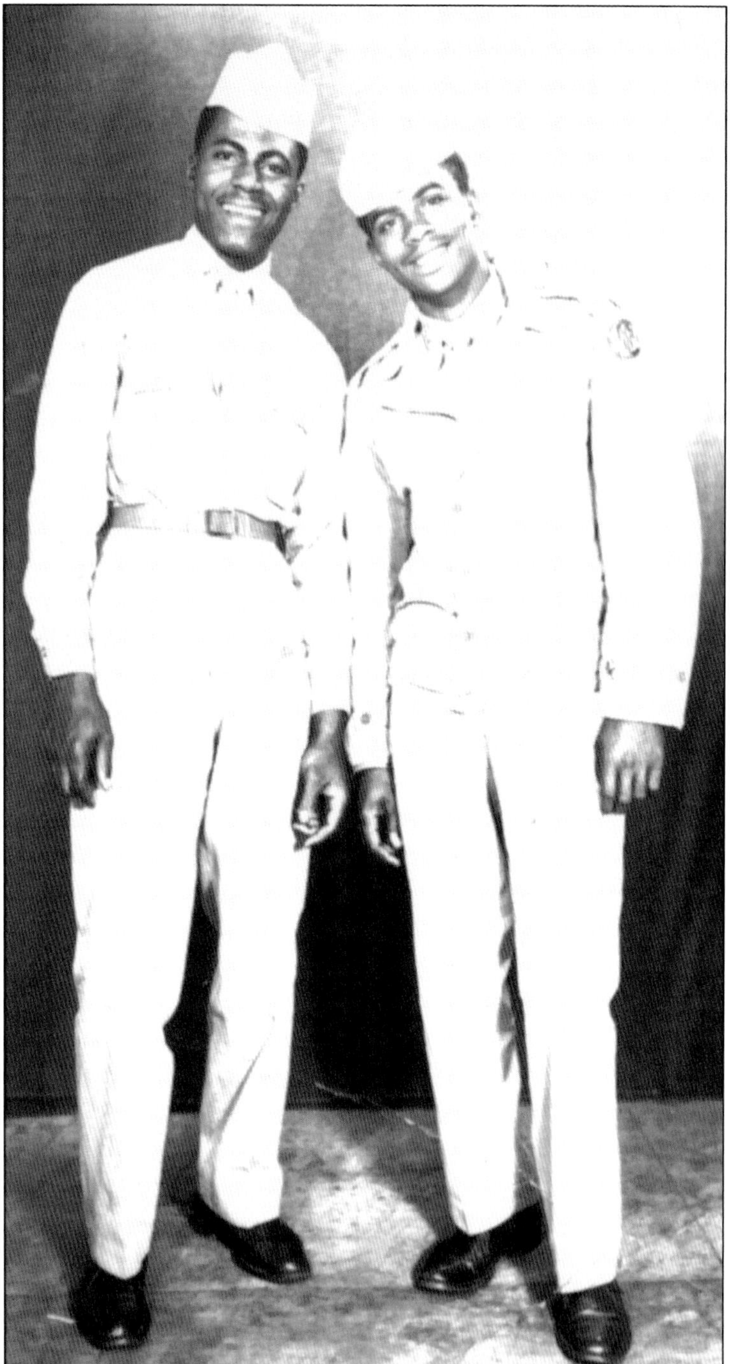

Black soldiers coming home were the cornerstone of the 1950s and 1960s civil rights movement. Black soldiers believed that defeating oppression in Europe and Asia would inspire a more just society in America. Pictured above are Richard Coles (left) and Eugene Burnett. Eugene would later become a key member of the NAACP. His activism was influenced by his time in the service and being rejected from buying a home in Levittown due to his race. (Eugene Burnett Collection.)

The NAACP had regional leaders and directors who focused on local issues. This system of leadership allows grassroots community organizing and support of other localized groups with the similar goals. Pictured here are "centennial members" (lifetime membership) of the NAACP. From left to right are Albert Breach, Austin Naylor, Gomez Paige, Nathan Jackson, Eugene Burnett, and Reginald Harewood. (Eugene Burnett Collection.)

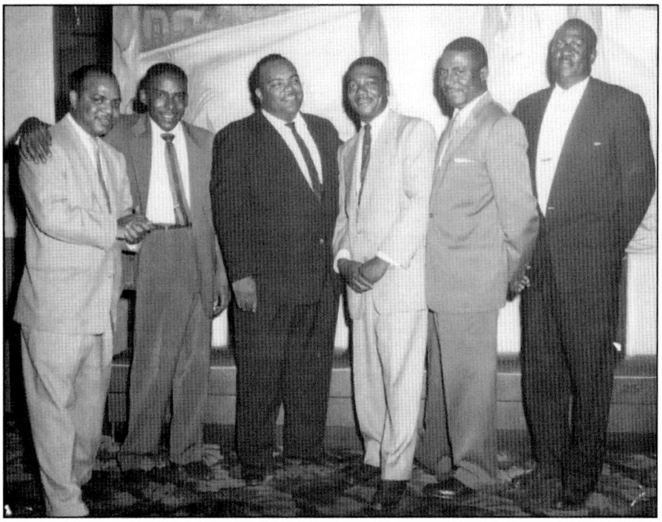

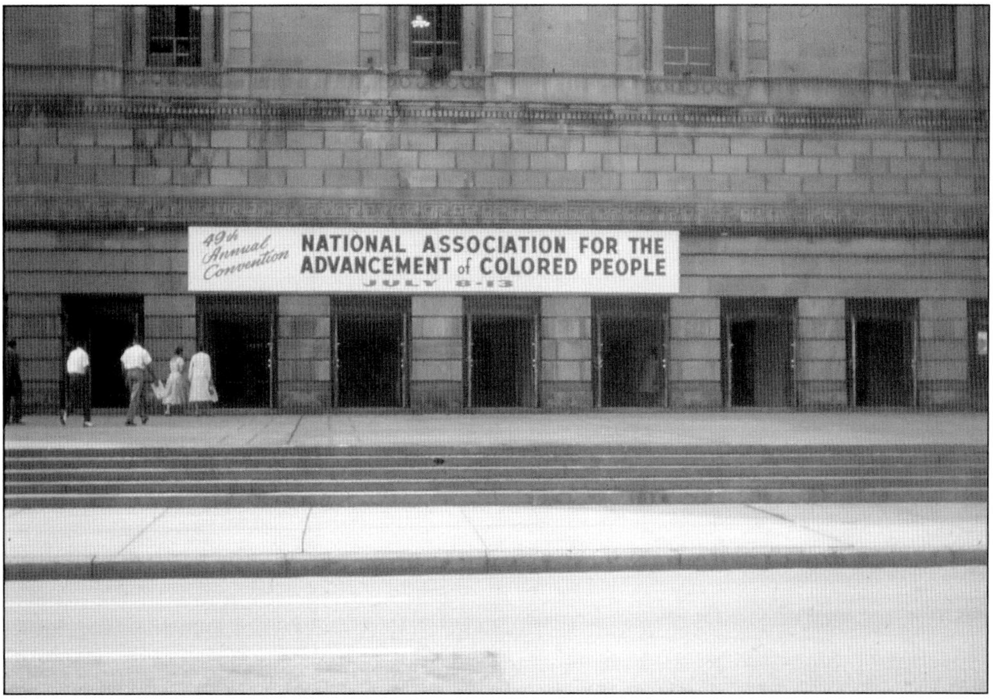

The NAACP conventions are the key component in carrying out grassroots activism. Conventions include opportunities for local delegates and regional leaders to collaborate on local and national civil rights issues. The 49th convention, July 8–13, 1958, in Cleveland, set national goals that included registering three million to vote, focusing on housing integration in Northern suburbia, and work with labor unions across the Northern states to promote fair employment opportunities. (Eugene Burnett Collection.)

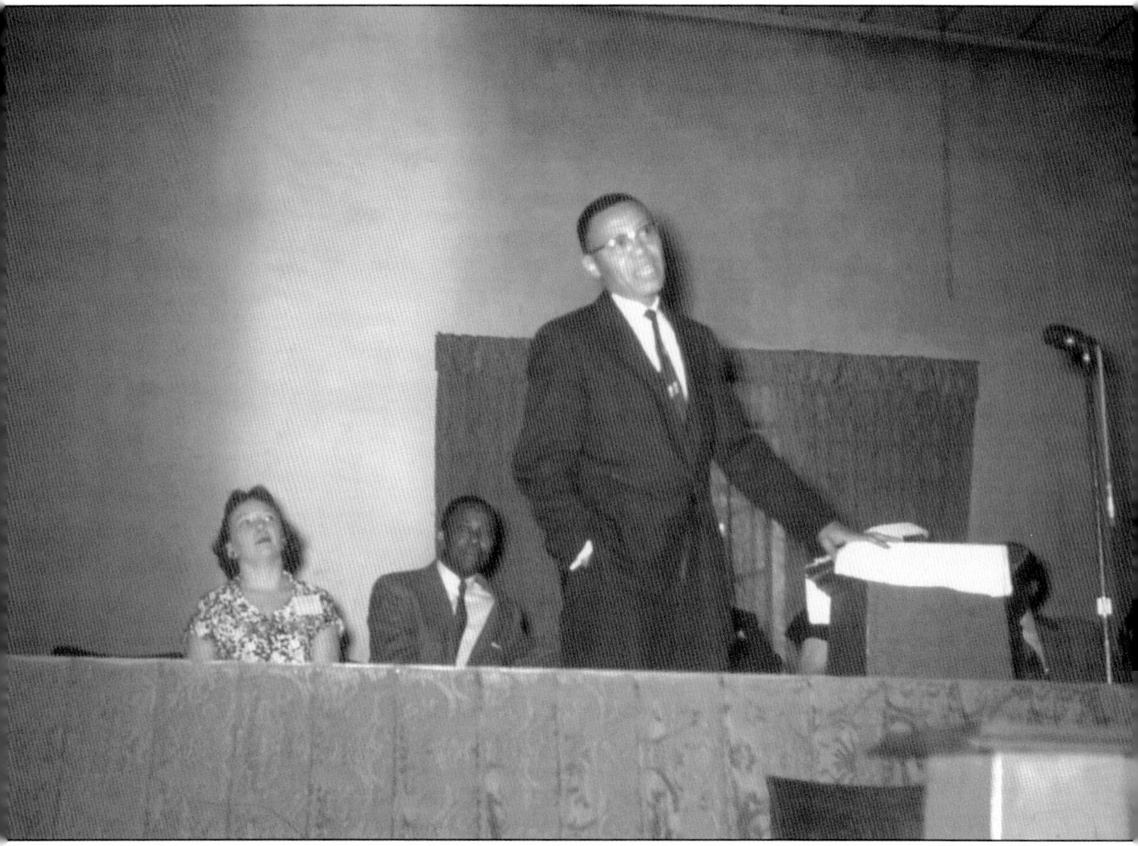

At the 1958 convention, Dr. Eugene Reed from Amityville held state and local leadership roles within the NAACP. Dr. Reed organized sit-ins and boycotts against Long Island housing and school segregation. Some of his accomplishments were getting rid of district-based elementary school in favor of the Princeton model with the Amityville School District and being a consultant on affirmative action within the town of Babylon. In the picture above, Dr. Reed is addressing de facto segregation at the convention. (Eugene Burnett Collection.)

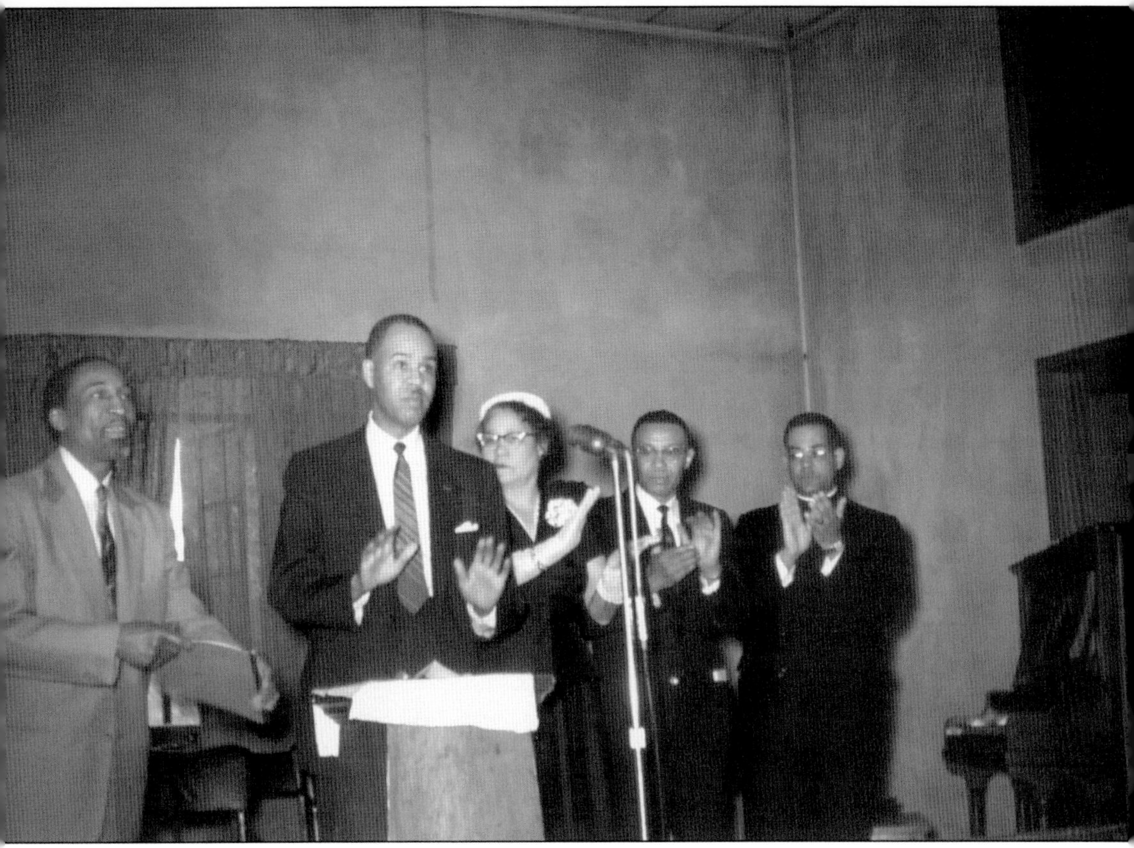

Roy Wilkins was the executive director of the NAACP during the peak years of the civil rights movement, from 1955 to 1977. Under his leadership, the NAACP created a small business loan fund for black businesses that were denied loans by biased lending practices. During the 49th convention, Wilkins organized workshops on how local chapters should collaborate with religious groups and how to effectively raise funds. (Eugene Burnett Collection.)

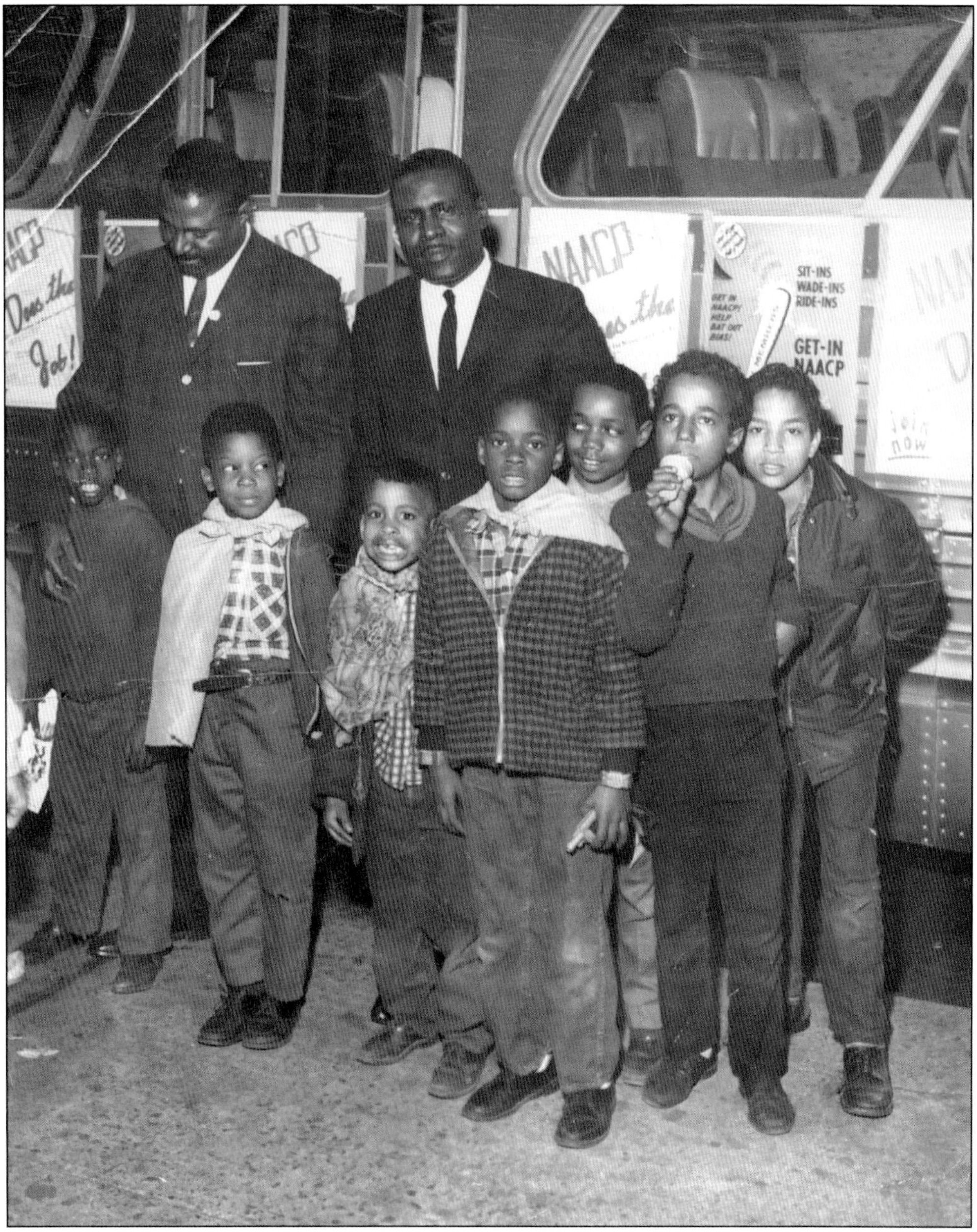

During mass migration to suburbia, the inner cities became poorer. Moving to Nassau or Suffolk Counties became a symbol for success. Long Island chapters of the NAACP encouraged members to revisit the neighborhoods they came from to do community service. Pictured above are Leroy (left) and Eugene Burnett (right) in a Harlem neighborhood. Eugene, originally from Harlem, joined the service and moved to Wheatley Heights. When he moved to Long Island, Eugene joined the Suffolk County Police Department, became a delegate to the NAACP, and opened a successful bar and restaurant. (Eugene Burnett Collection.)

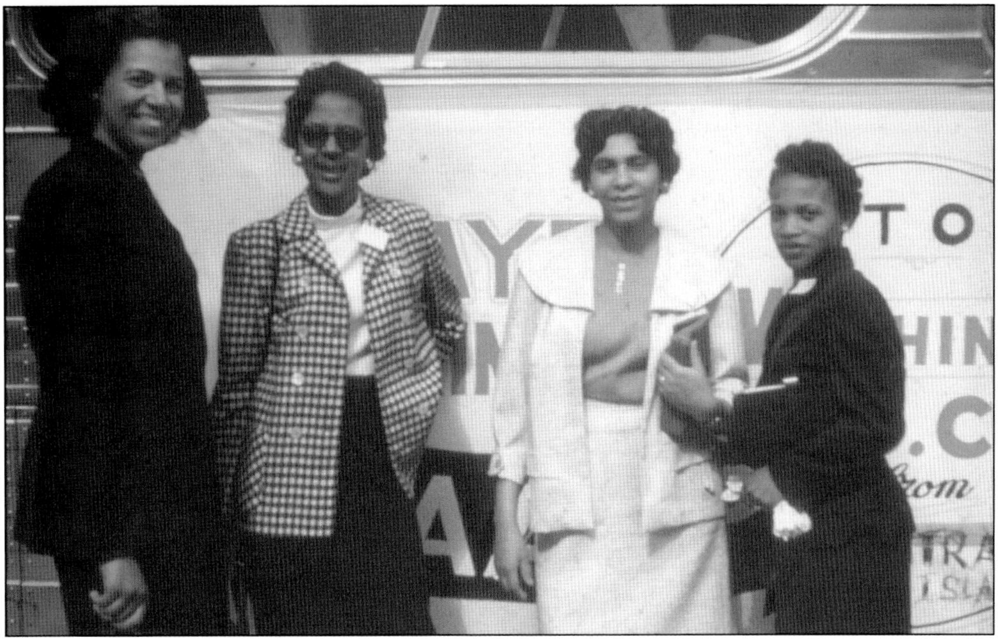

The civil rights movement has its roots in the church. The NAACP, CORE, and Committee to End Discrimination had strong support among religious communities. The Hollywood Baptist Church of Amityville organized prayer groups to visit other churches to promote civil rights. Pictured above is a Hollywood Baptist prayer group chartering a bus to go to the historic march on Washington, DC. (Eugene Barnett Collection.)

Local religious leaders were active in NAACP and CORE demonstrations and recruitment. Quaker minister Noel Palmer became the backbone of the Educational Opportunity Center (EOC). The goal of this organization is to provide college and career opportunities to students. Minister Palmer worked closely with the NAACP and Farmingdale State College to draw attention to educational gaps among urban poor and minority students. (Historical Society of the Westburys Photo Archive.)

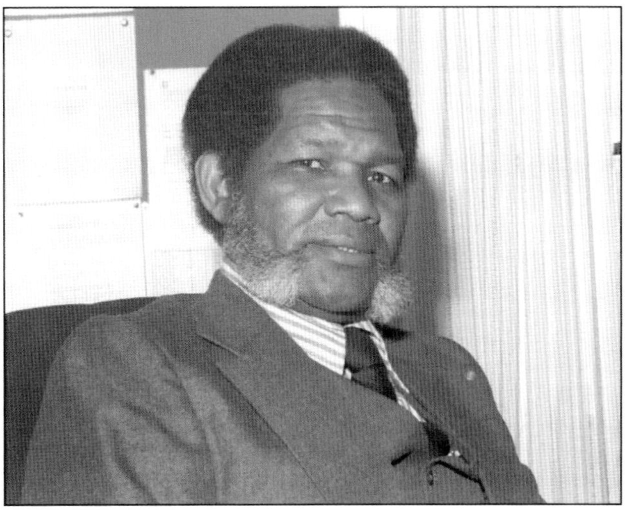

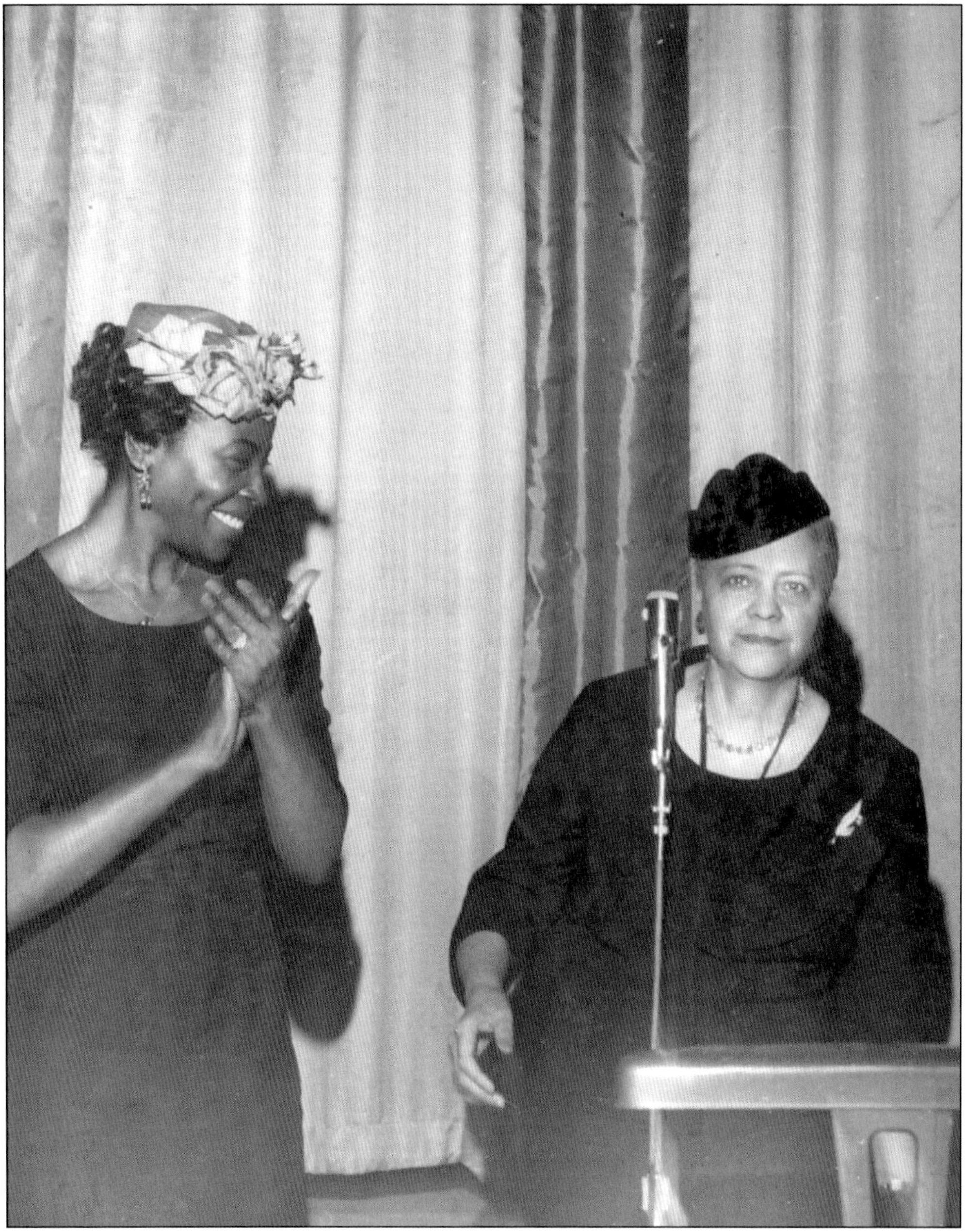

Women's rights groups assisted throughout the late 1950s, 1960s, and 1970s on NAACP and CORE campaigns. The League of Women Voters offered support to most of CORE's demonstrations and boycotts. National Organization of Women cofounder Anna Arnold Hedgeman (right) helped raise money and volunteers to boycott and demonstrate against local employment and educational discrimination. (Eugene Burnett Collection.)

Labor unions shared many of the civil rights movement's ideals. United Auto Workers Local 259 was a staple among the black working class. This union covered any unionized Long Islander who worked repairing or building cars. Under the leadership of Sam Meyers, blacks were put in leadership roles within the union and support was given to the NAACP for boycotts. (Eugene Burnett Collection.)

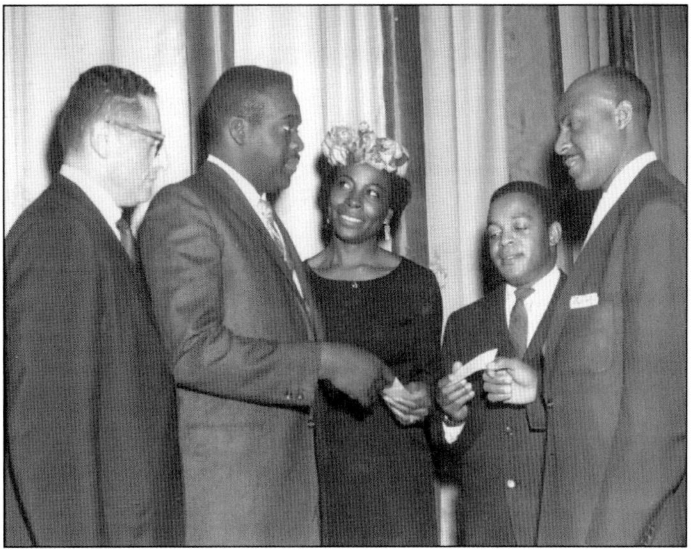

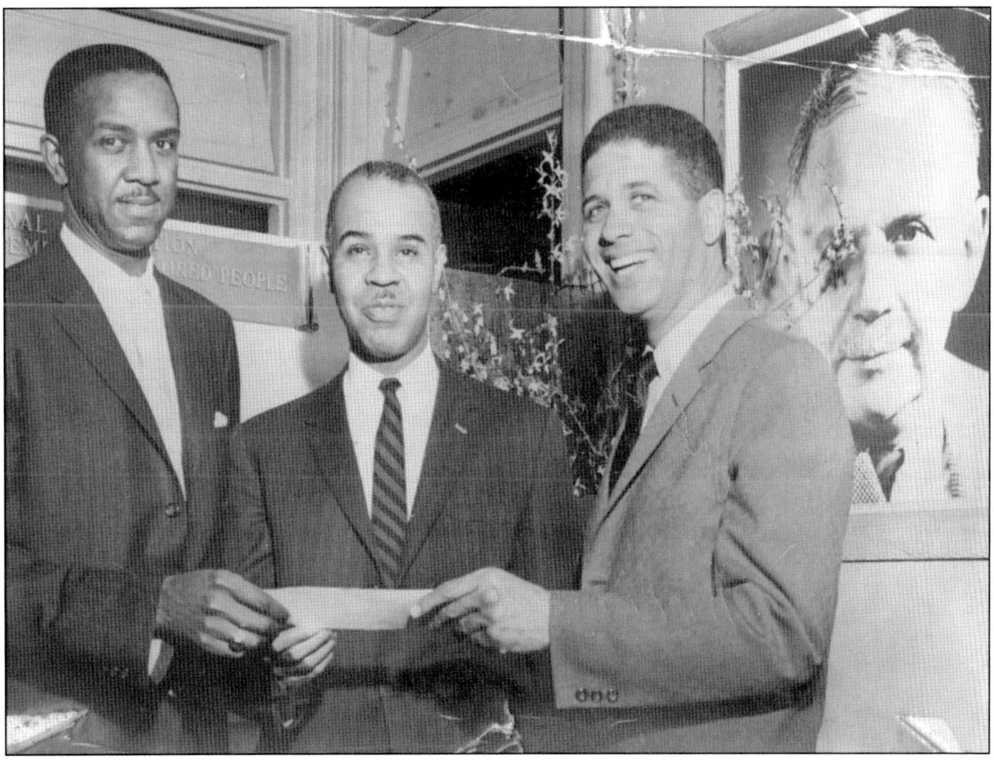

Local 259 not only boycotted and picketed with the NAACP, it also raised money for the organization. Above, Roy Wilkins accepts a $500 check from Local 259 to fund an employment equality campaign. Local 259 support was a two-way street. If 259 ever went on strike, the NAACP would provide support. (Eugene Burnett Collection.)

COMMITTEE TO END DISCRIMINATION IN LEVITTOWN 1951

POST OFFICE BOX 53, LEVITTOWN, LONG ISLAND, N. Y.

Dear Friend:

The Constitution says "yes"...The Supreme Court says "yes"...But William Levitt and Sons say "no."

By openly refusing to rent or sell homes to Negroes, the Levitt organization has run counter to American democratic thought, and has condemned Levittown in the eyes of all thinking Americans who believe that now, as never before, the fullest expression of democracy is mandatory.

Two years ago, our Committee was formed to halt Levitt's discriminatory practices. As a result of our joint action with groups like American Veterans' Committee, National Association for the Advancement of Colored People, American Civil Liberties Union and others, Levitt was forced to remove a restrictive covenant clause from his contracts. We have prevented, thus far, Levitt's attempted eviction of families who entertained Negro children in their homes...We have welcomed and helped successfully absorb into Levittown life the first Negro family to rent a house from a private owner...We have energetically publicized through the press, door-to-door visits and public meetings our Committee's efforts to end discrimination.

Community response to our program convinces us that Levittown sincerely believes in democracy. Nevertheless, we have not yet compelled Levitt and Sons to practice it...What remains for us to do? What final steps must we take? This is the urgent question we are now posing to hundreds of responsible organizations and individuals ...Will you, personally, or with your organization, join us in sponsoring a non-partisan, non-political Conference to find an answer to this problem? Will you participate in a Conference to focus public opinion on Levitt's dangerous practices?

We have scheduled this Conference for Thursday evening, June 7, at Hofstra College in Hempstead. Since we are eager to prepare our official Conference Call, will you tell us as soon as you can of your sponsorship and participation?

Help us realize Levittown's boast as "the Veterans' paradise - for all." Write to us - now.

Sincerely yours,

COMMITTEE TO END DISCRIMINATION

William G. Cotter

William G. Cotter, Chairman

By March 1949, the FHA told Levitt & Sons to get rid of the racial clause in renting and buying homes within the development. Levitt ignored the requests, and the FHA never followed through. William Cotter, director of the NAACP's Glen Cove chapter, challenged the white-only clause. Cotter formed the Committee to End Discrimination in Levittown in 1951. Cotter himself moved into 26 Butternut Lane in Levittown and challenged the racial clause in district court. After a lengthy eviction process, Cotter lost his appeal on August 1953. This is just one of many integration battles fought by the NAACP and CORE. (Levittown Library historical archives.)

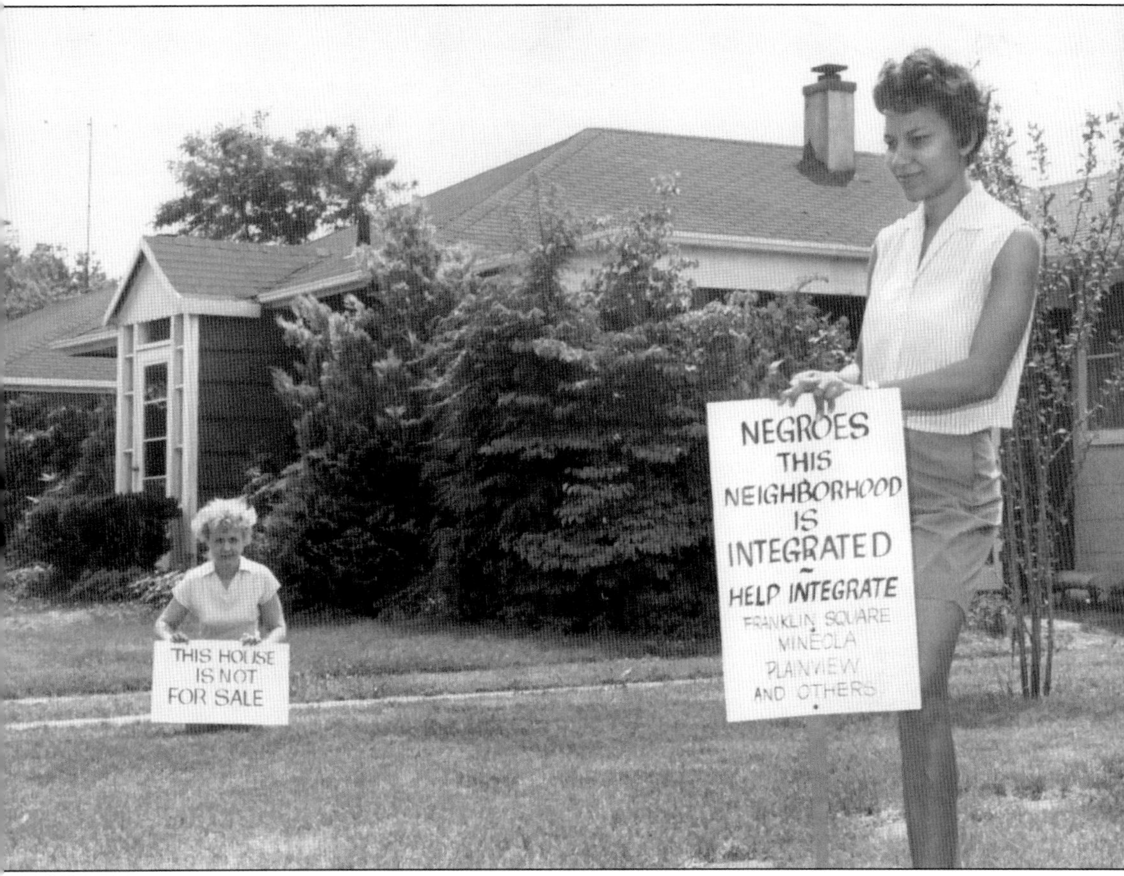

In this 1961 photograph, Mrs. Zaffe (left), a white resident of Lakeview, posts a sign that her home is not for sale. At right is Mrs. Lynch posting a sign for blacks to integrate other areas such as Plainview, Franklin Square, and Mineola. These signs were an attempt to create racial balance in Lakeview and prevent "white flight." (Newsday, LLC.)

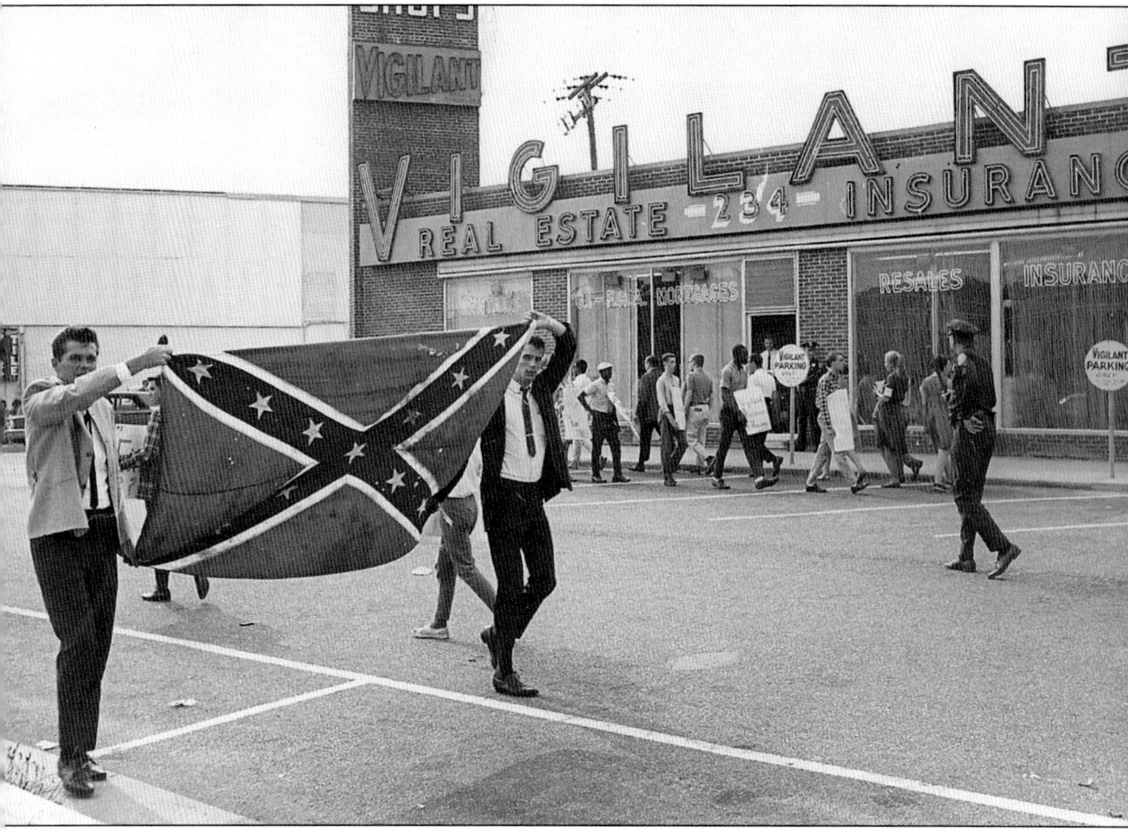

Local civil rights organizations such as CORE tested housing equality by encouraging blacks to buy homes in white areas. In August 1964, Vigilant Real Estate Company was accused of racially steering a black CORE member from a white area to buy a home. For eight days, CORE and religious leaders Rev. John Murphy of Rockville Center Diocese and Domenic Ciannella of Holy Trinity Episcopal Church picketed the realty company demanding a resolution. This protest attracted counter demonstrators from white racist groups. The total amount of demonstrators peaked at 900 people. (Newsday, LLC.)

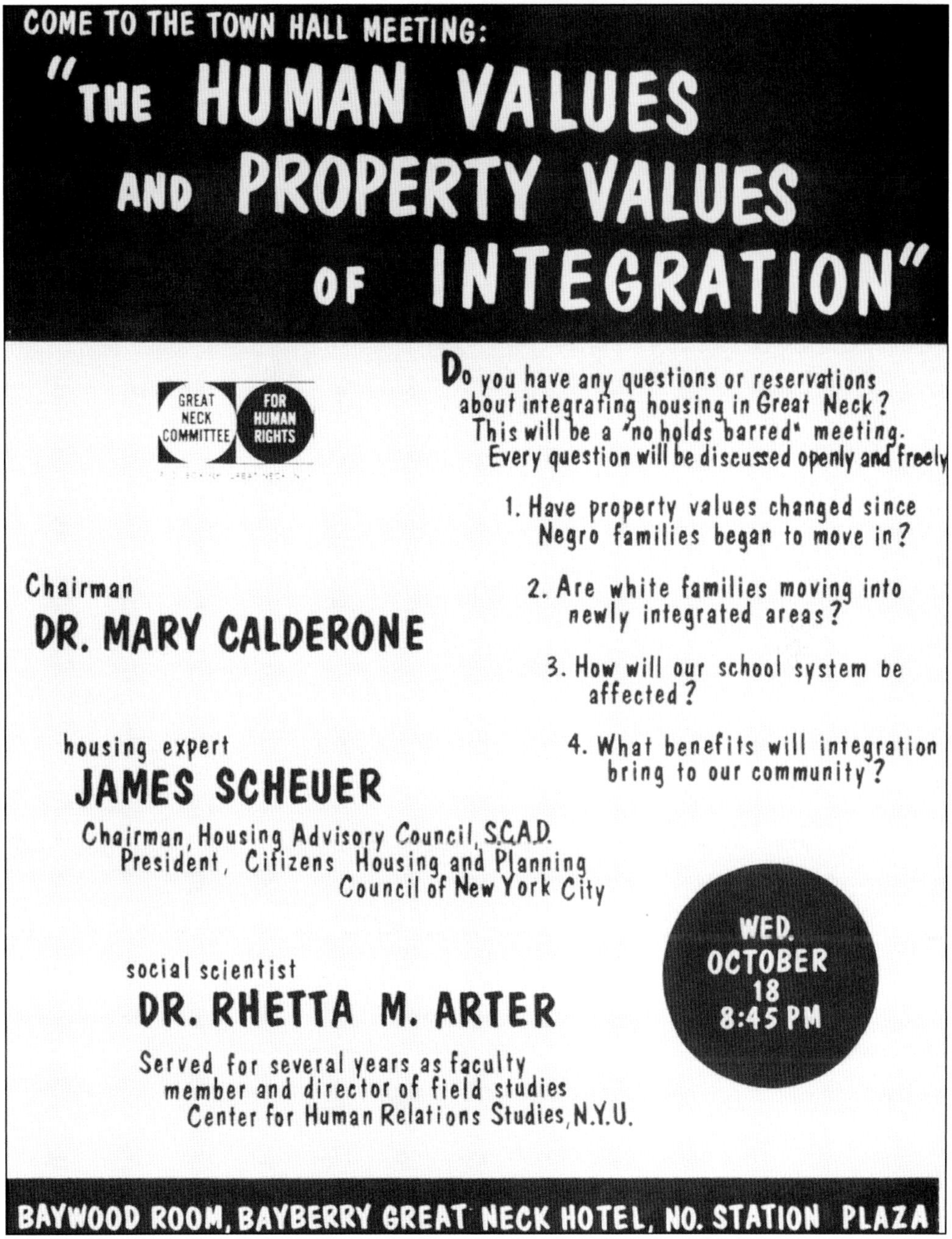

Town hall meetings were one of the most effective tactics to promote real estate integration. These meetings were held to identify a community's attitudes, beliefs, and biases on racial integration. Dr. Mary Calderone, chairperson of Great Neck's Human Rights Committee, extended her activism by becoming medical director of Planned Parenthood Federation of America. Dr. Calderone used her influence to promote racial equality. (Hofstra University Library Special Collections.)

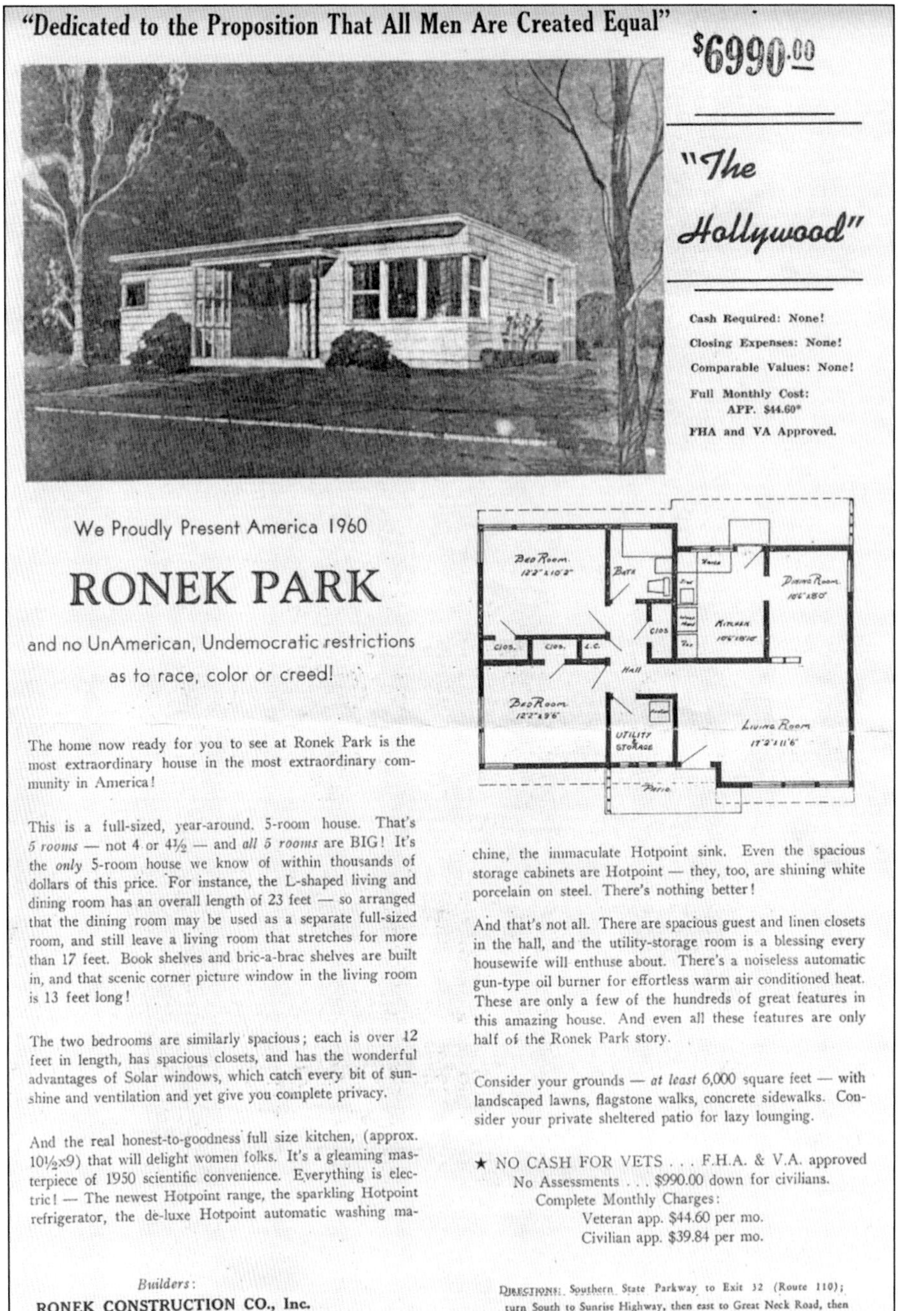

"Dedicated to the Proposition That All Men Are Created Equal"

$6990.00

"The Hollywood"

Cash Required: None!
Closing Expenses: None!
Comparable Values: None!
Full Monthly Cost: APP. $44.60*
FHA and VA Approved.

We Proudly Present America 1960

RONEK PARK

and no UnAmerican, Undemocratic restrictions as to race, color or creed!

The home now ready for you to see at Ronek Park is the most extraordinary house in the most extraordinary community in America!

This is a full-sized, year-around. 5-room house. That's *5 rooms* — not 4 or 4½ — and *all 5 rooms* are BIG! It's the *only* 5-room house we know of within thousands of dollars of this price. For instance, the L-shaped living and dining room has an overall length of 23 feet — so arranged that the dining room may be used as a separate full-sized room, and still leave a living room that stretches for more than 17 feet. Book shelves and bric-a-brac shelves are built in, and that scenic corner picture window in the living room is 13 feet long!

The two bedrooms are similarly spacious; each is over 12 feet in length, has spacious closets, and has the wonderful advantages of Solar windows, which catch every bit of sunshine and ventilation and yet give you complete privacy.

And the real honest-to-goodness full size kitchen, (approx. 10½x9) that will delight women folks. It's a gleaming masterpiece of 1950 scientific convenience. Everything is electric! — The newest Hotpoint range, the sparkling Hotpoint refrigerator, the de-luxe Hotpoint automatic washing machine, the immaculate Hotpoint sink. Even the spacious storage cabinets are Hotpoint — they, too, are shining white porcelain on steel. There's nothing better!

And that's not all. There are spacious guest and linen closets in the hall, and the utility-storage room is a blessing every housewife will enthuse about. There's a noiseless automatic gun-type oil burner for effortless warm air conditioned heat. These are only a few of the hundreds of great features in this amazing house. And even all these features are only half of the Ronek Park story.

Consider your grounds — *at least* 6,000 square feet — with landscaped lawns, flagstone walks, concrete sidewalks. Consider your private sheltered patio for lazy lounging.

★ NO CASH FOR VETS . . . F.H.A. & V.A. approved
No Assessments . . . $990.00 down for civilians.
Complete Monthly Charges:
Veteran app. $44.60 per mo.
Civilian app. $39.84 per mo.

Builders:
RONEK CONSTRUCTION CO., Inc.
TEL. AMITYVILLE 741

DIRECTIONS: Southern State Parkway to Exit 32 (Route 110); turn South to Sunrise Highway, then east to Great Neck Road, then North to the Exhibit home at Great Neck Rd., Amityville.

African Americans who were turned away from developments such as Levittown had very few options in achieving home ownership in Long Island. Builder Thomas Romano purchased 147 acres of land in North Amityville for the construction of over 1,000 homes. These homes were not to compete with Levitt & Sons but were marketed to people who shared the ideas of resisting the "Undemocratic restrictions as to race, color or creed." This development became known as Ronek Park. (Historic Photograph and Postcard Collection of the Town of Babylon, Office of Historic Services.)

The Ronek Park homes were five rooms on 5,000-square-foot lots. They came in a flat-roofed California-style model or a thatched-roof Cape Cod. The homes' starting price was $6,999, with financing provided. The Ronek community attracted black families from all across the five boroughs of the city. The community became a hotbed for local civil rights activism. Activists such as Dr. Eugene Reed of the NAACP and Irwin Quintyne of CORE exported the communities' founding principles across Long Island and the five boroughs. (Both, Eugene Burnett Collection.)

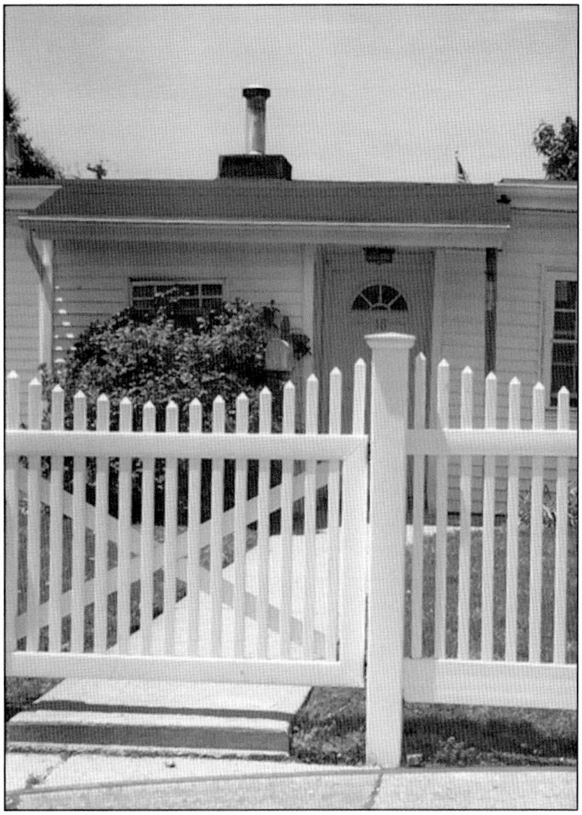

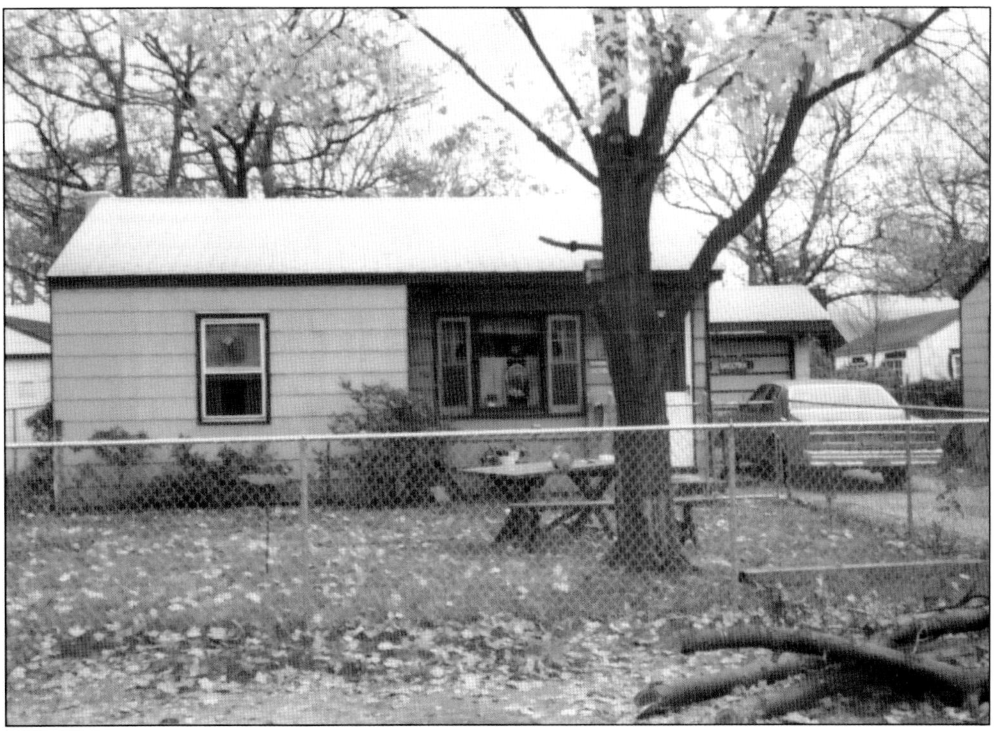

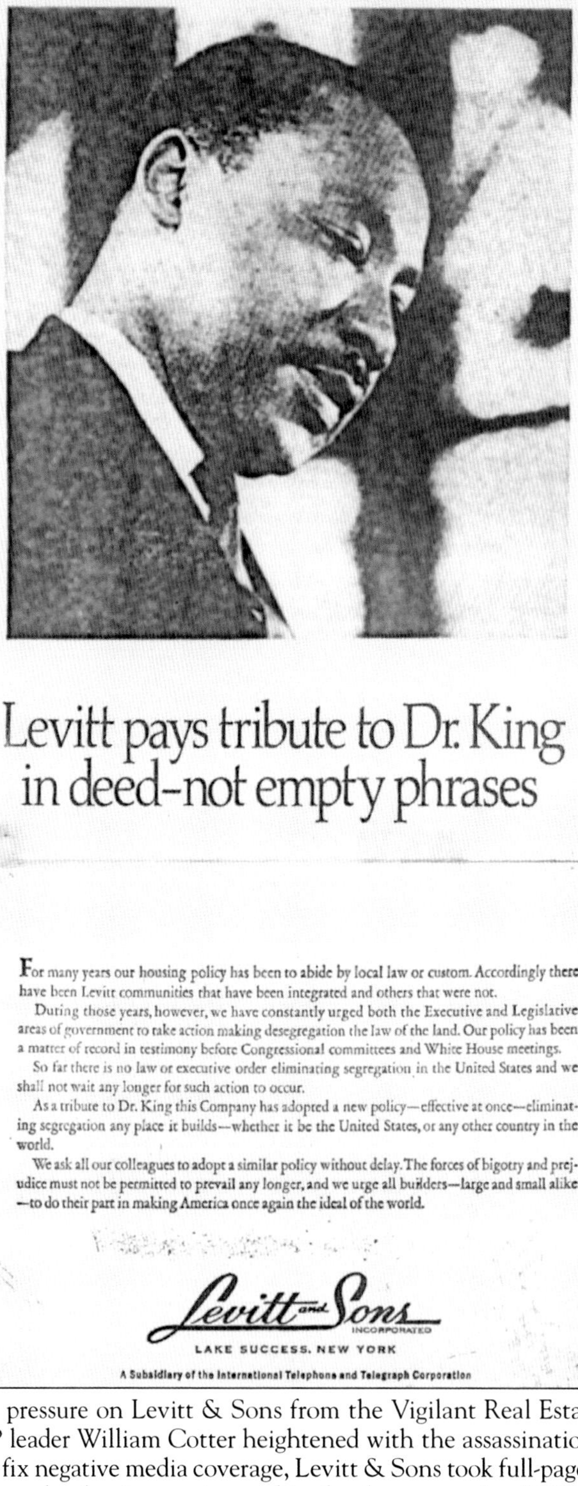

Social and political pressure on Levitt & Sons from the Vigilant Real Estate protests and the eviction of NAACP leader William Cotter heightened with the assassination of Martin Luther King. In an effort to fix negative media coverage, Levitt & Sons took full-page ads in local papers announcing a policy to develop integration within developments. As of 2010, Levittown is close to 90 percent white and less than one percent black. (Levittown Library historical archives.)

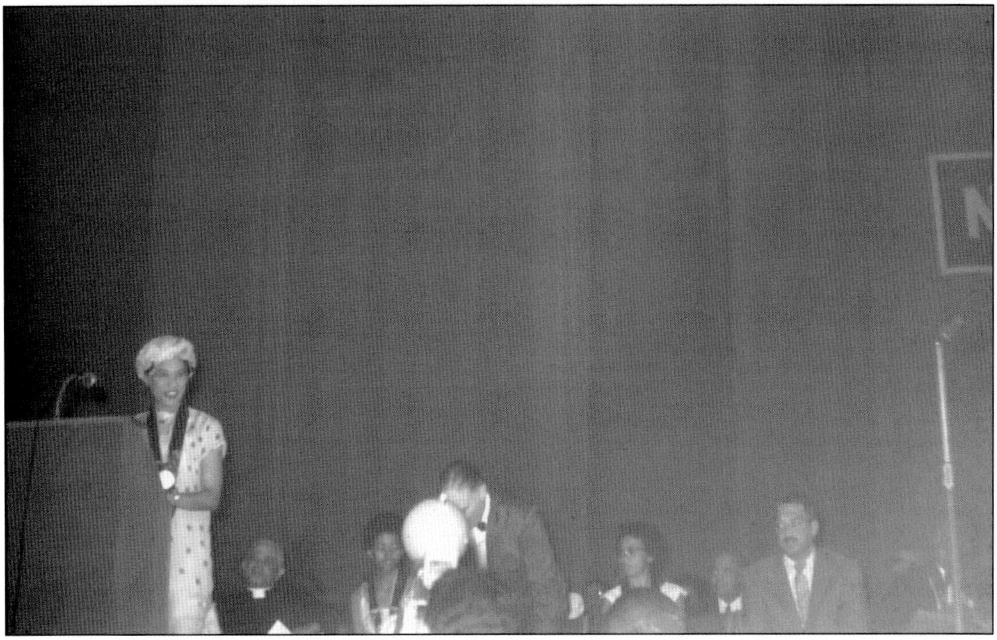

Catholic church St. Martin of Tours in Amityville hosted NAACP events and lecturers that brought awareness to racial and economic inequalities. The chief counsel for the NAACP, Thurgood Marshall, visited the parish in 1959. Eight years later, Marshall would become the first African American justice on the US Supreme Court. The lecturer was centered on the school segregation of Northern suburbia. Marshall's visit came during a local school integration battle that called for Amityville schools to get rid of zoned elementary schools. (Both, Eugene Burnett Collection.)

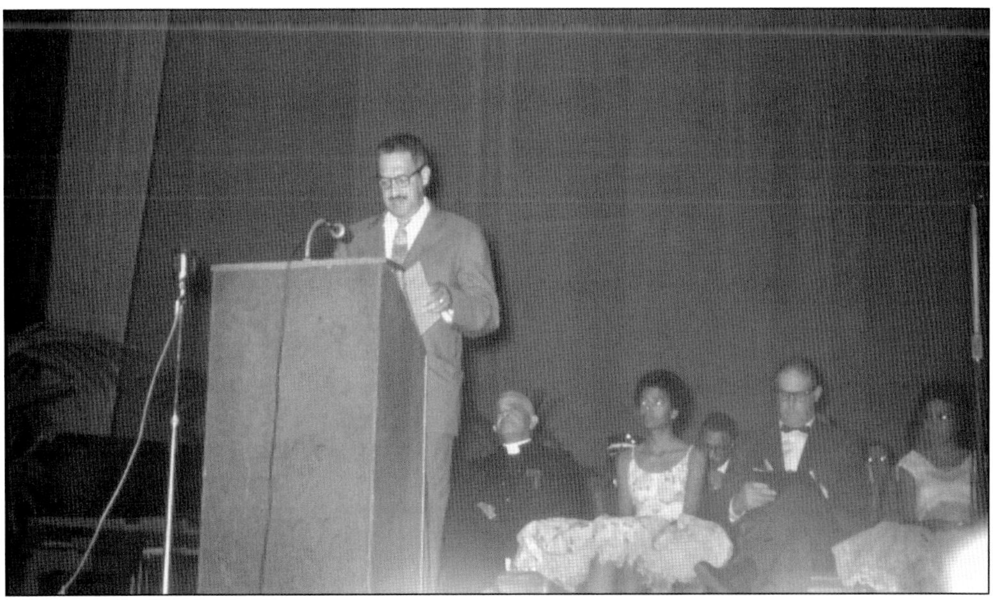

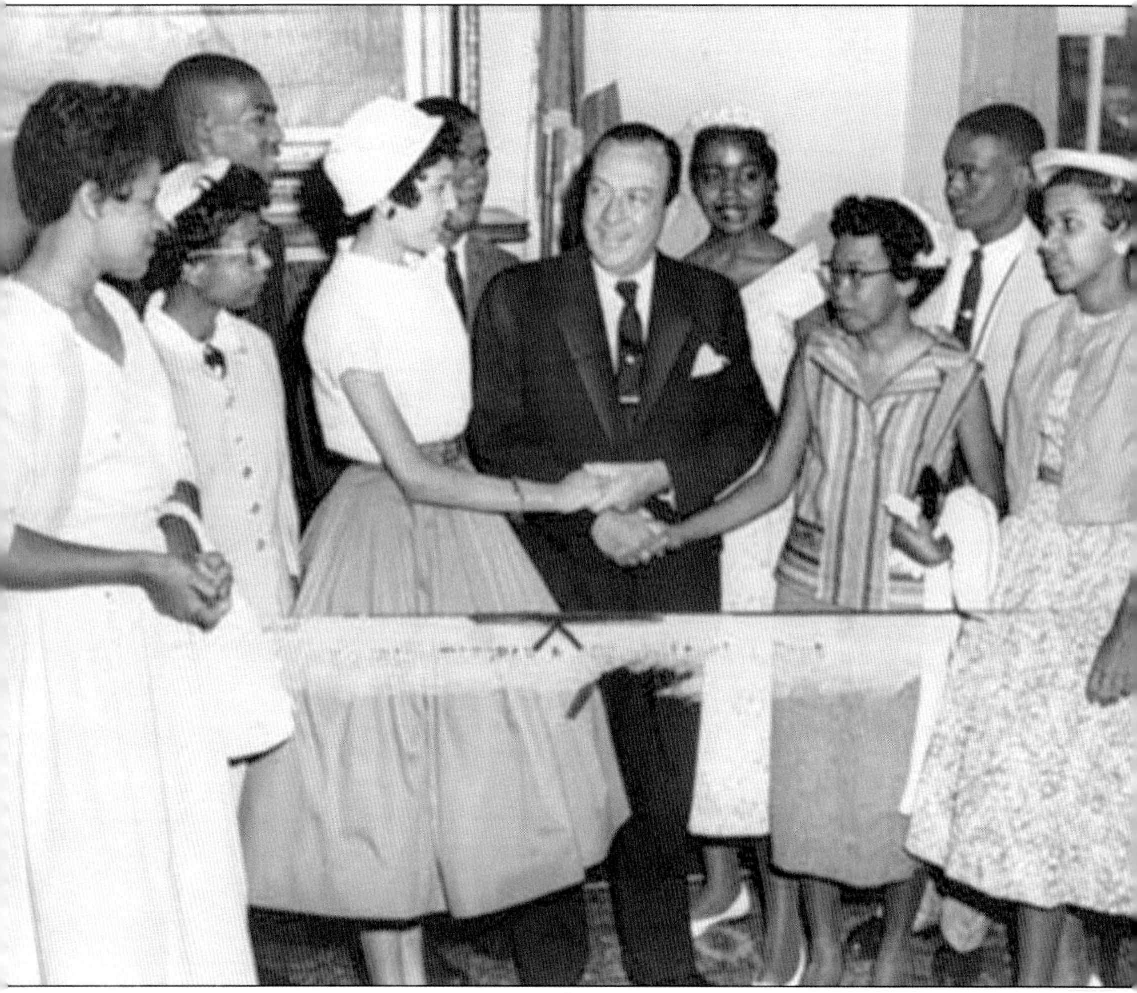

Pictured above, New York City mayor Robert Wagner greets the teenagers who integrated Central High School in Little Rock, Arkansas. While mayor of New York City, Wagner presided over white middle-class residents migrating to the suburbs, while blacks and Puerto Ricans were moving into the city with hopes of less racial discrimination. Blacks and Puerto Ricans started to pressure the mayor and state officials to create a school integration plan by boycotting to local schools. These boycotts and the growing diversity accelerated the population growth of Nassau and Suffolk Counties. (Library of Congress.)

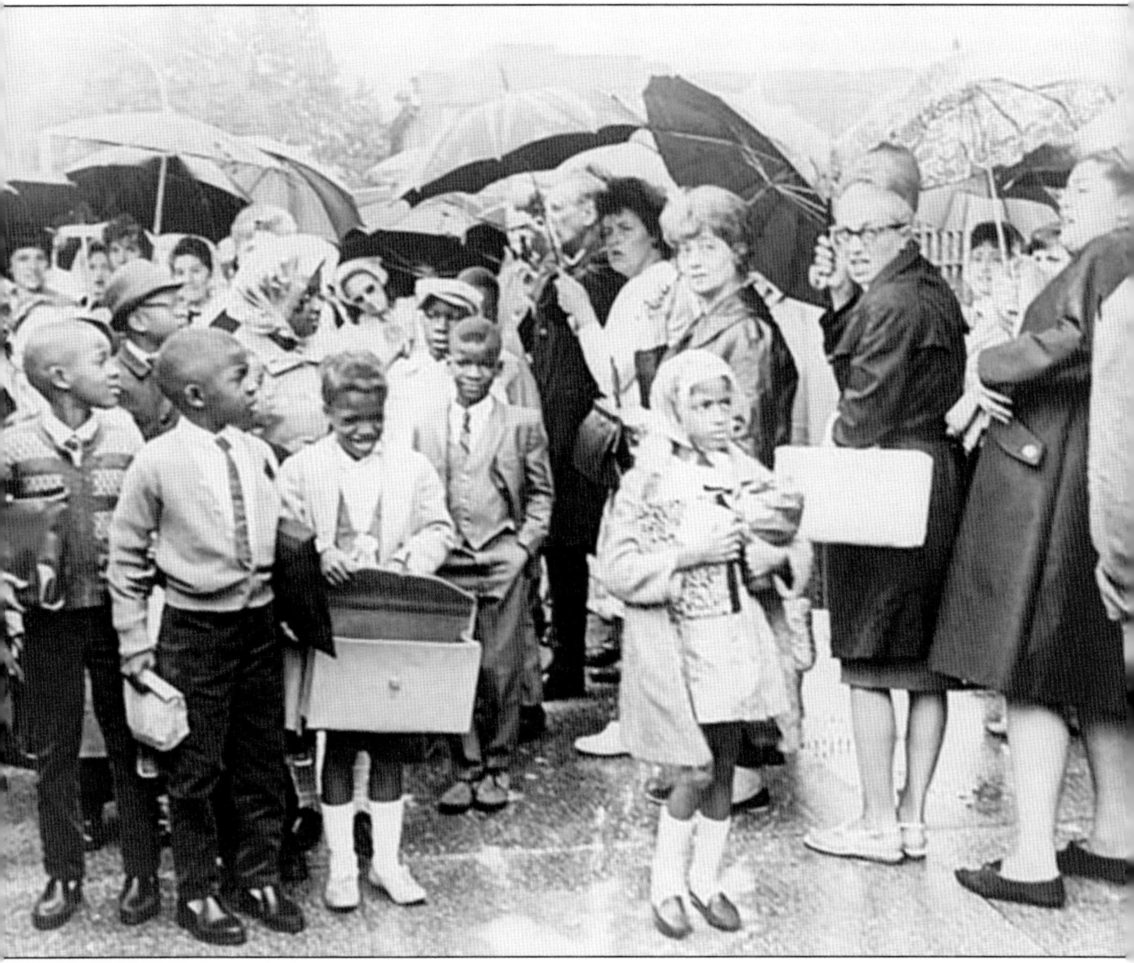

African American children are pictured on their way to school (Public School 204 at Eighty-Second Street and Fifteenth Avenue) while white mothers protest the busing of children to achieve integration. Mayor Wagner struggled to stay out of school integration issues. With pressure from New York State governor Nelson Rockefeller, Wagner's administration developed rezoning plans to create a racial balance. He was criticized by whites for breaking up neighborhoods and by blacks for integrating too slow. In the years to come, elected officials across Long Island were going to face the same dilemmas. (Library of Congress.)

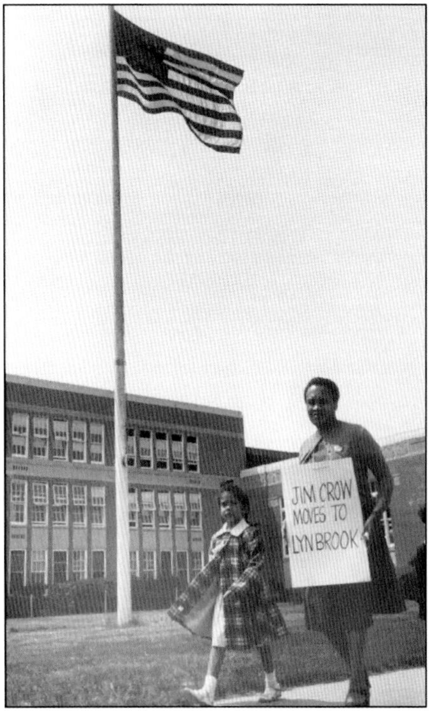

Long Island schools are zoned along residential borders. These boundaries in most cases reflect the racial demographics of neighborhoods; zoned schools create segregated schools. Malverne School District became highly contested due to the racial demographics of the two areas the school serviced. Lakeview is an African American neighborhood and Malverne a white neighborhood that shared the same district but had zoned elementary schools that kept the districts segregated. The image at left shows Mrs. Walter A Parker picketing with five-year-old Katheryn Parker. The Parkers are demanding Malverne create a plan for a racially integrated district. (Newsday, LLC.)

Woodfield Road School within Malverne District was 80-percent African American. Most of the students at the school were residents of Lakeview. The community organized against segregation in the school with the help of the NAACP, CORE, the United Committee for Action Now, and various religious groups. Below, students picket the Woodfield Road School. (Newsday, LLC.)

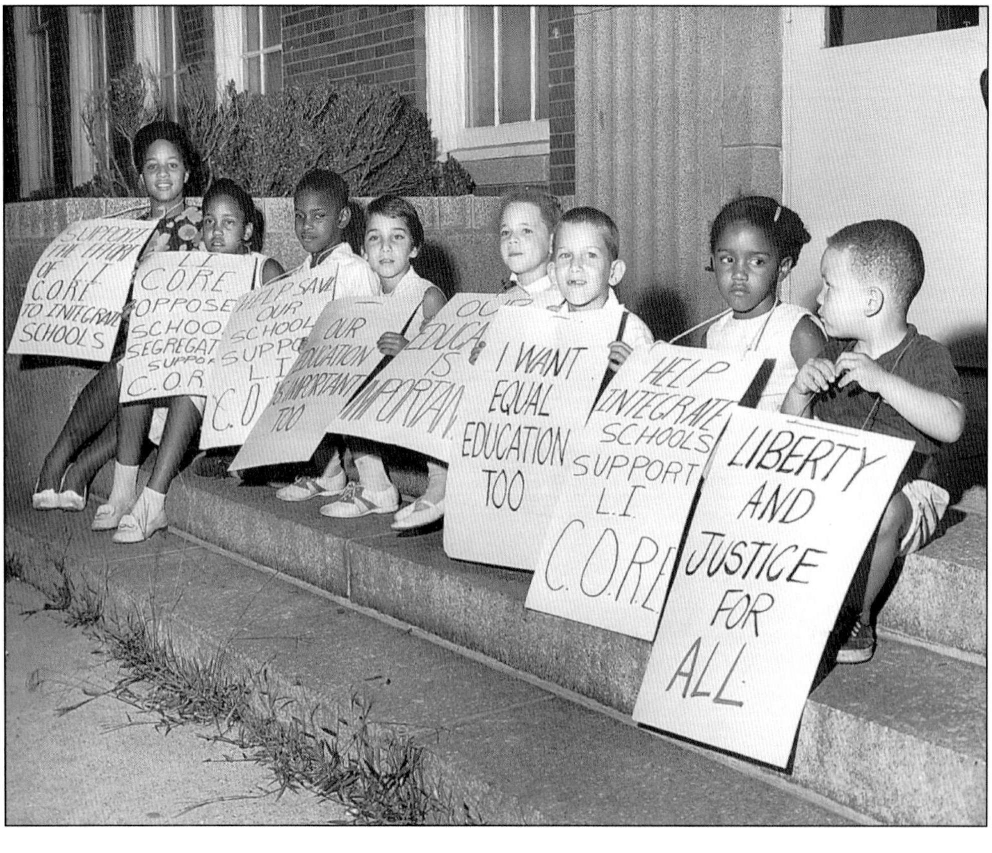

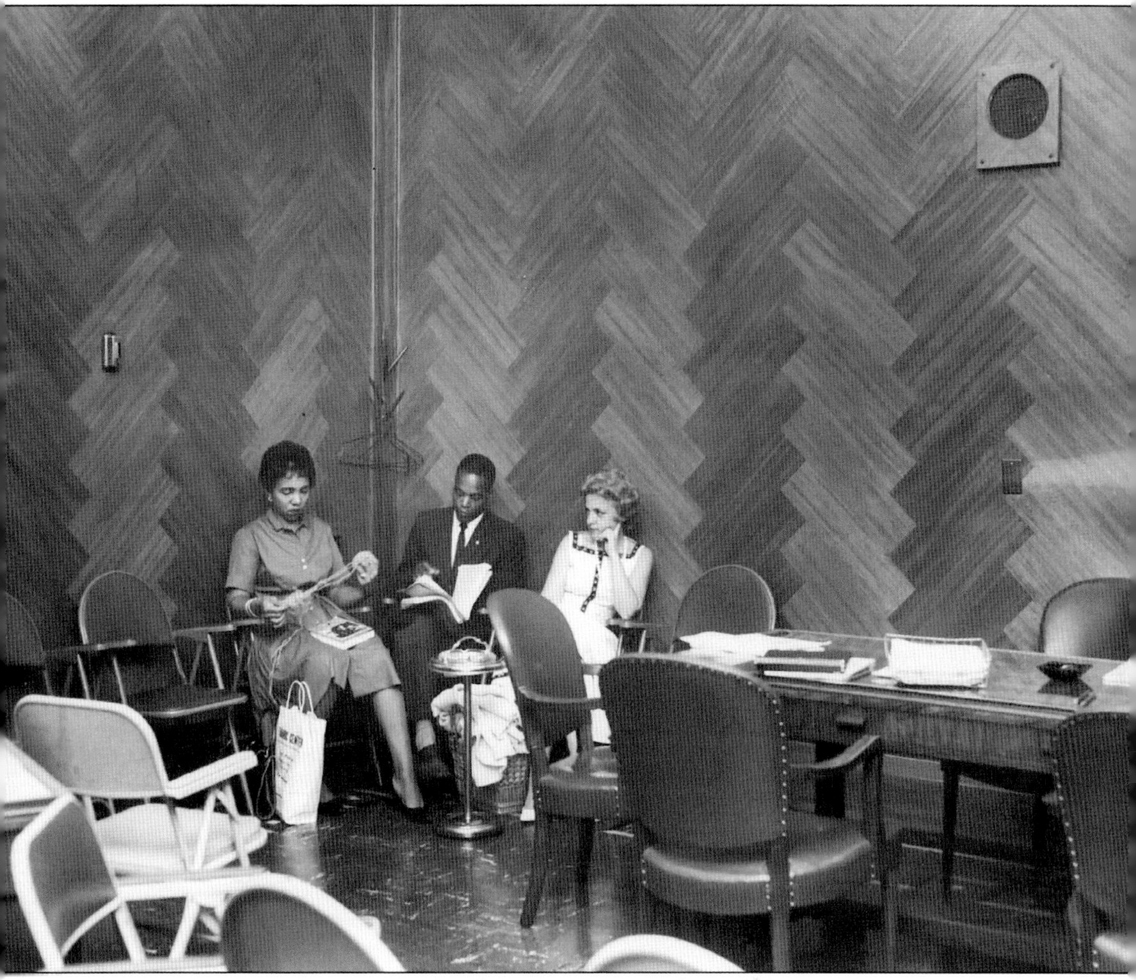

To attract attention to the issue of school segregation, members of the Lakeview community and CORE staged a hunger strike at Malverne High School. Pictured above is Joyce McCroy, Lincoln Lynch, and Bea Zaffe conducting their strike. Media attention of the picketing and hunger strikes forced Dr. James Allen, state commissioner of education, to formulate a plan for integration. Malverne School District was ordered to adopt the Princeton model. This model is based on students' grade levels in schools as compared to the residential zoning of schools. (Newsday, LLC.)

TAP Taxpayers And Parents, asso.

P. O. BOX 231
MALVERNE, NEW YORK

October 27, 1965

Dear Neighbor,

Since it involves your home and children I am sure you know that the Supreme Court has refused to listen to our appeal. This means that Commissioner Allen has the power to force us to adopt the Princeton Plan, as he ordered us to do over two years ago.

Of course the plan will fail. But it will do more than just fail--it will destroy the presently integrated Malverne School District and create in its place, a "resegregated" school district.

A "resegregated" district is one that has passed from being predominately white to being predominately Negro.

Acting Supt Said Plan will Succeed

In the last three years the very threat of the Princeton Plan has changed Malvern School District #12 dramatically.

Now more than 50% of the pupils in the combined lower grades and Junior High School are Negro--and that percentage grows day by day.

Acting Supt Said Not So

Only the prospect of the institution of the Princeton Plan was enough to cause white people with children of school age, with rare exception, to refuse to move into our district, (unless their children were expected to go to private schools). Look around you--see what kind of families move out of our school district,--and see what kind move in. The normal replacement of older families with grown children by younger families with school-age children is simply not taking place.

Acting Supt Said Not So

Even though not a single Negro family has moved into the Lynbrook or Malverne sections of our school district and white adults outnumber Negro adults more than two to one, Negro children have become the majority in our schools! And the percentage grows day by day!

Unless the threat of the Princeton Plan is removed forthwith this trend will continue, until a white child in the public schools will be an oddity.

Parents simply will not tolerate their children being bussed out of their neighborhoods involuntarily!

Commissioner Allen found that out in New York City when white children "evaporated" from his "integrated" bussed Princeton Plan School districts.

No court can prevent white parents from moving out of school districts, nor Negro parents from moving in. While lawyers were arguing and judges deliberating that's just what has been happening in Malverne School District #12. But, once the Princeton Plan is implemented, what has been the wind of change will become a hurricane of destruction. That's how it happened elsewhere and that's what must happen here.

No Negro live in Malverne

And that is why the Princeton Plan is "dead" in New York City, with NAACP and CORE consent and approval.

But the school areas in New York City on which it was tried are "dead" too--that is, dead to integration, they have become predominately Negro areas.

Must this happen to Malverne School District #12?

Must we become a "resegregated" Negro School District?

Not necessarily.

Not if Commissioner Allen withdraws from backing the Princeton Plan in Malverne, as he withdrew from backing the Princeton Plan in New York City.

And how can this happen? If, in any way, it can be caused by your letters. All you parents and taxpayers, white and Negro, must write Commissioner Allen demanding that he kill the Princeton Plan. If you don't, you will have no one to blame but yourself when you end up with a segregated all Negro Malverne School District #12. The address is:

Dr. James E. Allen, Jr.
Commissioner of Education
State Education Department
Albany, New York

Charles W. Reardon, Pres.
Taxpayers and Parents Association

Malverne community members formed a segregationist group called Taxpayers and Parents Association. This group rallied the white residents to collectively file lawsuits to halt the plan. In response to the white community of Malverne, state senator Norman Lent proposed amendments to state educational law that barred transporting children to create integration. Above is a pamphlet arguing that the Princeton Plan will make Malverne School District resegregated by a black majority student population. (Library of Congress.)

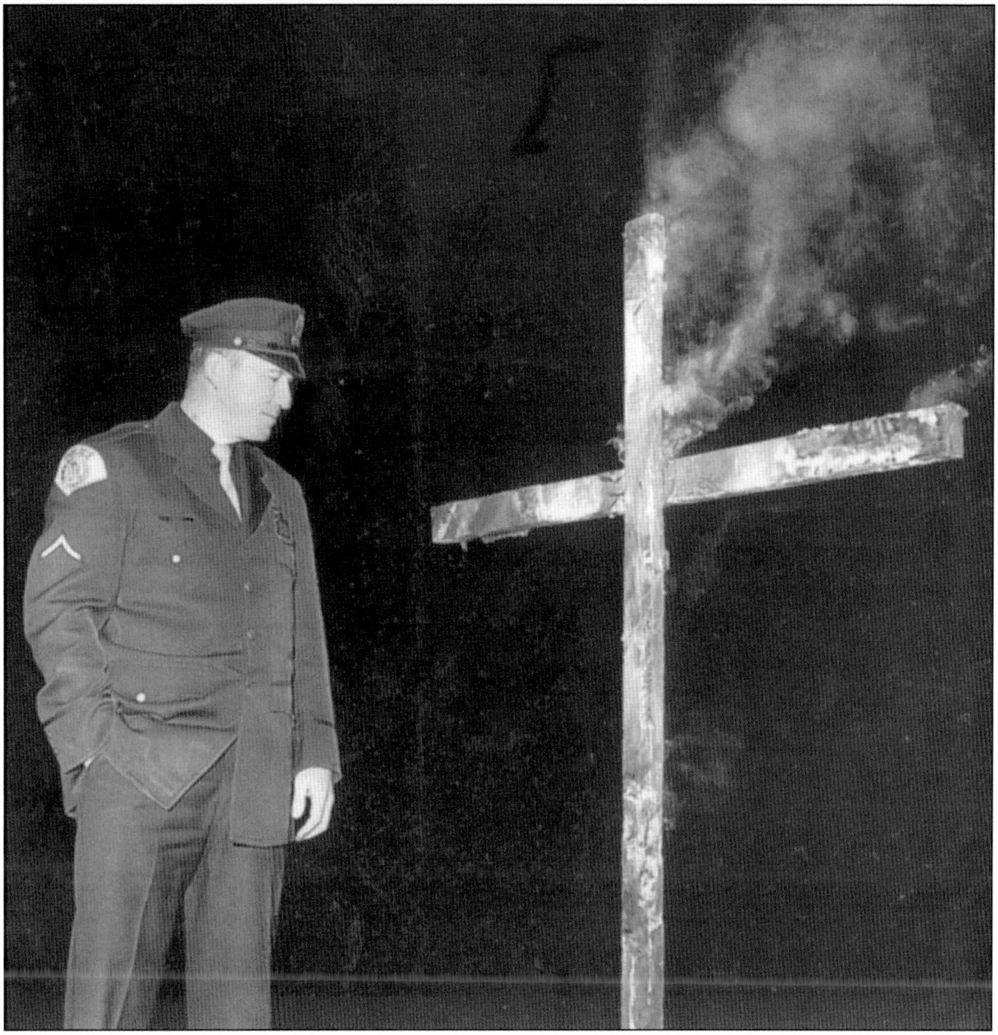

Following three years of failed Supreme Court appeals and lawsuits, the community resistance became national news. To avoid further media attention, Commissioner Allen's order to integrate the school was agreed on by the Malverne Board of Education. Following the approval, local residents burned a cross in front of the high school to intimidate the African American community. (Newsday, LLC.)

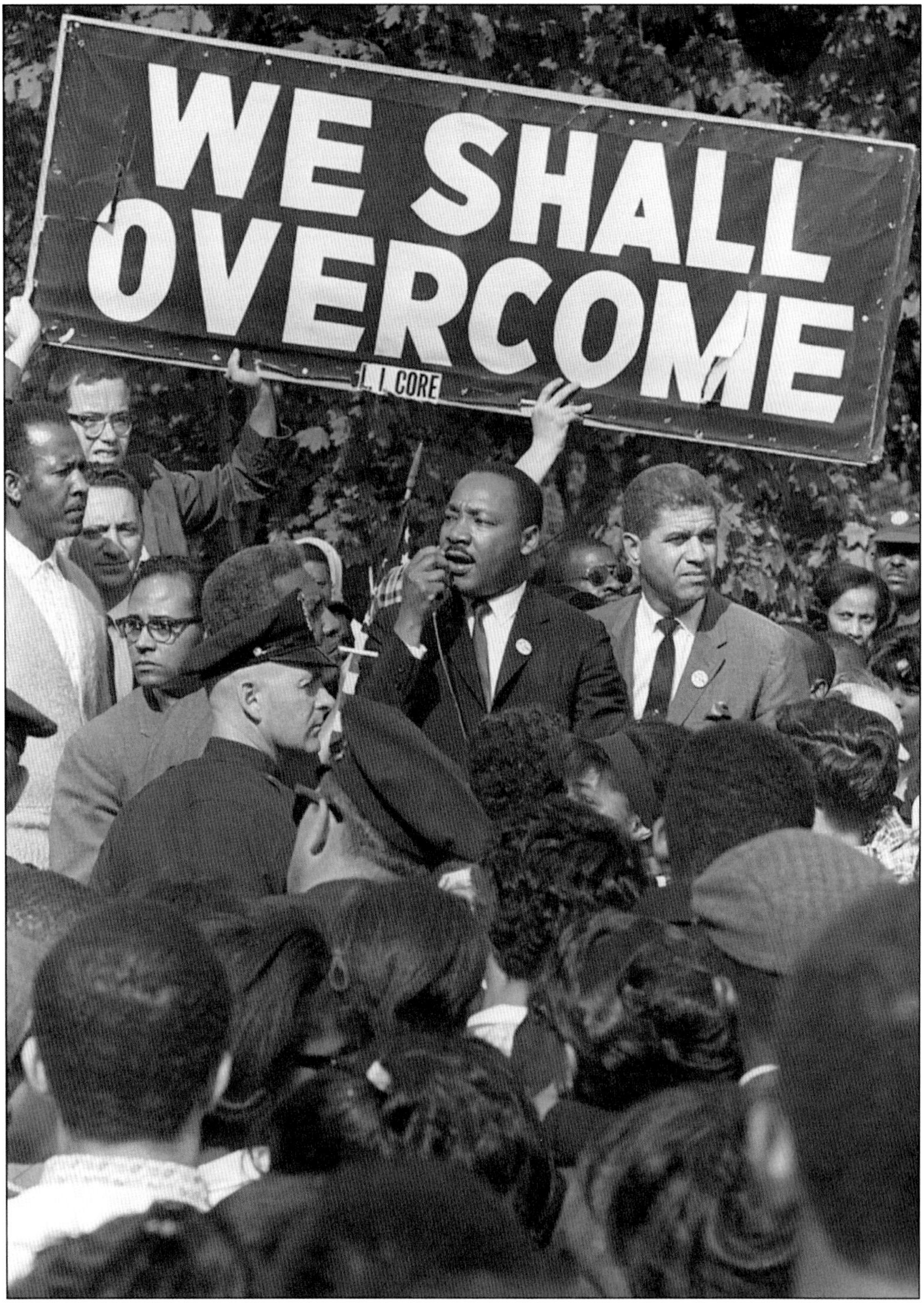

Malverne School District brought the attention of national civil rights figure Rev. Martin Luther King. This was the first of many notable visits of Reverend King. While visiting, King toured communities such as Lakeview that were struggling with de facto segregation. During his visit, he announced his support for CORE and their goals. His endorsement helped to raise more volunteers and money for the activists' campaigns. (Newsday, LLC.)

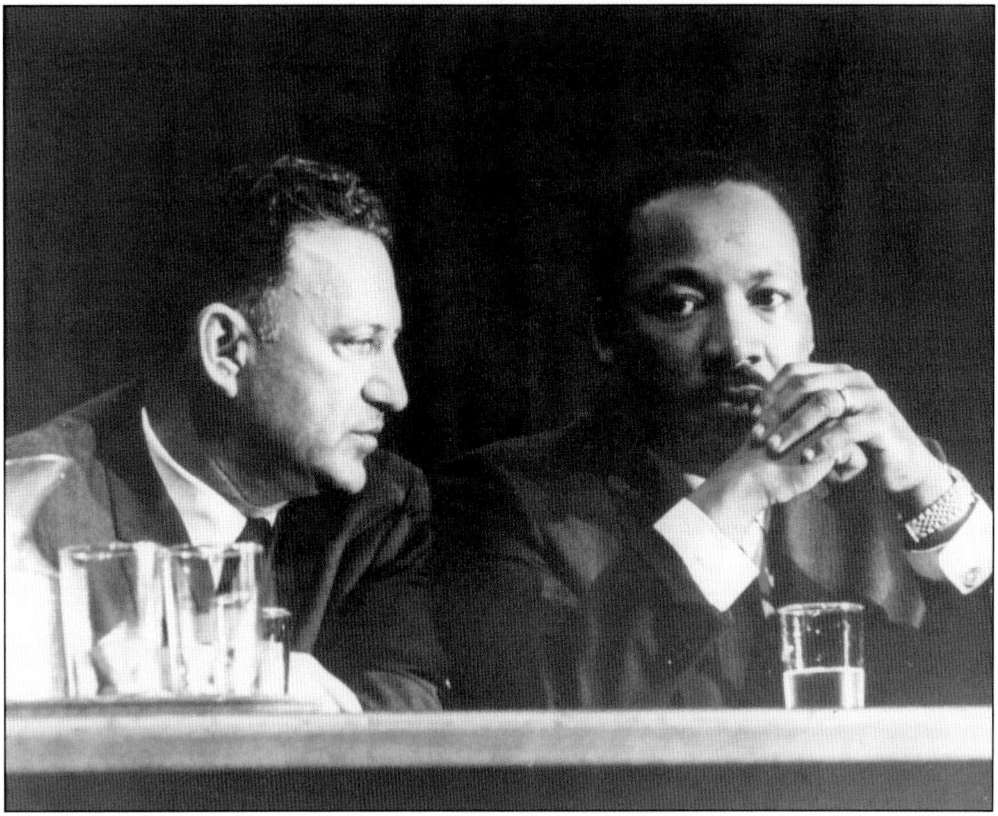

Civil rights activism was not confined to community grassroots organizations or church groups but played a key role among academic communities as well. Hofstra University became a hub in civil rights activists' recruitment. Faculty member Harry Wachtel became known for being Martin Luther King's attorney. His work inspired students to become active in national campaigns such as the march in Selma, Alabama. Pictured above are Harry Wachtel and Martin Luther King. (Hofstra University Library Special Collections.)

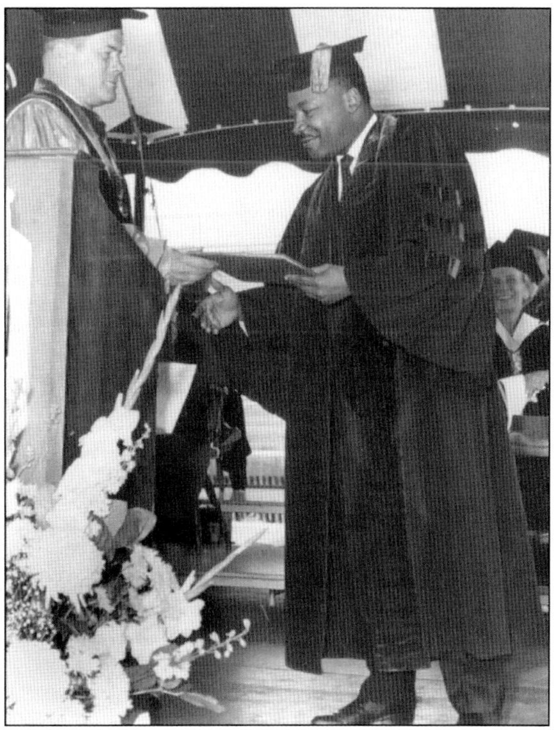

The 1965 graduating class and faculty of Hofstra University presented Martin Luther King with an honorary doctorate. During the commencement ceremony, he discussed de facto segregation and the power of student activism. (Hofstra University Library Special Collections.)

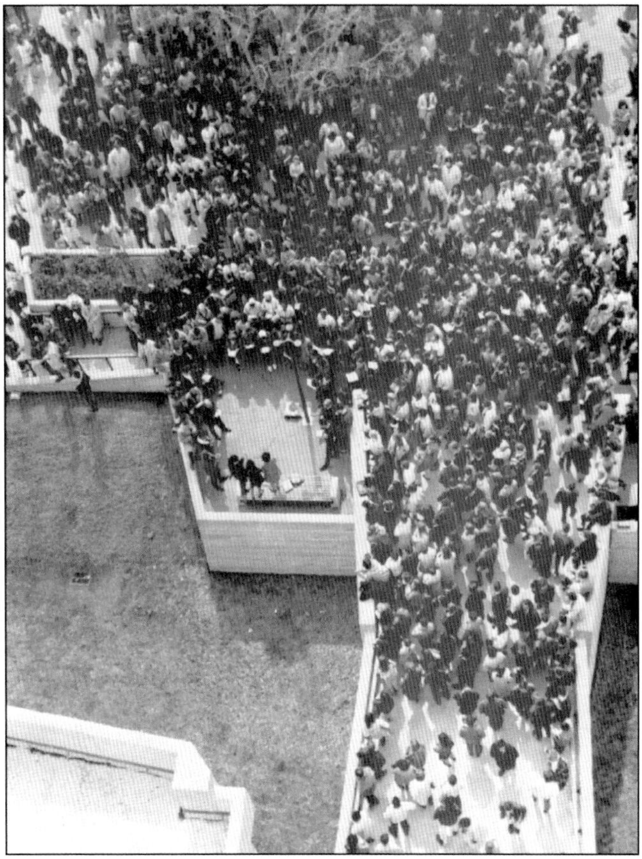

The late 1960s brought student unrest among college campuses throughout the country. Hofstra University faced the same challenges. In the spring semester of 1969, students against the Vietnam War and black rights groups collectively boycotted, took over buildings on campus, and staged marches down Hempstead Turnpike expressing their discontent with the university curriculum. Students' demands included adding classes that reflected growing social issues, canceling ROTC classes, increasing diversity among faculty members, and providing resources that would represent all ethnic and racial groups of the college community. (Both, Hofstra University Library Special Collections.)

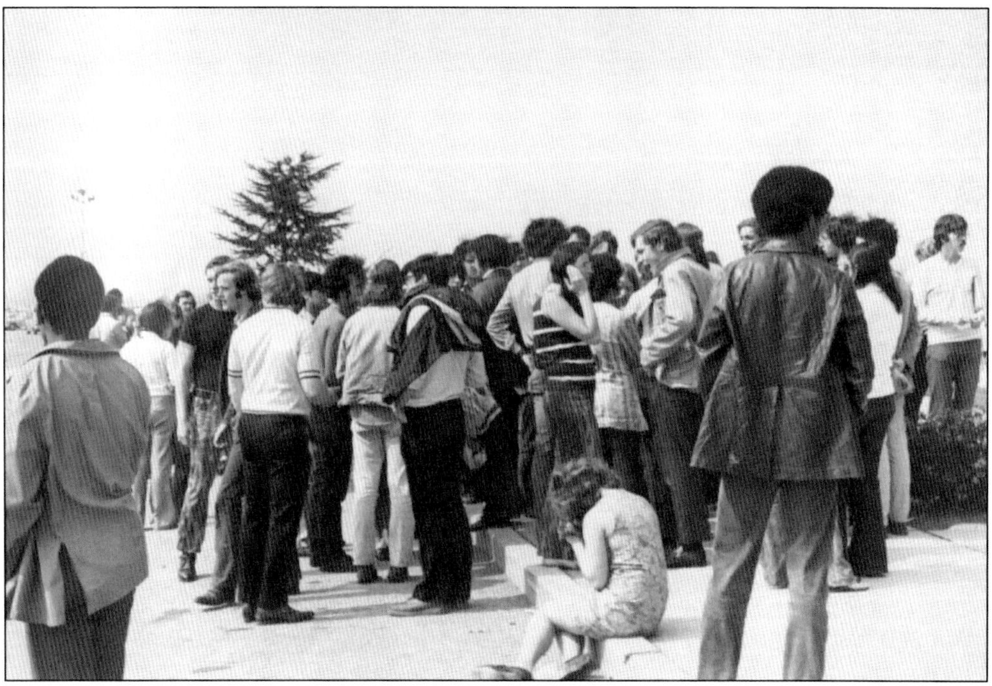

OBC

ORGANIZATION OF BLACK COLLEGIANS

(Student Center-Rm. 206)
Hofstra University
Hempstead, N.Y. 11550

To: Department Chairmen
From: Mr. Frank Smith, Minister of Foreign Affairs - O.B.C.
Re: Recruitment of Black Faculty

In a memo dated February 5, 1969, to the students and faculty of Hofstra University, President Lord " urged the chairmen of the academic departments to give special consideration to the addition of qualified Blacks to the faculty."

The Organization of Black Collegians considers the hiring of Black faculty of paramount importance; therefore, we are asking each department chairman what he has done to comply with President Lord's request. Your reply, which is imperative that O.B.C. have before September 28, 1970, can be sent to our Student Center address.

We are thanking you in advance for an anticipated early reply.

Respectfully,

Frank Smith, Minister of Foreign Affairs

cc: Clifford Lord
Canute Parris

RECEIVED
SEP 28 1970
Office of President

Student academic organizations such as the Organization of Black Collegians (OBC) focused on having the university reflect African American culture. OBC petitioned the administration to hire black faculty members, purchase more books on black literature, create degree programs in African American culture, and accept more blacks to the freshman class. The letter above is a request from OBC to hire more qualified black faculty. (Hofstra University Library Special Collections.)

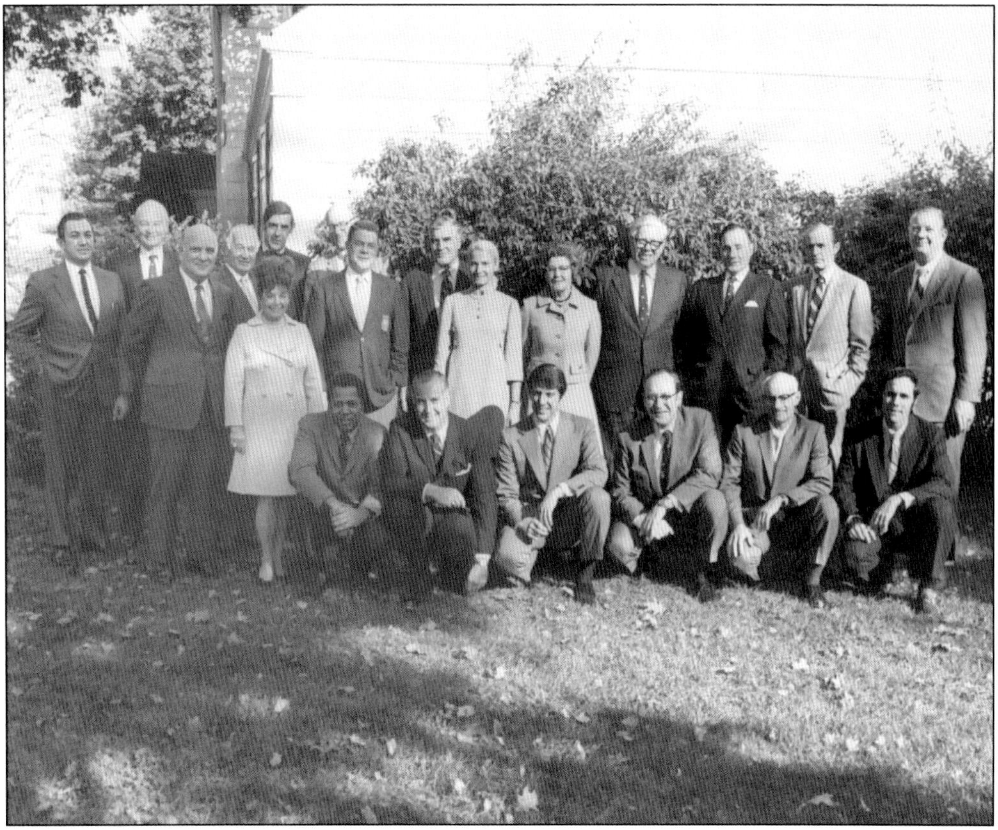

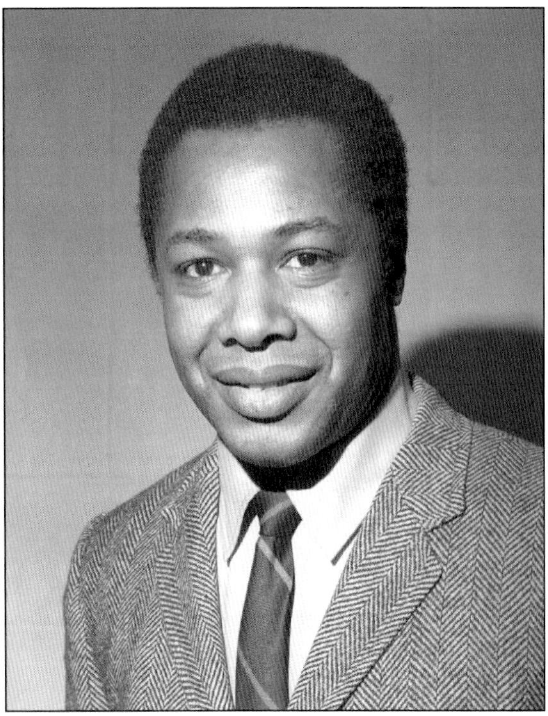

OBC was successful in its demands for diversity among the Hofstra faculty. In March 1970, Lamar Cox became the first black trustee of Hofstra University. Lamar severed as a trustee from 1970 to 1976. Cox's social activism background includes establishing the Long Island Council for Integrated Housing, chairing of Long Island CORE and the Alliance of Minority Leaders, and directing Hempstead's Employment Opportunity Corporation. Cox assisted in organizing CORE leadership schools across local colleges and universities. These leadership programs trained students to coordinate large-scale boycotts and civil disobedience campaigns. The photograph above shows the 1970 Hofstra Board of Trustees. (Both, Hofstra University Library Special Collections.)

Louis Lomax is known for being the first African American television journalist. Lomax's freelance work included articles related to the Nation of Islam, Black Panther Party, and other Black Power groups or movements. Hofstra administration was petitioned by OBC and other student groups to hire Lomax as a full-time faculty member. The administration agreed and hired Lomax, but his career was short lived due to his fatal car accident in 1970. (Hofstra University Library Special Collections.)

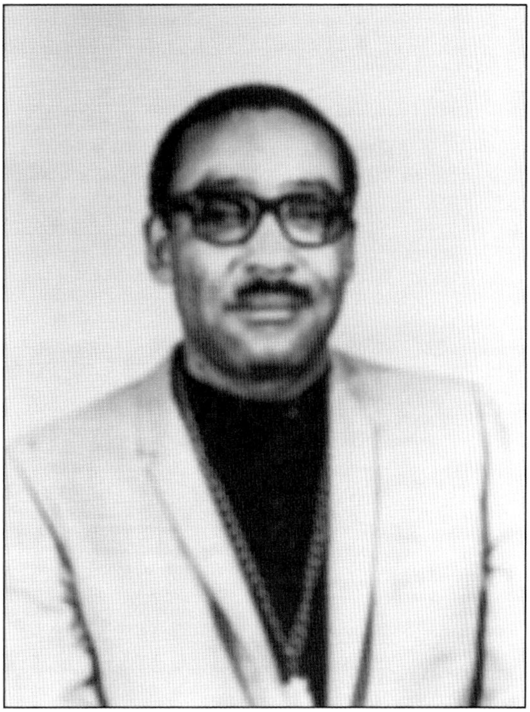

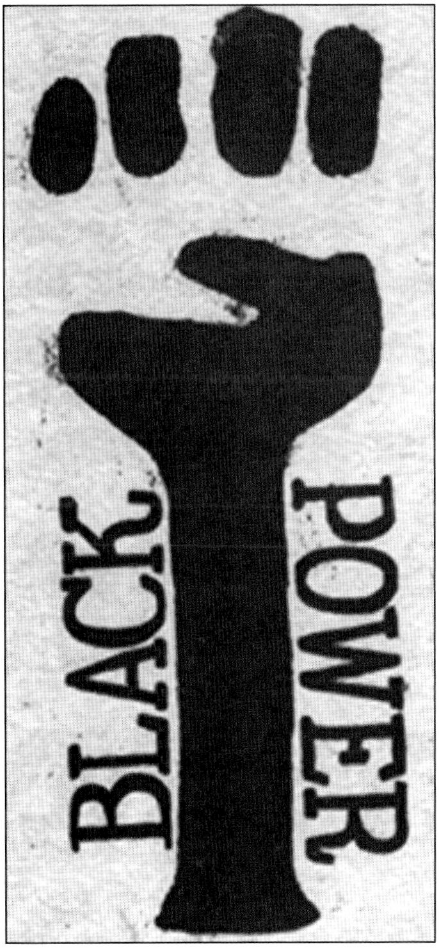

With the rise of student activism, Black Power started to be embraced. Members of OBC organized a section in the *Hofstra Chronicle* called Black Power. This section was focused on embracing local and national black culture. It conducted interviews with black leaders such as Shirley Chisholm. (Hofstra University Library Special Collections.)

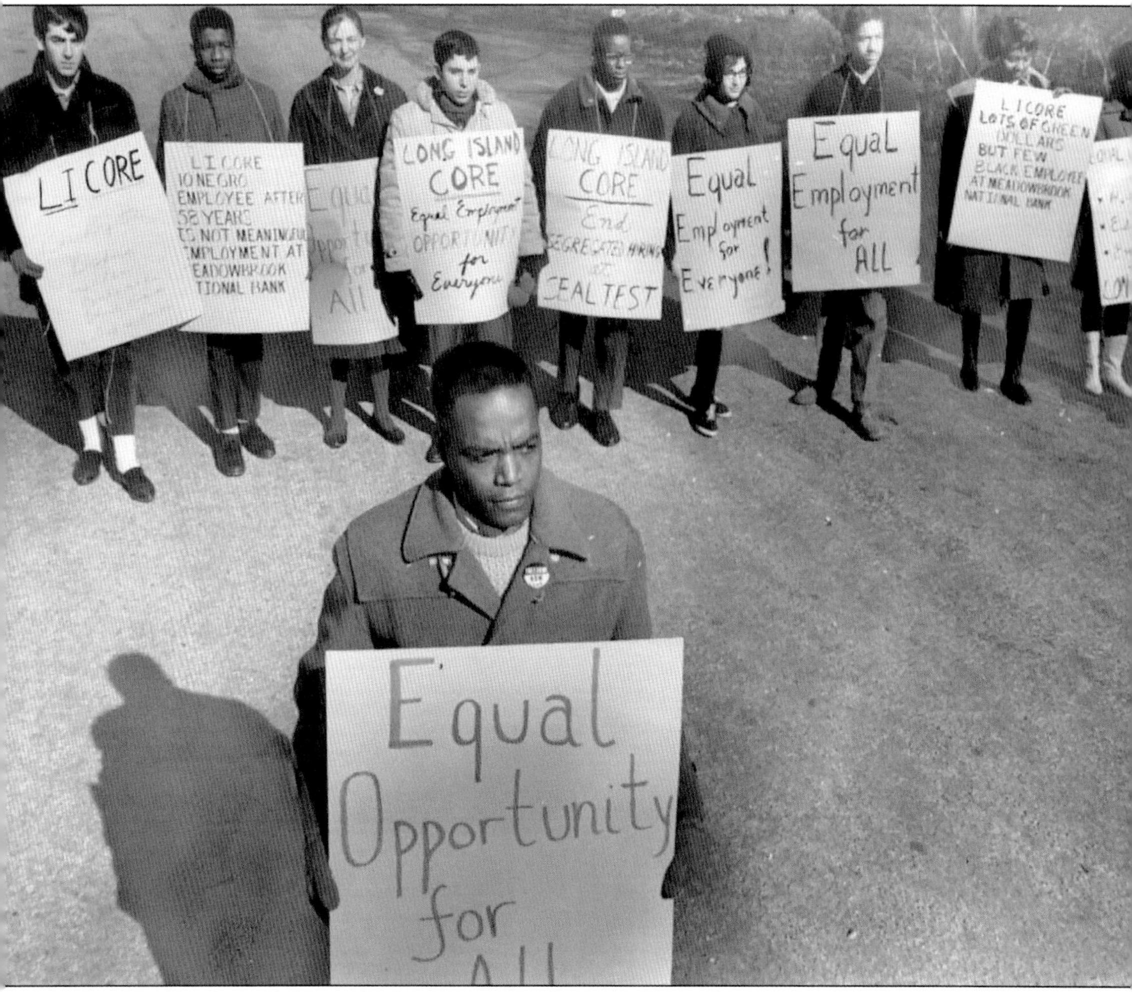

Local banks and the civil rights movement historically conflicted. Banks using unethical lending practices to prevent construction and restricting employment have been contested by CORE and the NAACP. Franklin National Banks employed an estimated 1,200 people, but only 15 were black or Latino. CORE picketed and boycotted Franklin National, demanding that 50 percent of all new hires be black or Latino. Following success against Franklin, Meadow Brook National Bank was targeted next to change its hiring policies. Pictured above is the Meadow Brook National Bank protest and boycott. (Newsday LLC.)

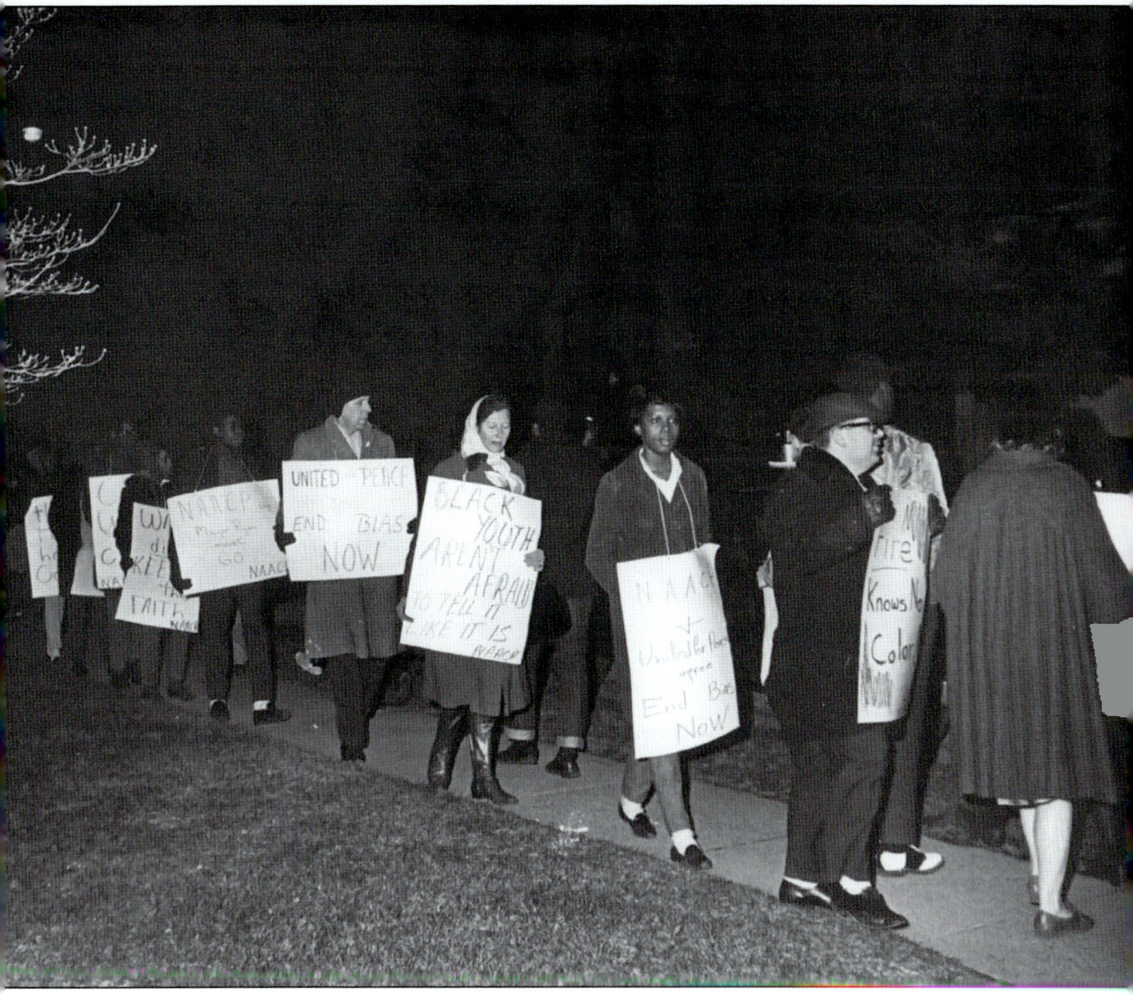

Discrimination in local fire departments was widespread throughout Long Island. Nassau County had only one black fireman. Gordon Heights, Suffolk County, was the first integrated fire department in New York State. The racial gains of Gordon Heights were limited due to the lack of tax revenue from a small commercial tax base. CORE conducted demonstrations at firefighter tournaments and local politicians' offices to demand fire departments accept nonwhite recruits. Above, CORE is demonstrating in front of Hempstead mayor Walter Ryan's house. Hempstead's fire department was the slowest department in a black community to integrate. (Newsday, LLC.)

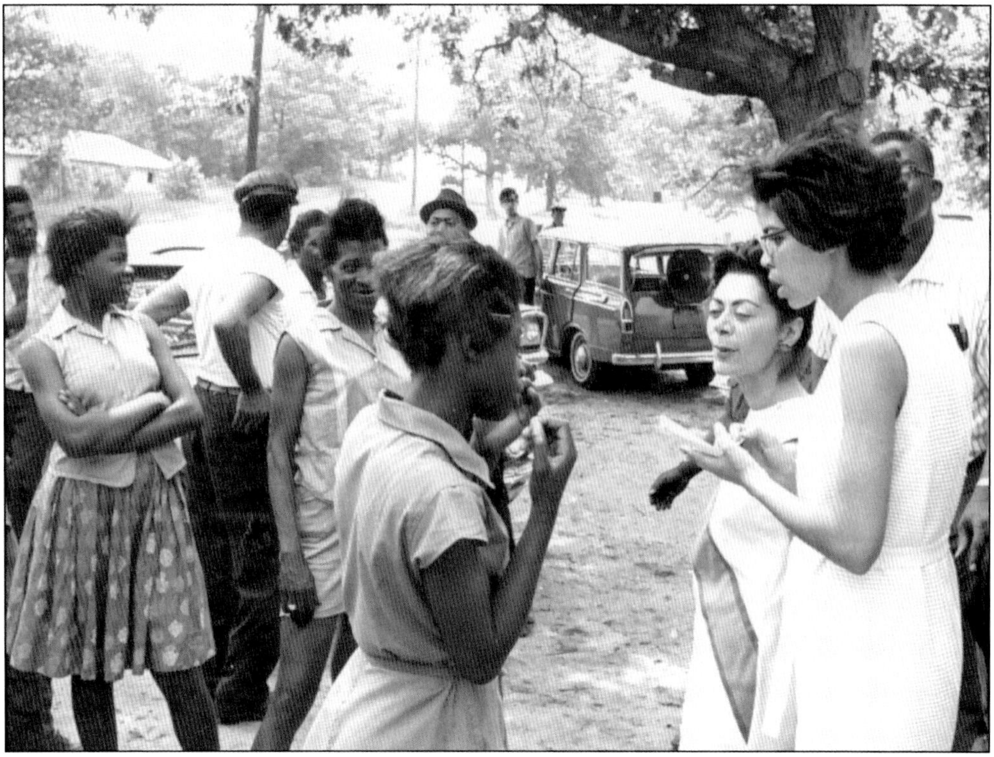

The east end of Long Island was home to several duck farms. Hollis Warner Duck Farm raised 500,000 ducks a year with the use of exploited migrant workers recruited from Southern farm communities. Advertisements in the local papers made claims that Hollis Warner Farm would provide a better quality of life for laborers and their families. Once the workers came to the farm, they were faced with the reality of 12-hour workdays, living in hazardous company homes, and isolation from the locals. Above, CORE members Ruth Schwartz (left) and Delores Quintyne (right) register migrant workers to vote. The conditions of Hollis Warner Duck Farm got the attention of local and national officials. Pres. Lyndon Johnson sent aides to investigate. The investigation found that the living and working conditions were some of the worst in the country and recommended that local officials respond. County executive Lee Dennison ordered the county to condemn and knock down the company homes. (Delores Quintyne Collection.)

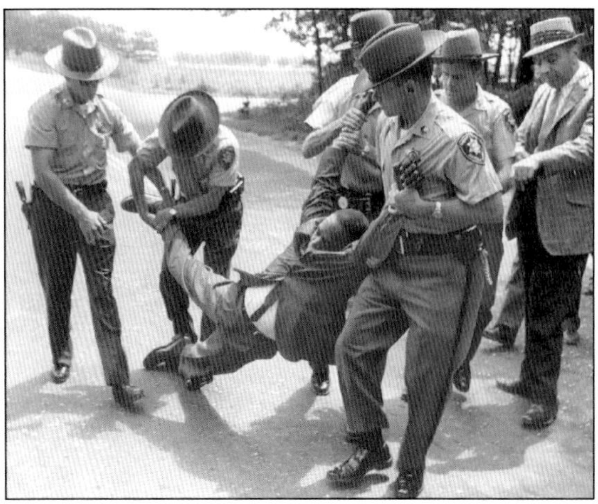

The relocation of hundreds of workers became CORE's top priority. Demonstrations became more aggressive to relocate the workers into proper living conditions. Here, Lincoln Lynch of CORE is being arrested at one of these demonstrations. (Newsday, LLC.)

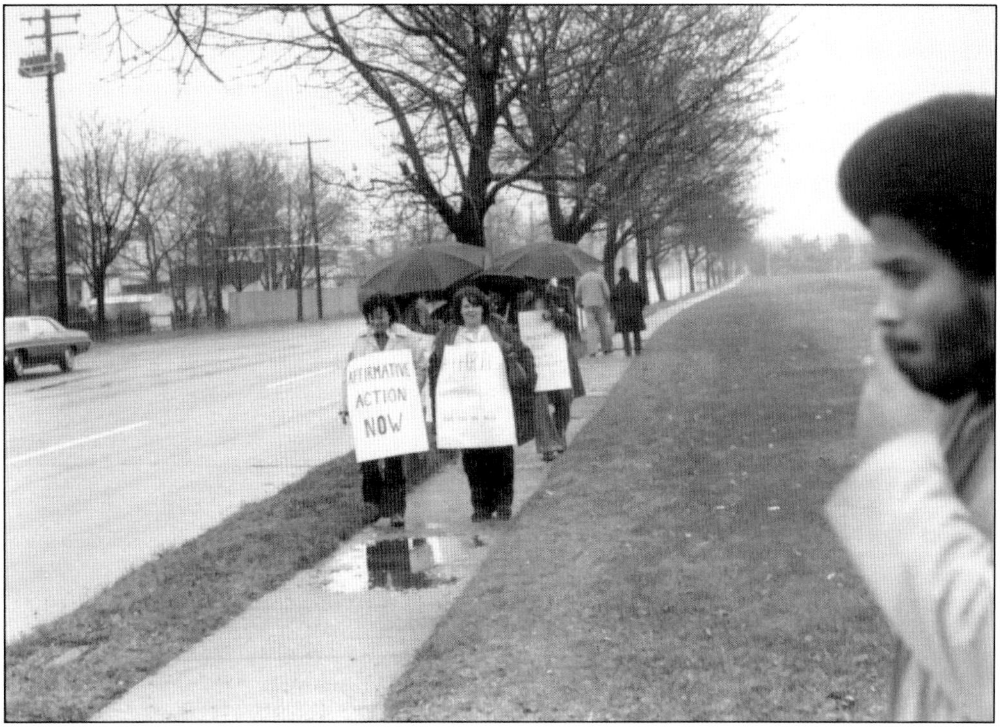

Suburban public works companies became the largest employers on Long Island. LILCO was at the center of employment discrimination suits. The first suit, filed in 1974, alleged that LILCO refused to hire an applicant based on his Pakistani origins. A closer look revealed that LILCO's hiring of higher-paid engineers was dominated by white applicants. This discrimination suit and others that followed attracted CORE's civil rights activist Irwin Quintyne to picket LILCO Suffolk County headquarters. (Both, Delores Quintyne Collection.)

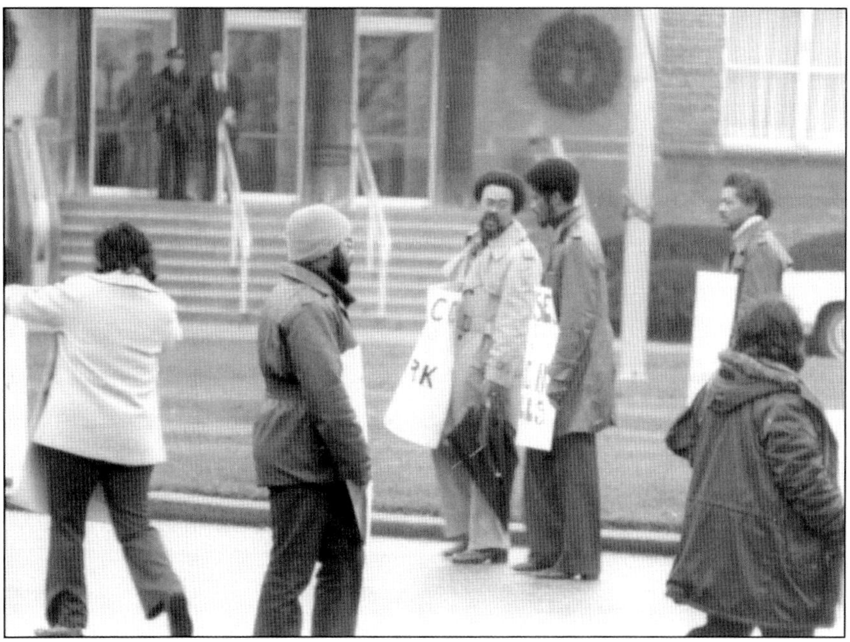

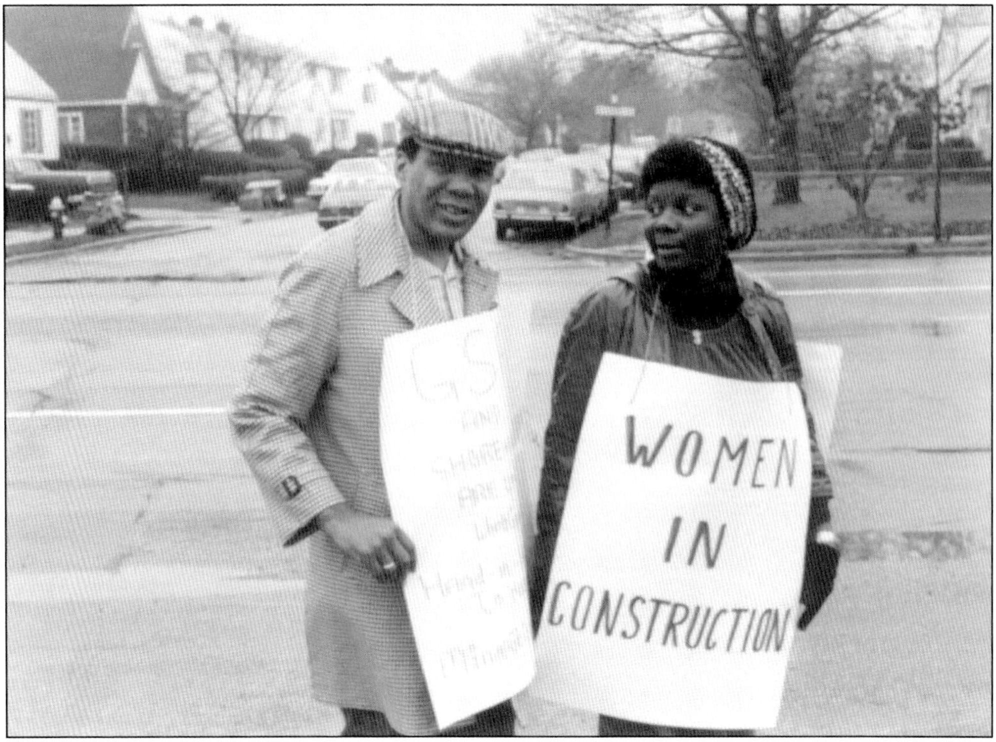

CORE formed alliances with women's rights groups such as the League of Women Voters. These groups worked together aggressively to achieve the goals of employment equality. The LILCO campaign was not just based on racial hiring practices but also on gender and age discrimination. The demonstration had limited success, but later lawsuits awarded applicants as much as $2 million in lost wages and forced employment reforms. (Both, Delores Quintyne Collection.)

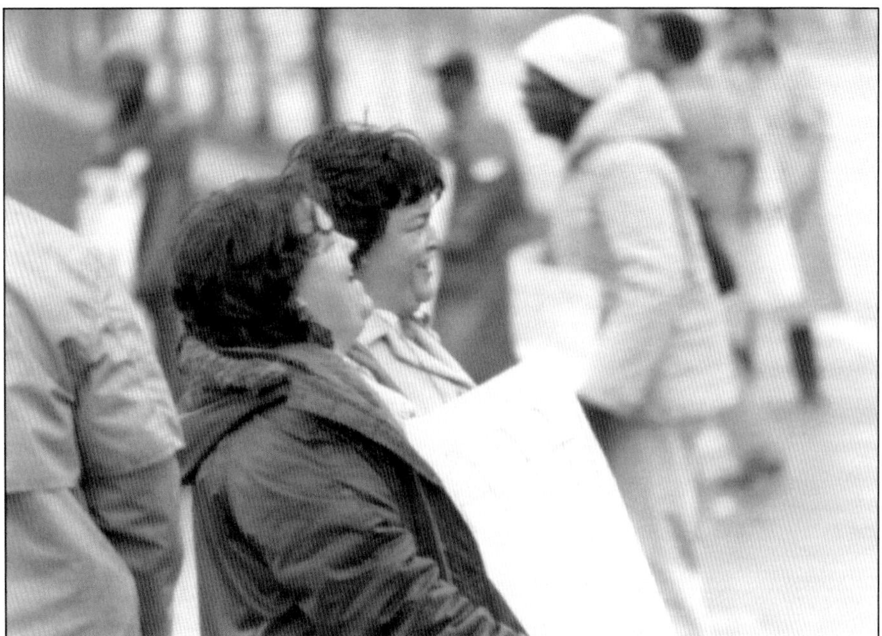

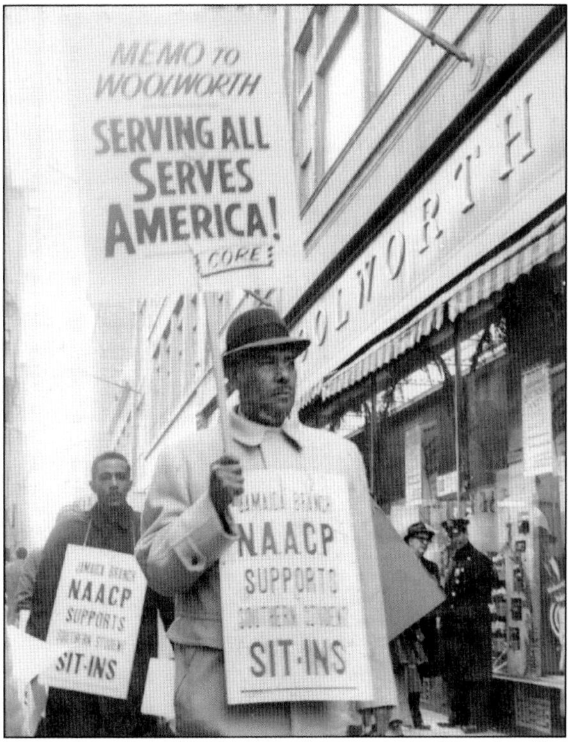

The Woolworth department store in Greensboro, North Carolina, became a battleground for integration. Lunch counters within the Southern stores enforced segregation. These segregated counters were the focus of sit-ins by the Southern branch of CORE. Woolworth stores in New York City and Long Island faced mass demonstrations and boycotts against the segregationist policies of the Southern stores. The NAACP and CORE picketed the Jamaica Queens and Nassau County Woolworth stores. CORE and the NAACP worked together on national issues. On local issues, CORE took the lead, but the NAACP provided support to CORE by obtaining lawyers for activists who got locked up during demonstrations. (Both, Eugene Burnett Collection.)

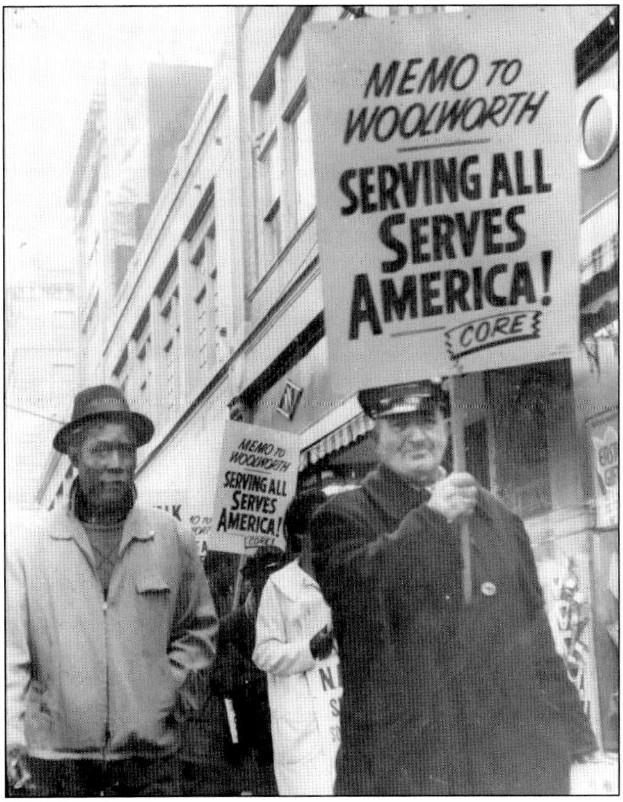

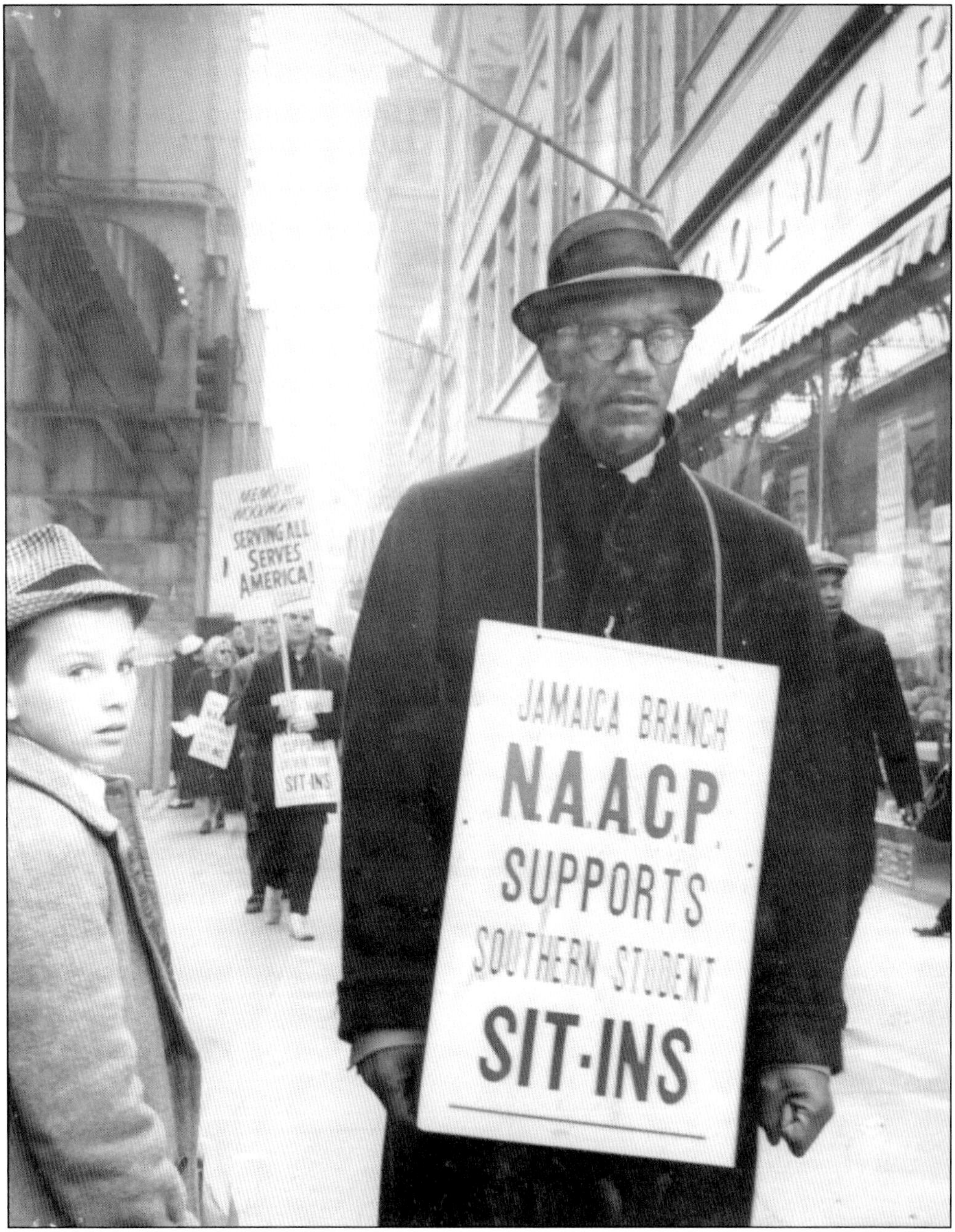

Picketing in this picture is John Burnell, NAACP's Labor and Industry Committee chairman. This position within the NAACP locally enforces employment equality, investigates discrimination and employment needs of minority areas, and liaises with private corporations and labor unions. John Burnell's main focus within the NAACP was to promote membership within organized labor. (Eugene Burnett Collection.)

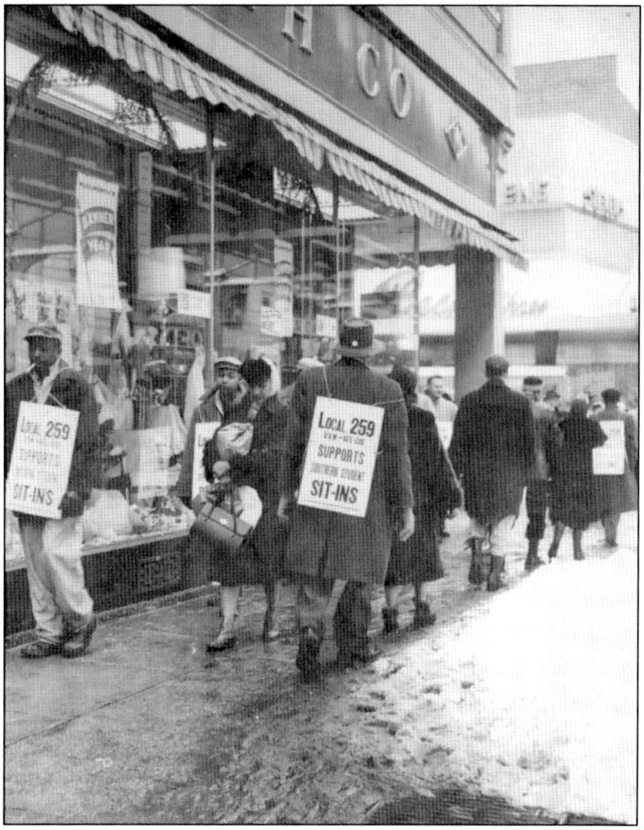

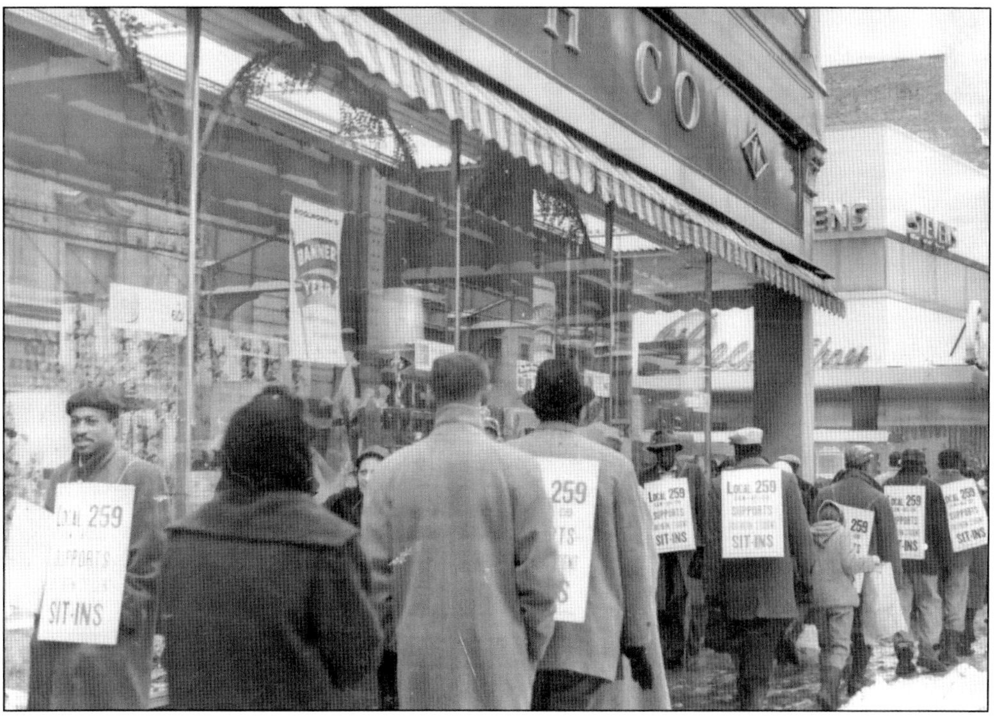

Groups that provided support to the NAACP and CORE included labor unions. Organized labor influenced the goals of CORE, which inspired campaigns such as the Hollis Warner Farm workers' struggle for livable wages and safe living and working conditions. United Auto Workers Local 259 was vital for financial support in bankrolling activist campaigns. Local 259's other support included sending members out to participate in picketing and boycotts. Collective efforts from labor unions, CORE, and the NAACP forced Woolworth to remove its segregationist policies. (Both, Eugene Burnett Collection.)

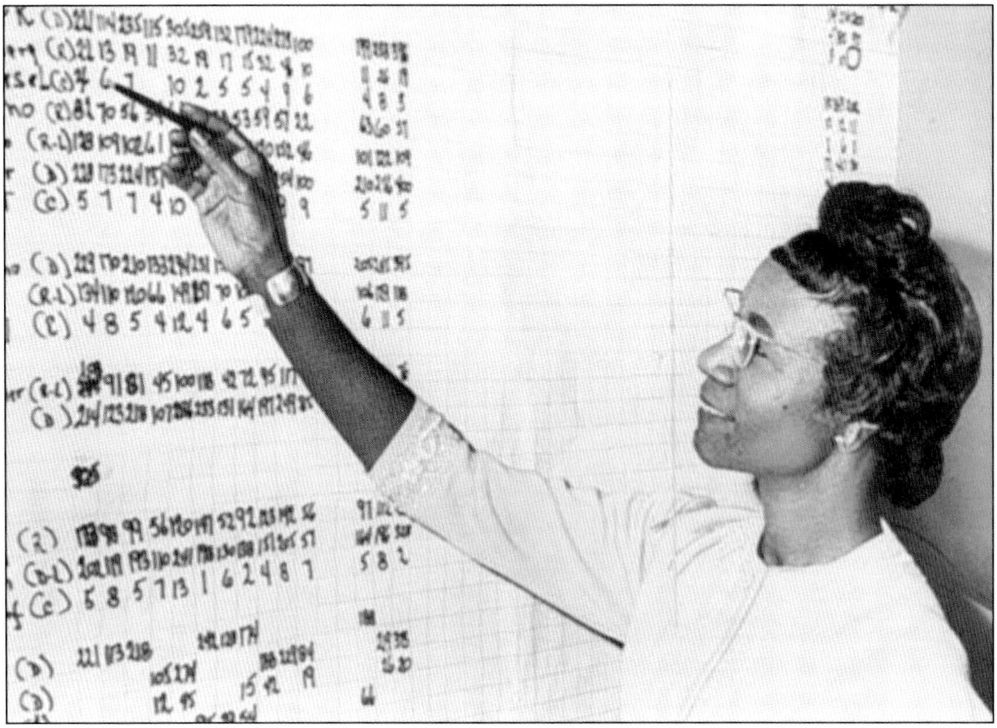

At the close of the 1960s, New York civil rights groups witnessed a historic success. Shirley Chisholm became the first African American women to be elected to Congress. Chisholm was elected from New York's 12th Congressional District. This district encompasses eastern Brooklyn and Western Queens. Her successful election was a result of grassroots efforts and a platform that mirrored civil rights goals such as expanding educational opportunities and providing a minimum wage and unemployment benefits for domestic workers. Her election and successful legislative career served as a catalyst for black communities across Long Island to seek black political representation. (Library of Congress.)

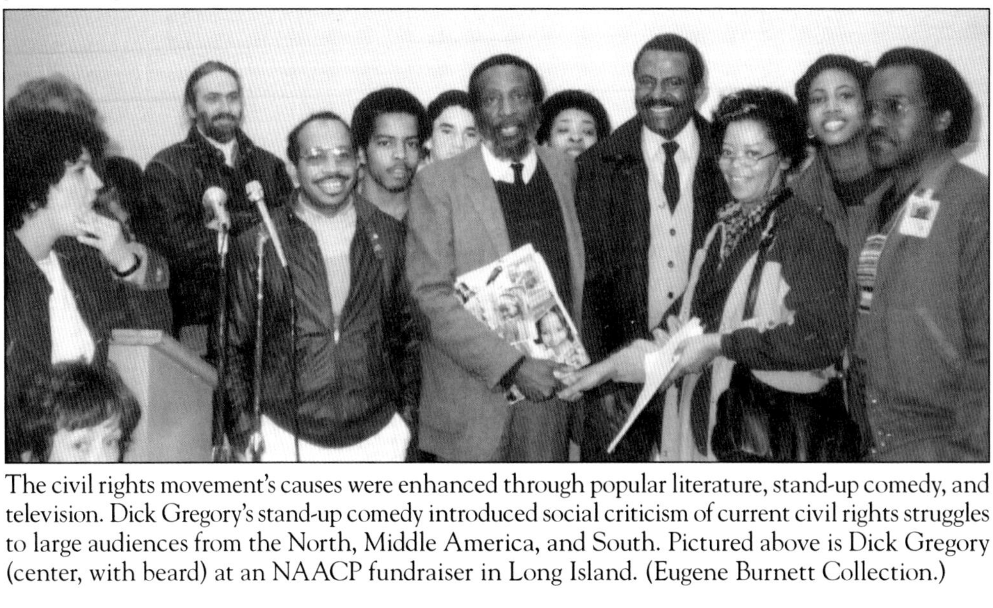

The civil rights movement's causes were enhanced through popular literature, stand-up comedy, and television. Dick Gregory's stand-up comedy introduced social criticism of current civil rights struggles to large audiences from the North, Middle America, and South. Pictured above is Dick Gregory (center, with beard) at an NAACP fundraiser in Long Island. (Eugene Burnett Collection.)

Five

Milestones and Current Fights on Long Island's Civil Rights Movement

During the 1980s, the civil rights movement across Long Island started to slow. The momentum of the 1960s and 1970s stalled due to the disputed leadership of Roy Innis within CORE and the rising conservative movement. The fight for racial equality had to reinvent itself for the new struggles of the decades to come. The civil rights movement across New York City and Long Island turned to historic black churches as a way to harness collective support or focused on the popularity of hip hop culture. Churches such as Hollywood Baptist Church of Amityville became centers for meetings with Al Sharpton and fundraising powerhouses for the NAACP. Hip hop culture brought current issues of race, poverty, and crime to a mainstream audience that crossed racial boundaries.

The slowdown to reinvent the movement did not affect the strong desire for blacks to reclaim their state and local governments. Voter participation in areas such as Hempstead led to James Garner becoming the first black mayor elected on Long Island. His successful election bid was dwarfed by the election of David Dinkins, first black mayor of New York City. Local political battles included district council systems versus the current at-large system. The district council system is based on local hamlets or towns within the township electing council members. Most of the townships had the at-large system, in which the township as a whole votes for candidates. Promoting district-based candidacy enabled the first black council person and county legislator for Babylon. With the success of black leadership, blacks joined the middle and upper class in larger numbers.

These historic gains have only put a dent in the fight for equality. Current struggles include integration of public schools. Despite the efforts of the 1960s and enforced Princeton Plans, Long Island schools remain some of the most racially segregated in America. Policing throughout Long Island utilizes racial profiling, which is reflected in the racial demographics in Nassau and Suffolk County jails. The civil rights movement has no time to become complacent. Battles have been won, but the war is still in progress with causalities such as broken education systems and racial profiling within county policing.

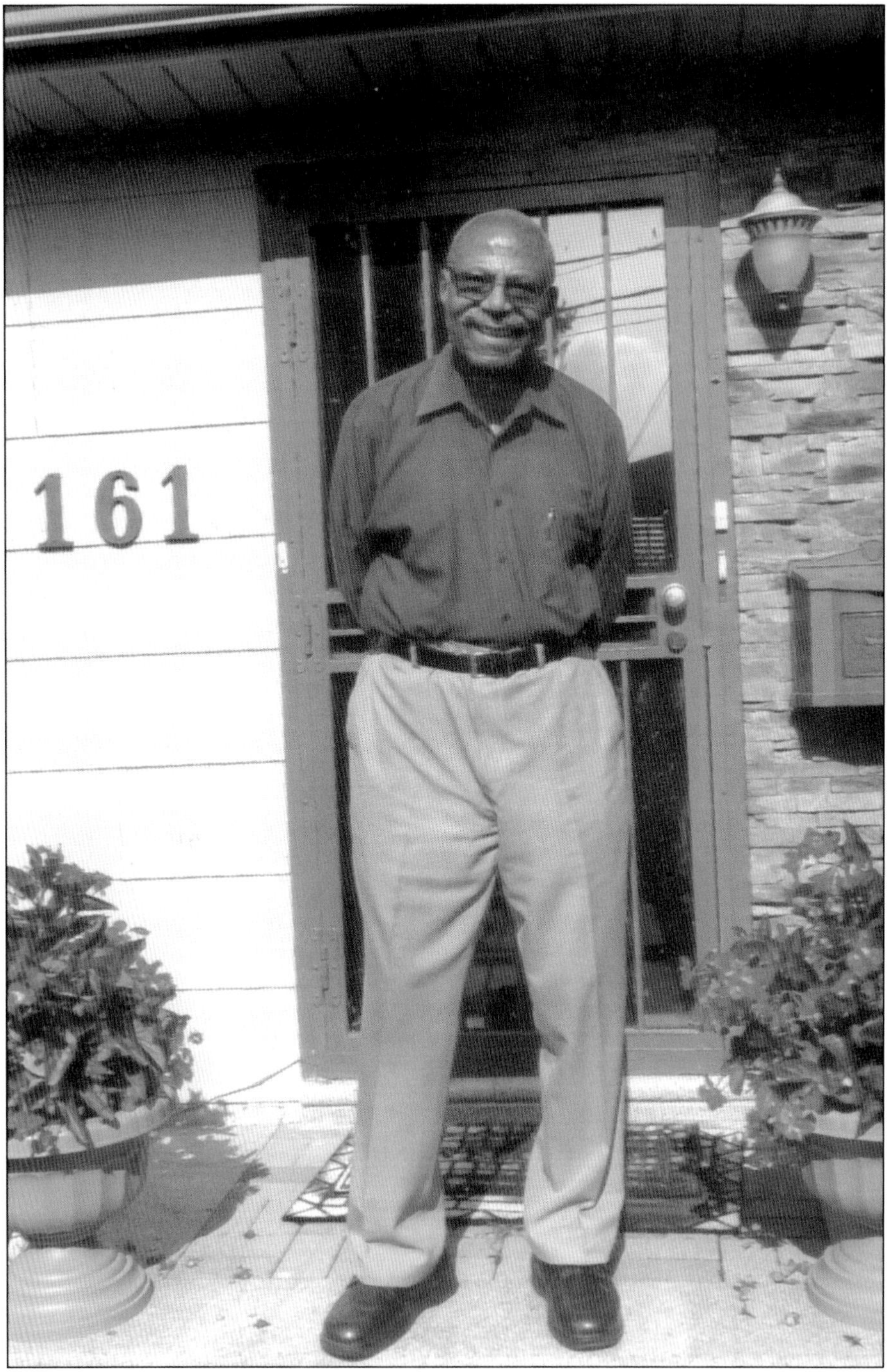

Returning home from World War II, Eugene Burnett was refused a house in Levittown. This frustration motivated Eugene to become active in the local civil rights movement to desegregate schools and neighborhoods. The area Eugene moved to was Wheatley Heights. The Burnett family became the first black family to move there. Despite the threats from neighbors who told him to leave, he stayed. His kids benefitted from a great school system that propelled them into successful careers. After more than 55 years, Eugene still lives in Wheatley Heights.

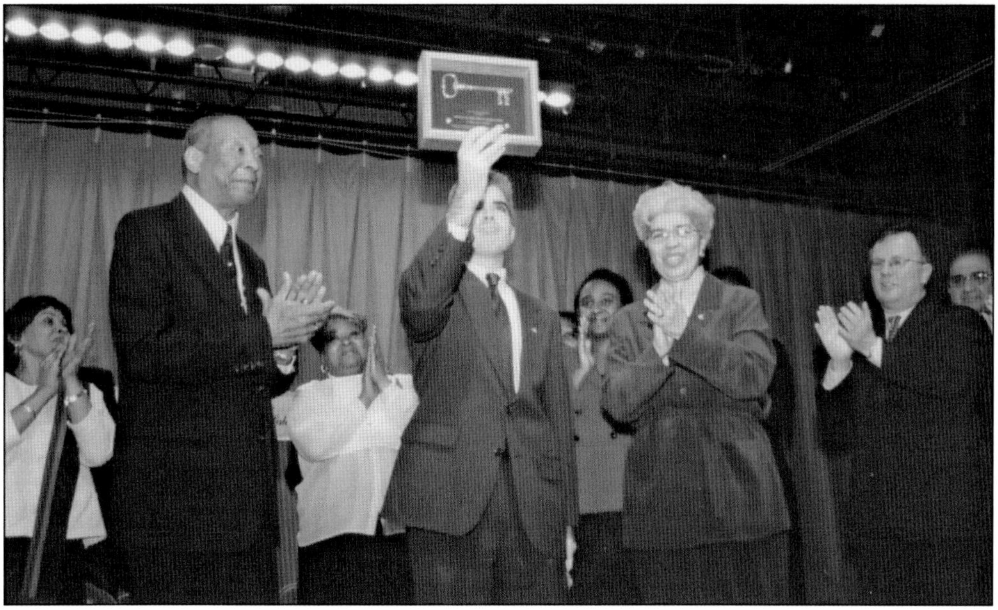

Civil rights activists were celebrated in the later years for being on the right side of history. In this image, Irwin and Delores Quintyne of North Amityville are being honored by Babylon town supervisor Steve Bellone. Delores and Irwin collaborated with CORE on demonstrations against housing, educational, and employment discrimination. (Historic Photograph and Postcard Collection of the Town of Babylon, Office of Historic Services)

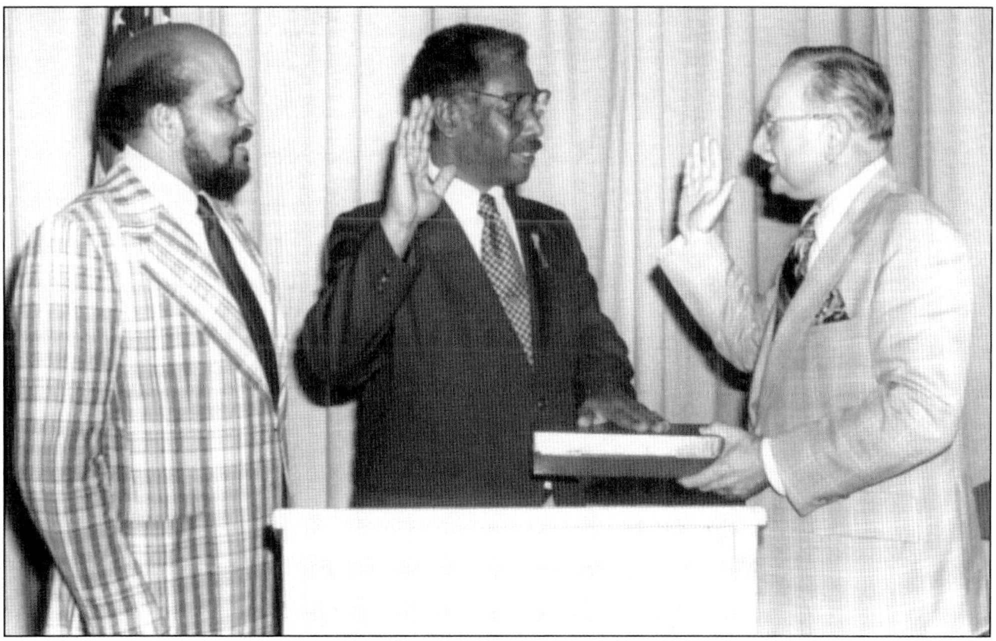

After a century of being discouraged from participating in local community politics and housing associations, black communities started assuming a role in their own community affairs. With a growing middle class within black communities, homeownership increased. The picture above shows the first black person to be elected to serve head of Westbury's Sherwood Civic Association. (Historical Society of the Westburys Photo Archive.)

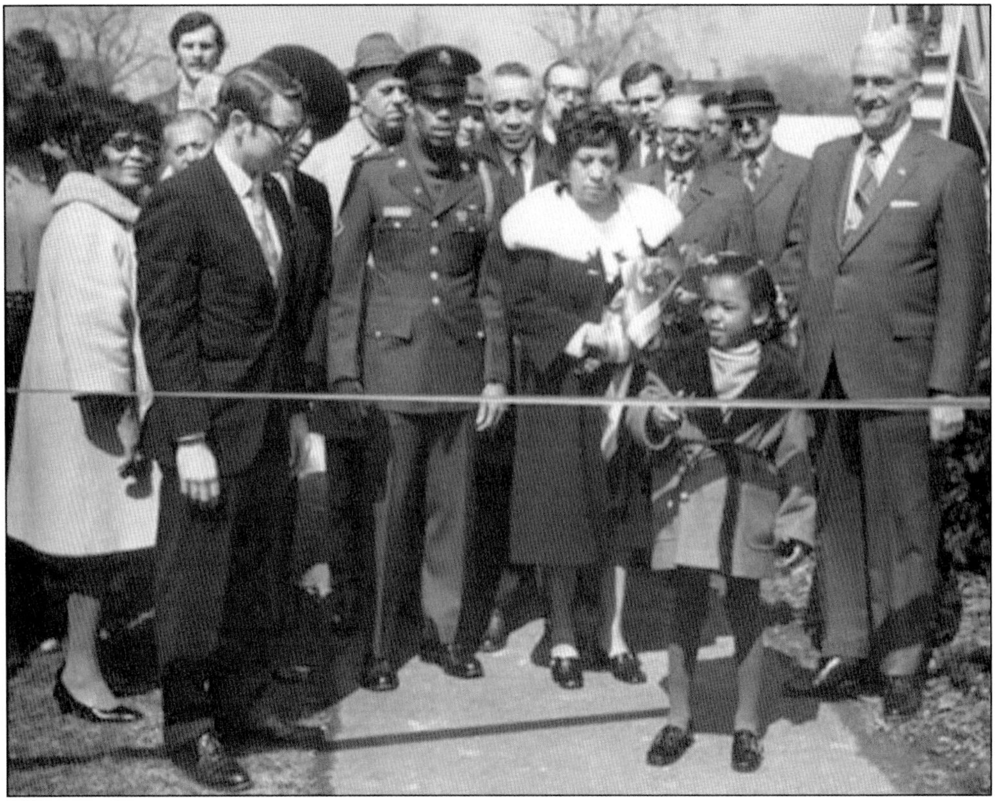

Towns and villages that had African American populations but white control of their governments included Hempstead Village. Local parks and buildings reflected white community members. African Americans were mostly left out of the building and park dedications. By 1970, African American home ownership within Hempstead increased. This changing demographic forced a change within the community to reflect local culture. Parks and public buildings were renamed after locally known African Americans. In 1971, Harold Mason Memorial Park was named after a local African American killed in combat during the Vietnam War. (Both, Historic Memories Collection of Hempstead Library.)

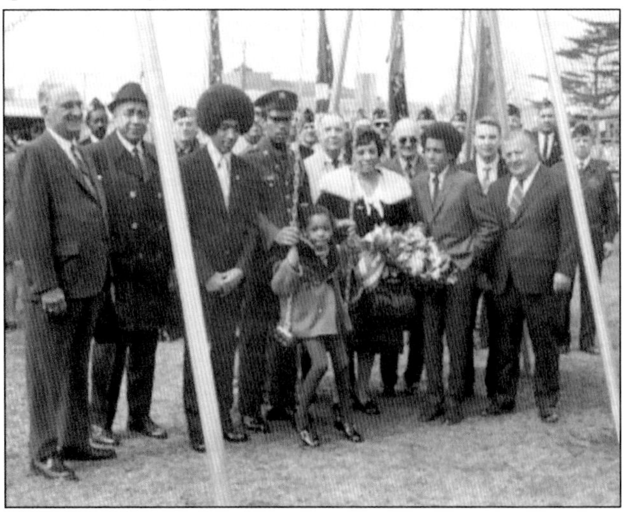

Wyandanch, like Hempstead, named community landmarks and buildings in commemoration of well-known locals. La Francis Hardiman Elementary School was named after a local resident and Vietnam War hero. La Francis Hardiman was a member of the 173rd Airborne Brigade who died in combat on November 13, 1967.

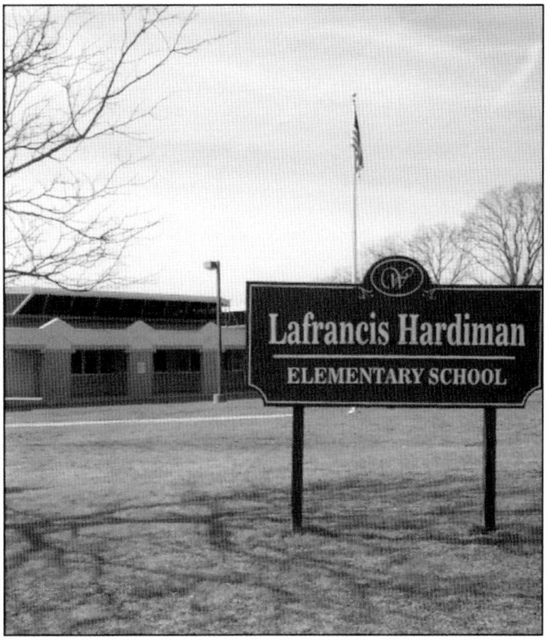

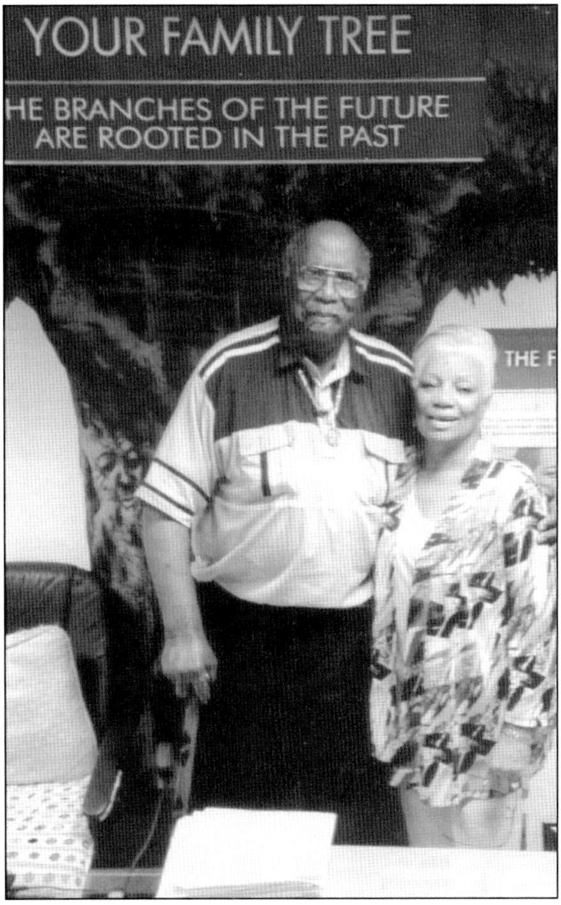

Naming buildings and parks was only a small step in preserving and embracing the local African American culture. In 1968, Prof. Leroy Leonardo Ramsey created black history exhibits at Nassau Community College. These exhibits expanded into the development of the African American Museum of Nassau County. This museum has become a cultural hub of African American culture with a genealogical service for locals to better understand their heritage. Pictured here are museum and genealogical service coordinators Joysetta and Julius Pearse.

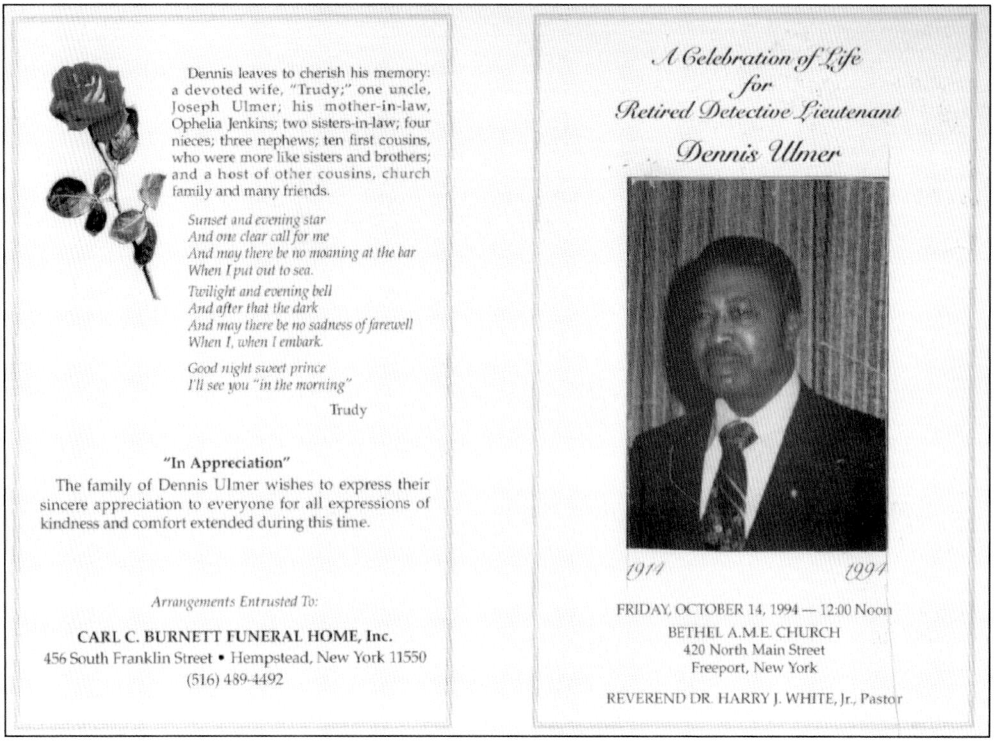

Dennis leaves to cherish his memory: a devoted wife, "Trudy;" one uncle, Joseph Ulmer; his mother-in-law, Ophelia Jenkins; two sisters-in-law; four nieces; three nephews; ten first cousins, who were more like sisters and brothers; and a host of other cousins, church family and many friends.

Sunset and evening star
And one clear call for me
And may there be no moaning at the bar
When I put out to sea.

Twilight and evening bell
And after that the dark
And may there be no sadness of farewell
When I, when I embark.

Good night sweet prince
I'll see you "in the morning"

Trudy

"In Appreciation"

The family of Dennis Ulmer wishes to express their sincere appreciation to everyone for all expressions of kindness and comfort extended during this time.

Arrangements Entrusted To:

CARL C. BURNETT FUNERAL HOME, Inc.
456 South Franklin Street • Hempstead, New York 11550
(516) 489-4492

A Celebration of Life
for
Retired Detective Lieutenant
Dennis Ulmer

1914 1994

FRIDAY, OCTOBER 14, 1994 — 12:00 Noon
BETHEL A.M.E. CHURCH
420 North Main Street
Freeport, New York

REVEREND DR. HARRY J. WHITE, Jr., Pastor

The Nassau County Police Department's color barrier was broken by Dennis Ulmer. Dennis became Nassau County's first black cop in 1945 and retired in 1969. Over his 24-year career, Dennis was a detective, sergeant, and lieutenant. He opened the door for other African Americans to obtain well-paying jobs and the opportunity to police their own community.

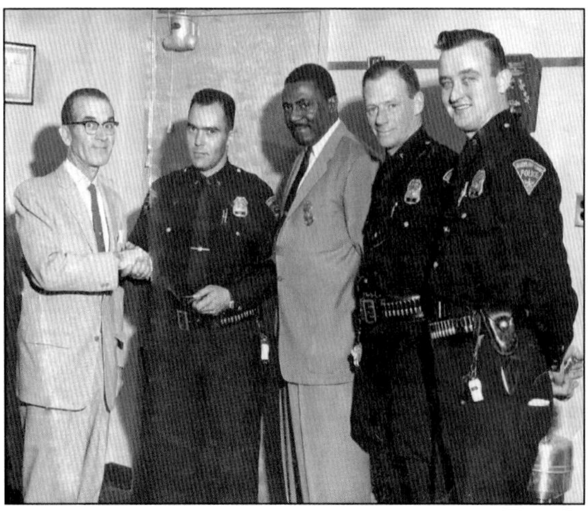

Suffolk County Police Department was formed in 1960 as a result of growing suburban developments. Babylon, Brookhaven, Huntington, Islip, and Smithtown voted to merge within the newly formed department. Eugene Burnett, originally part of Babylon Police Department, was promoted to the rank of sergeant when the town merged with Suffolk. This promotion made Burnett the first black sergeant in Suffolk County. Here, Burnett is being awarded his sergeant's shield. (Historic Photograph and Postcard Collection of the Town of Babylon, Office of Historic Services.)

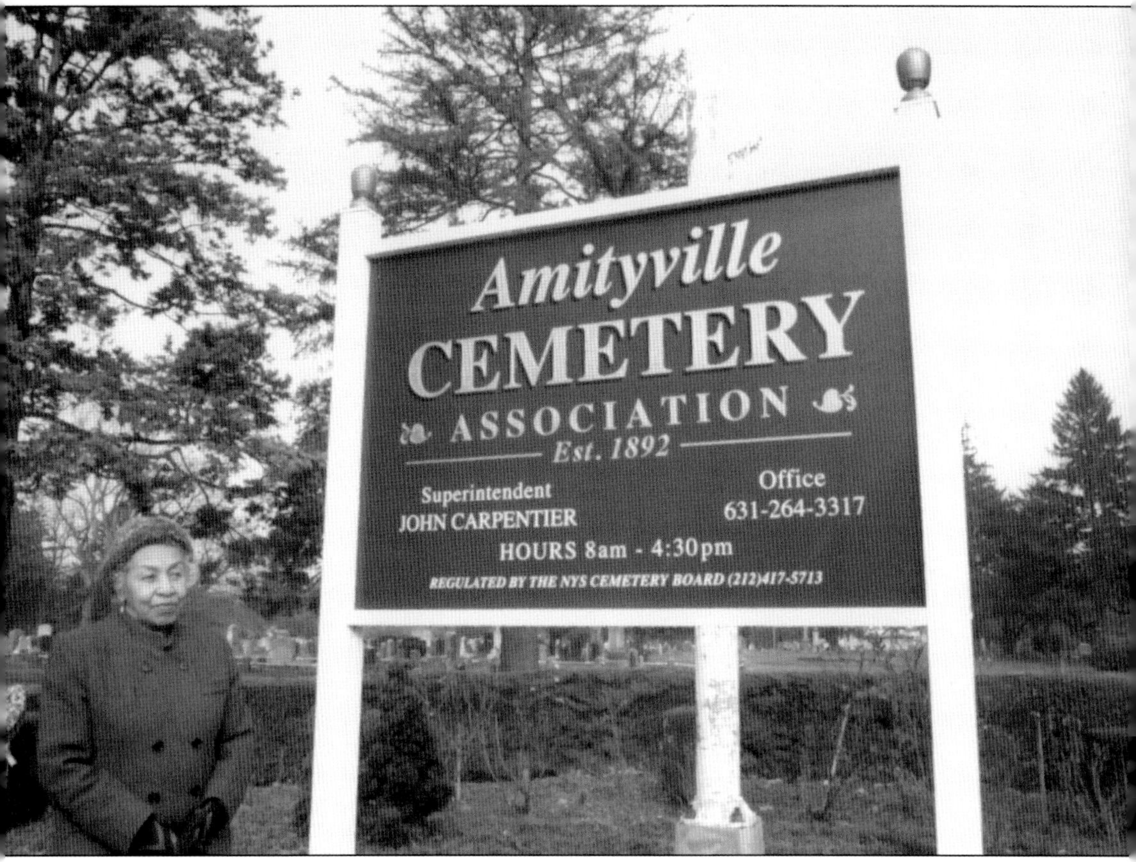

The black community attempted to integrate not only police departments and civic associations but also public works. The Amityville Cemetery was run and operated by white management since 1892. While under white leadership, it was rumored that blacks were buried in the back and whites were buried in the front of the cemetery. By 2002, John Carpentier became the first black superintendent of the cemetery. (Joe Turner Collection.)

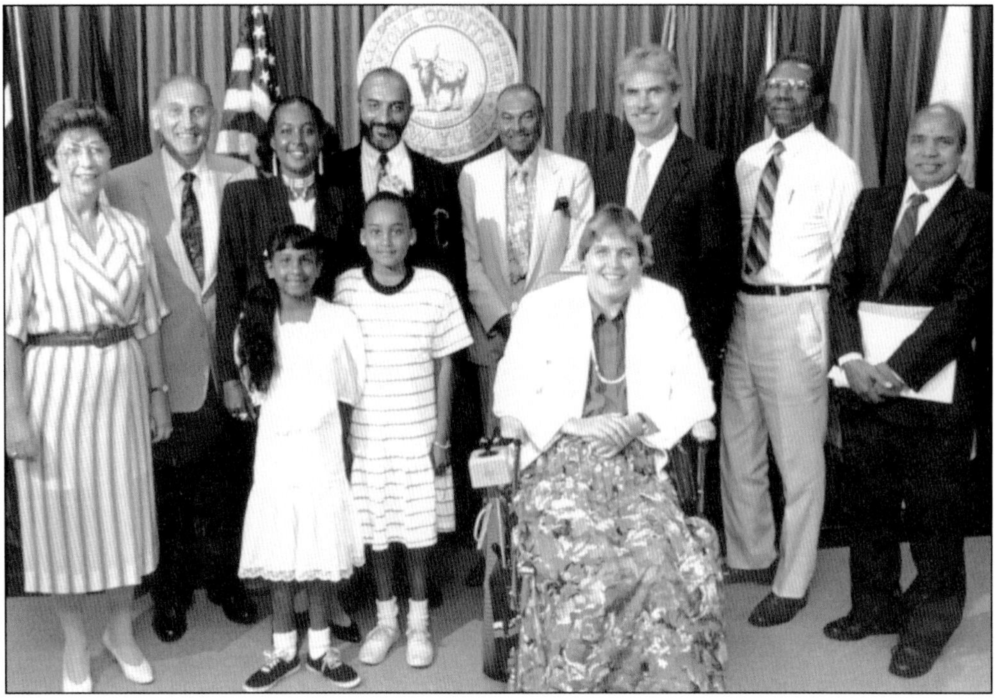

By 1963, Suffolk County formed a human rights commission. This commission comprises 15 members who oversee laws and violations that discriminate against a person's race, religion, gender, sexual orientation, disability, or former military service. Local activists who participated in these commissions include Dr. Eugene Reed of the NAACP and Irwin Quintyne of CORE. Pictured above is the 1990 Human Rights Commission under Suffolk County executive Patrick Halpin. (Eugene Burnett Collection.)

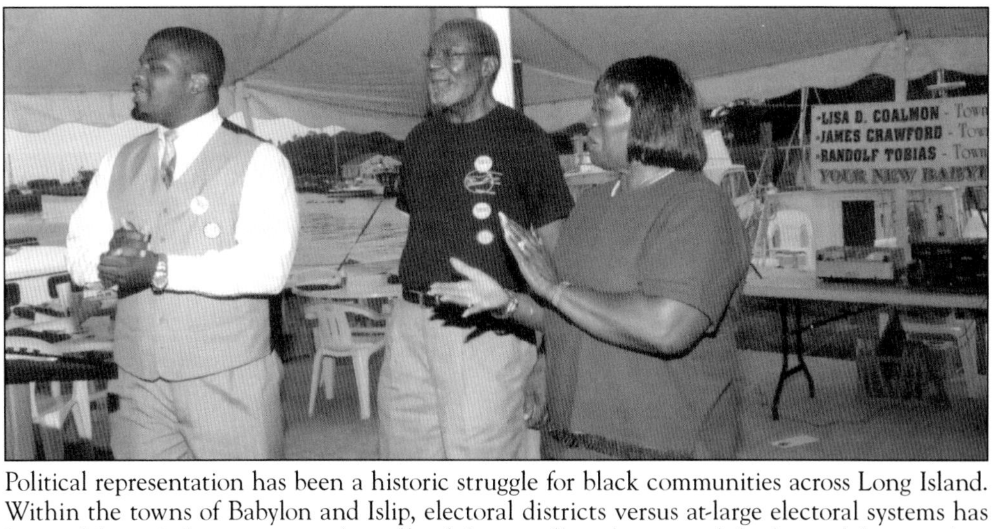

Political representation has been a historic struggle for black communities across Long Island. Within the towns of Babylon and Islip, electoral districts versus at-large electoral systems has been a debate. At-large systems select officials by overall poplar vote, while electoral districts elect members from within a subdivided election district to represent the people of that community. The at-large system leaves black areas like North Amityville underrepresented. The photograph above shows, from left to right, councilmember candidate James Crawford, Eugene Burnett, and Hempstead councilmember Dorothy Goosby. (Joe Turner Collection.)

Despite the Town of Babylon not giving in to replace the at-large system with electoral districts, political gains were made by the African American community. In 1999, Janice Tinsley Colbert became town clerk and the first elected African American town official. Pictured at right is the election night victory of her campaign. Janice is the woman in gray on the right. (Joe Turner Collection.)

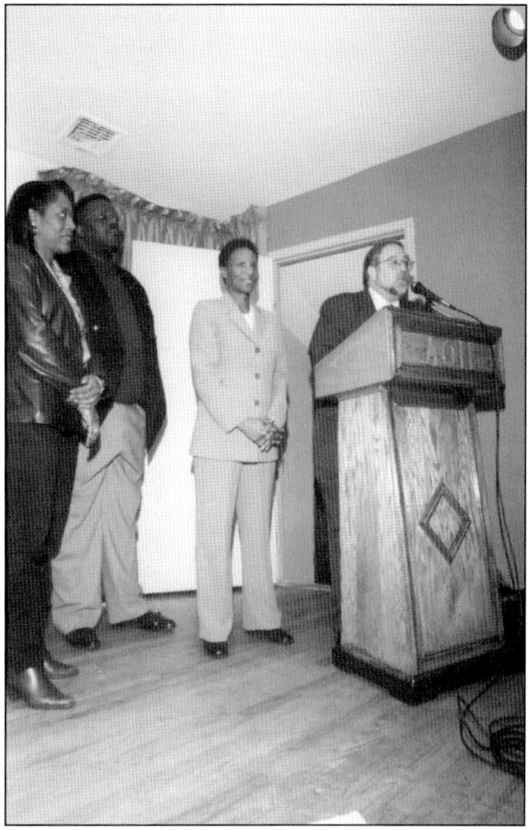

Prior to being elected to Babylon town clerk, Janice Colbert had a successful career as a lawyer. Her experience and respected reputation pushed her into local politics. Below, Steve Bellone congratulates Janice on her successful election. (Joe Turner Collection.)

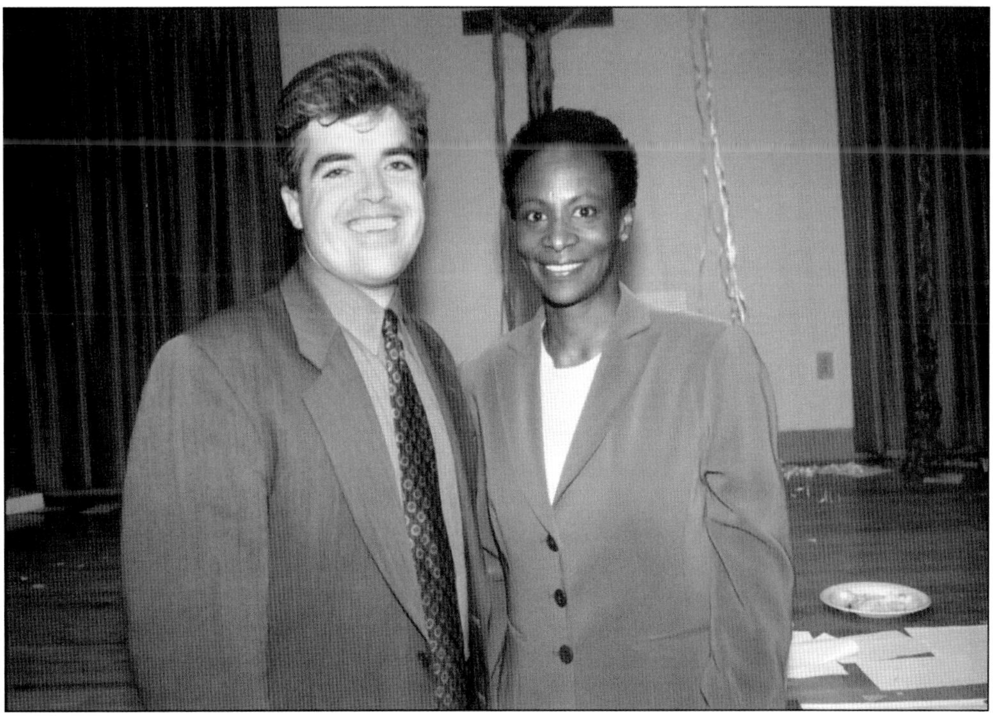

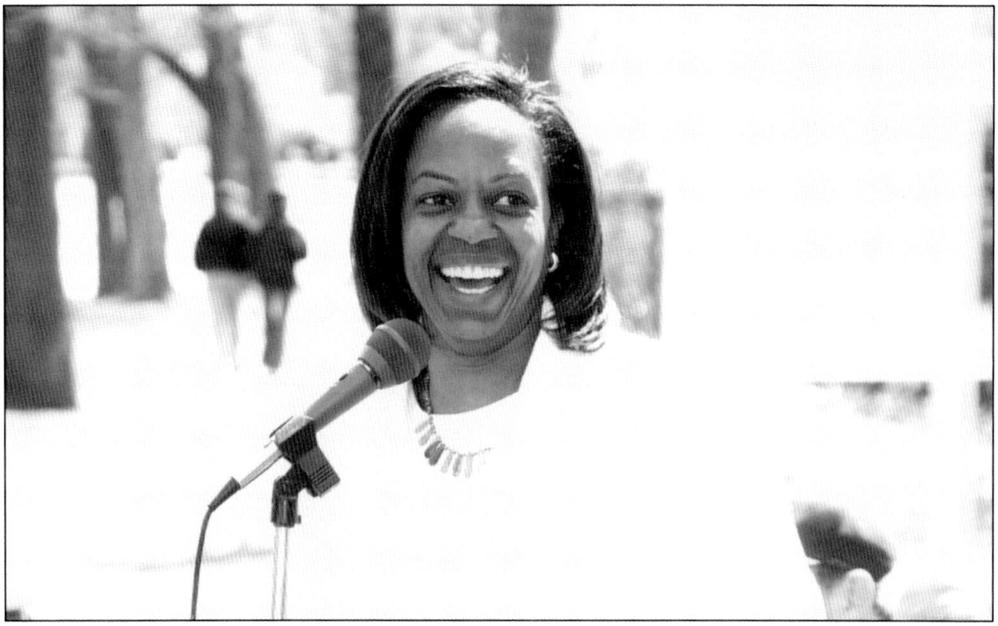

Jacqueline Gordon is one of the first elected black Babylon town officials. Gordon sits on the executive board for the Association of Long Island Vocational Educators (ALIVE) and coordinates the Ujima Summer Minority Internship Program. Pictured above, Gordon is at the ceremony for the historical designation of the Cuban Giants baseball field in Babylon. (Joe Turner Collection.)

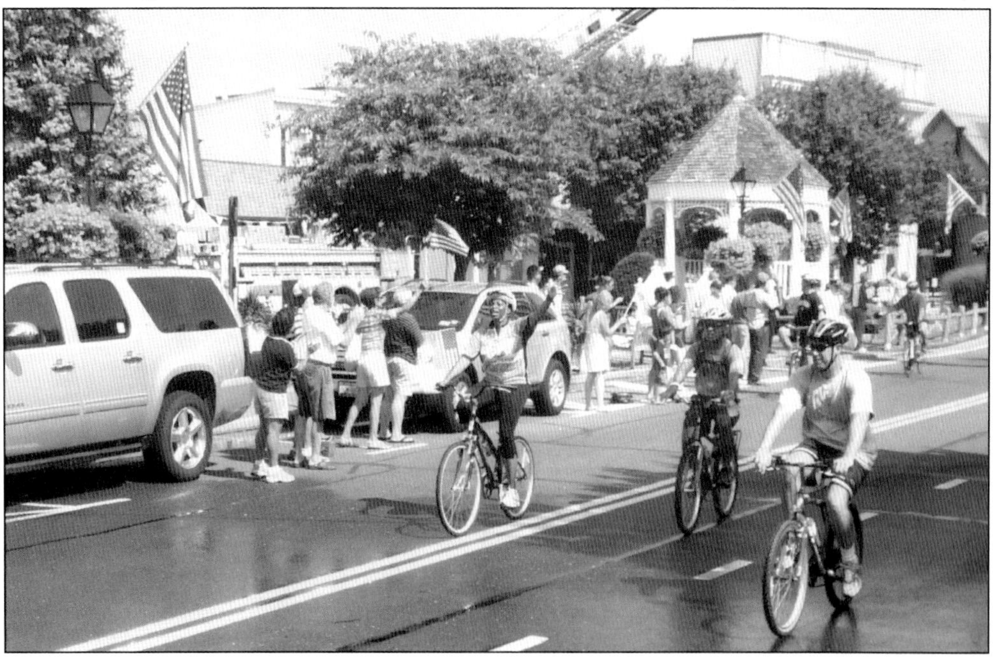

Jackie Gordon has been dedicated to causes regarding returning soldiers. Gordon herself is a veteran of the US Army and was deployed four times in Iraq and Afghanistan. Jackie collaborates on Wounded Warriors Project events. One event is the Annual Soldier Ride, which raised up to $500,000. In this photograph, Jackie Gordon is at the finish line of the Soldier Ride in the village of Amityville. (Joe Turner Collection.)

In 1988, the village of Hempstead elected its first black mayor. James Garner remained mayor until he was defeated in 2005 by Hempstead's second black mayor, Wayne J. Hall. Under Hall's leadership, the village of Hempstead rebuilt its downtown through beatification initiatives and expanded affordable housing. Pictured is Mayor Wayne J. Hall. (Mayor Wayne J. Hall.)

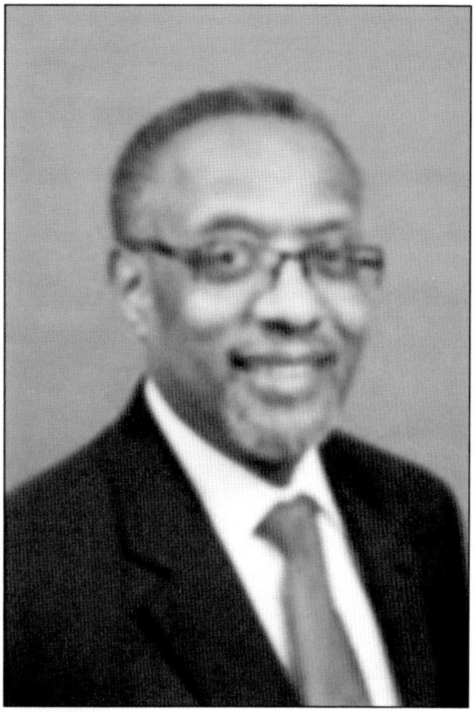

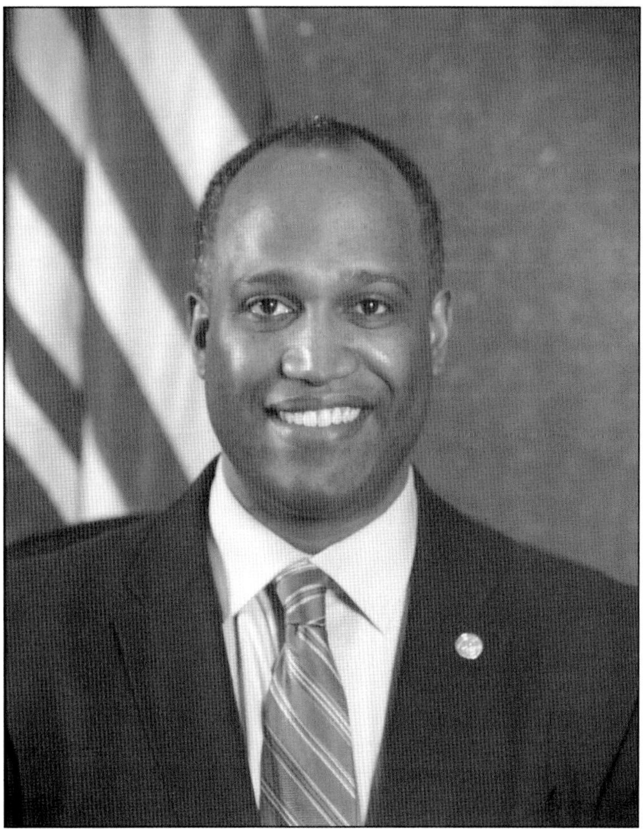

In 2008, Du Wayne Gregory was elected to the Suffolk County Legislature's 15th District seat. Suffolk County 15th District includes Wheatley Heights, Wyandanch, North Amityville, the village of Amityville, Copiague, West Babylon, and North Babylon. Since being elected, Gregory has become the first black majority leader and the first black person elected as presiding officer of the Suffolk County Legislature. (Du Wayne Gregory.)

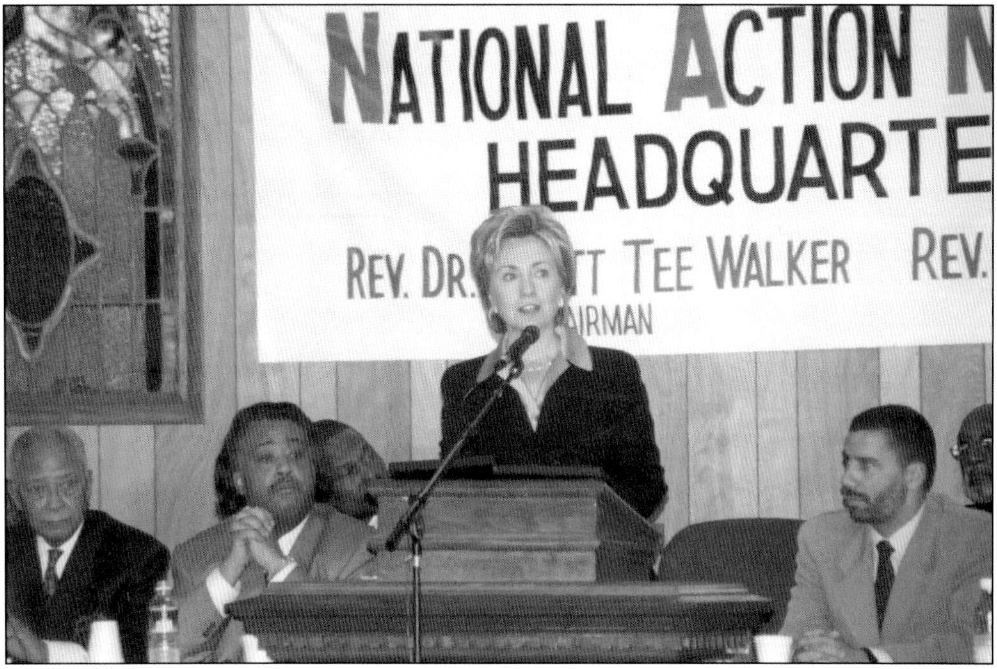

On March 17, 2008, David Patterson became the first African American governor of New York. Patterson has his roots in Hempstead, Long Island. In 1971, David Patterson graduated from Hempstead High School, becoming the first disabled/legally blind person to graduate within the district. Patterson went on to earn whis law degree from Hofstra University in 1983. Pictured above are, from left to right, David Dinkins, Rev. Al Sharpton, Hillary Clinton, and David Patterson. (Carol Marino Collection.)

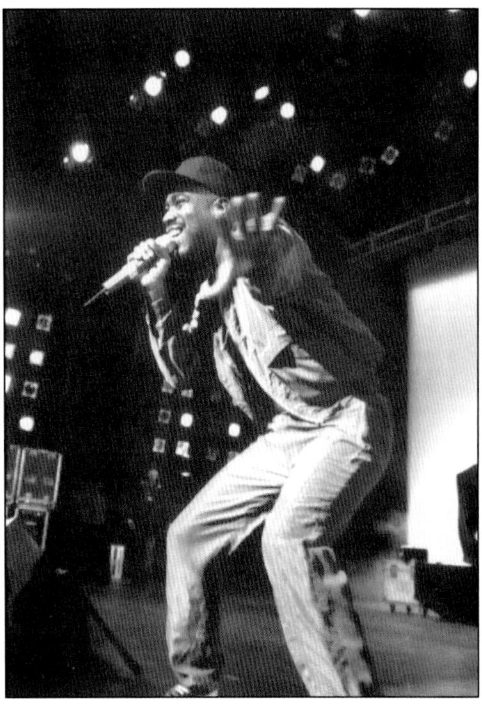

Hip hop has its roots in the South Bronx and all across the urban backdrops of New York City. The civil rights movement was evolving from promoting ideals within church meetings to pop culture. The art of hip hop was embedded in realities of racial inequalities, crime, and poverty. Hip hop pioneer Kurtis Blow was born in Harlem but lived on Long Island during his adolescent years. Blow's music was centered on bringing to light the racial inequalities in society. (Carol Marino Collection.)

Inspired by local rappers such as Kurtis Blow and Rakim, EPMD rose to fame. Founding members Parrish Smith and Erick Sermon attended Brentwood High School together. Their experiences within the local communities inspired the lyrics to some their songs. (Carol Marino Collection.)

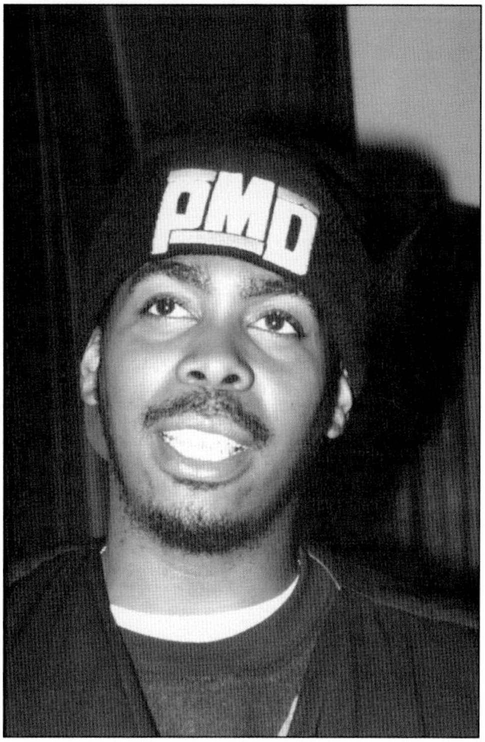

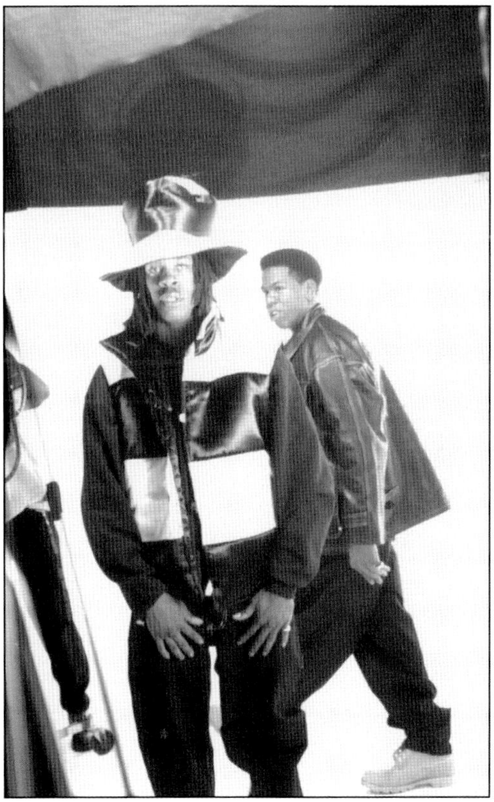

One of the many successful hip hop icons from Long Island is Trevor Tahiem Smith Jr., better known as Busta Rhymes. Smith moved to Uniondale at the age of 12 and graduated from Uniondale High School. Here, Busta Rhymes is on the left and Brentwood native Craig Mack on the right. (Carol Marino Collection.)

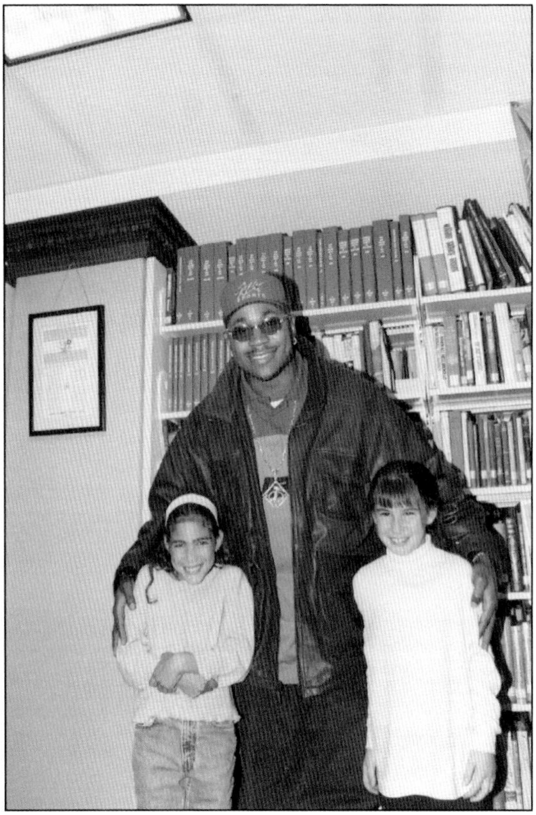

James Todd Smith, better known as LL Cool J, has achieved success pioneering hip hop and perfecting popular characters in movies and prime time TV. Born in Bayshore, Suffolk County, but raised in Queens, Smith got his start making and selling mix tapes from his grandparents' house. After achieving commercial success, Smith focused on social causes, including helping disadvantaged or at risk-youth, urban poverty, and promoting the arts. Like many other hip hop artists, Smith focused on social activist causes through philanthropy. Here, LL Cool J is receiving a proclamation from city council members for his community service and posing with young fans. (Both, Carol Marino Collection.)

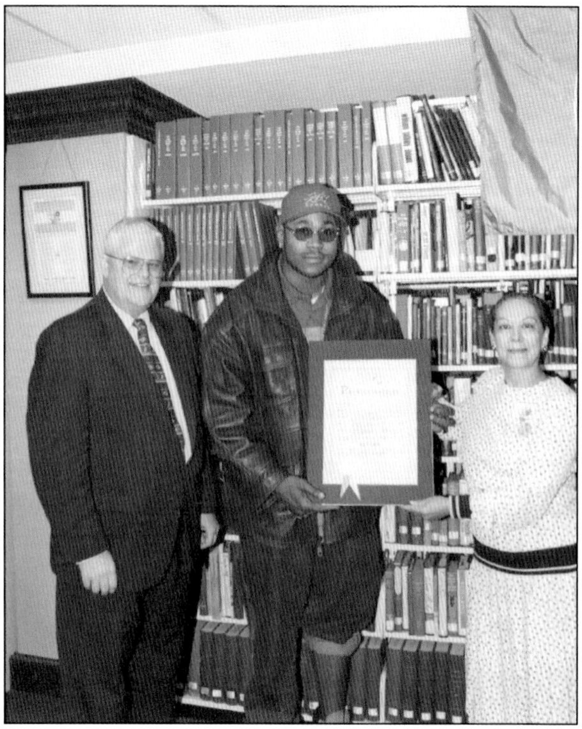

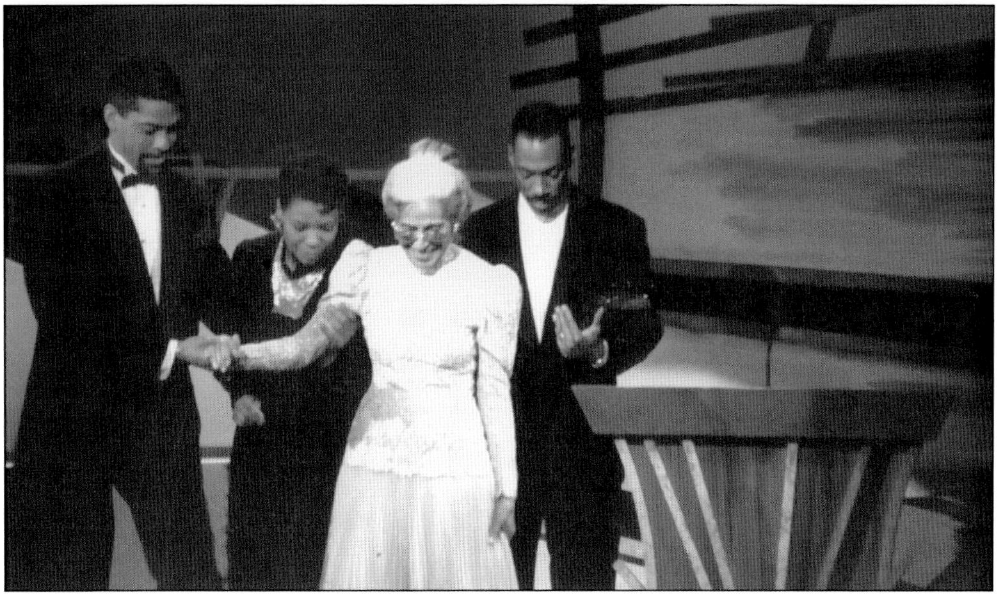

Long Island was home not only to some of the most iconic hip hop pioneers but also to innovative stand-up comic and Academy Award–nominated actor Eddie Murphy. Born in Brooklyn, Eddie Murphy was raised in Roosevelt, Nassau County. In this photograph, Eddie Murphy escorts Rosa Parks to the 1993 Essence Awards. (Carol Marino Collection.)

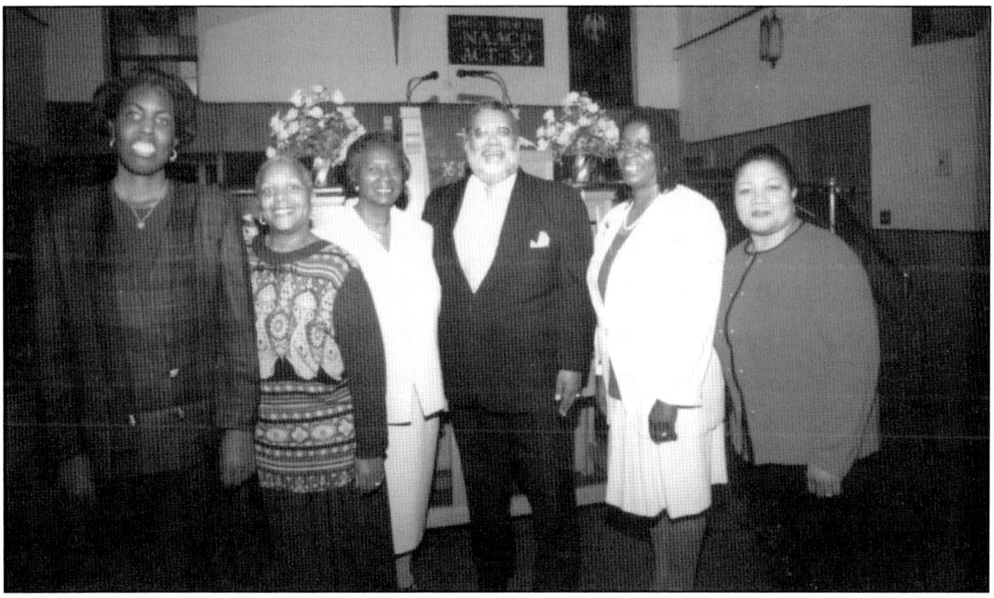

The church has been a hub for community activism. The Holy Trinity Church, located on Albany Avenue in Amityville, has had an active role in the NAACP and local political campaigns. Since Reverend Crayton had the church obtain a lifetime membership with the NAACP in 1985, the church has been a lifeline for recruitment and fundraising. Pictured above from left to right are 10th Judicial District judge Toni Bean (left); Earlene Dixon, treasurer of the Central Suffolk NAACP; and Mrs. Brown, former president of the Central Suffolk Chapter. In the center and at right are church elders and parishioners. The event documented is the annual fundraiser and member drive. (Joe Turner Collection.)

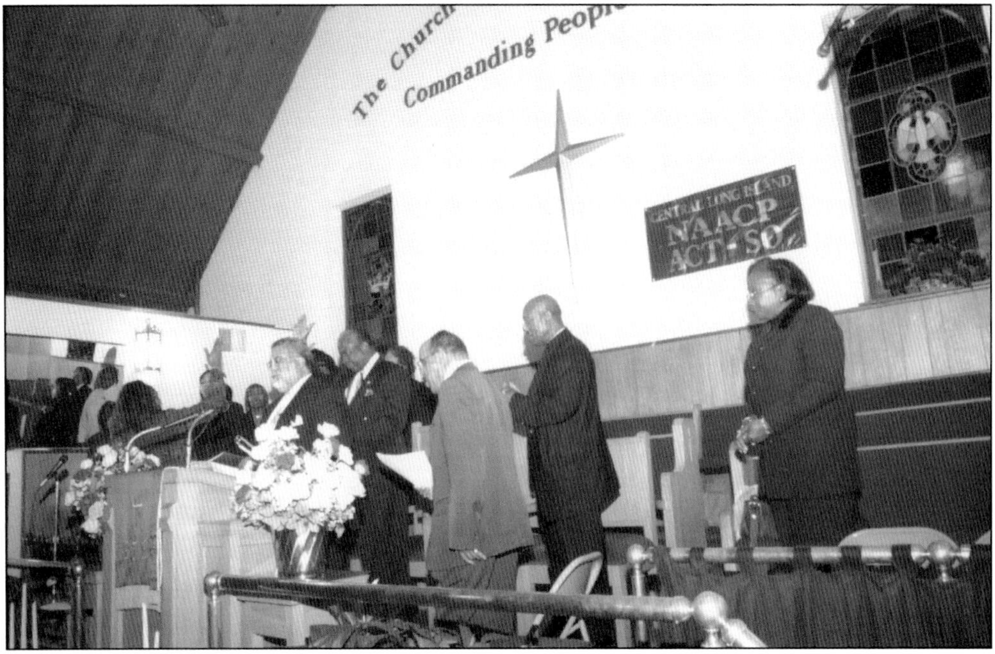

Holy Trinity Church of Amityville not only hosts NAACP meetings but also the Freedom Fund dinner. The Freedom Fund's goal is to raise money for international campaigns and scholarships. Historically, this fund has paid for the lawyers for CORE members who were arrested during protests, court battles to desegregate Levittown, and implementing the Princeton Plan for Malverne School District. (Joe Turner Collection.)

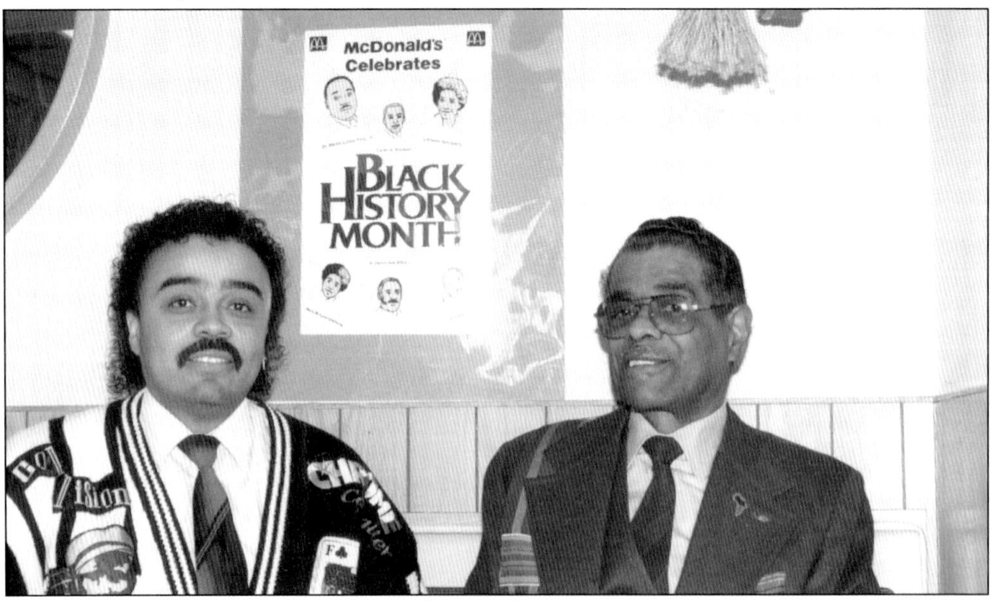

The NAACP's main goal is to obtain political, educational, and economic equality for all. The growing Latino population across Long Island has faced many challenges. These challenges include bias attacks and exploitation of labor. The Eastern Long Island NAACP actively campaigns against these injustices. Pictured above are NAACP Eastern Long Island former leaders Eveny Collins (left) and Harold Brown (right) during a 1998 NAACP luncheon. (Joe Turner Collection.)

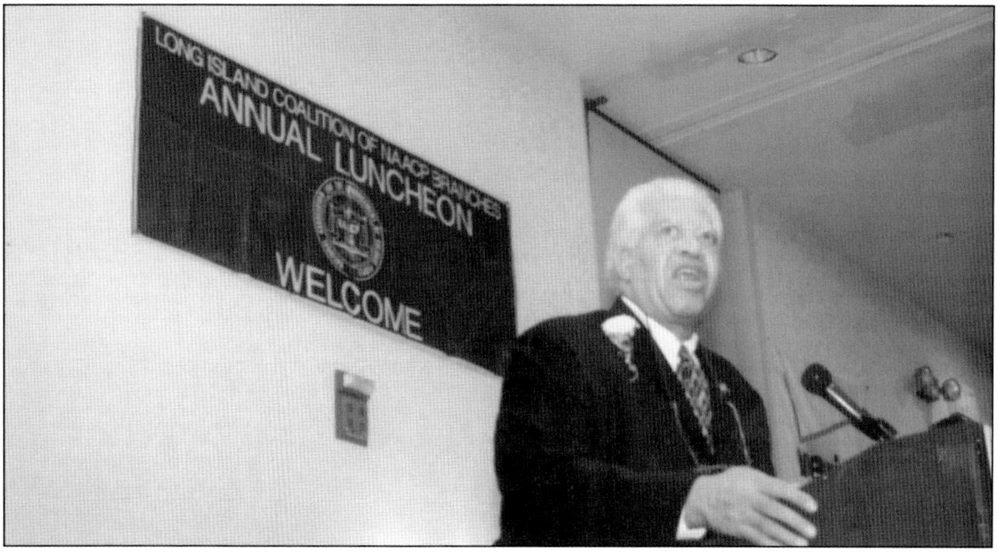

The current NAACP Eastern Long Island president is Lucius Ware. Under the leadership of Lucius Ware, the NAACP's focus was on educational and employment discrimination within the Hampton townships. In 1999, three percent of the town of South Hampton's workforce was black. With the aggressive review of affirmative action agreements, the town's workforce is now 17 percent black. Educational reforms include racial disparity report cards of eastern school districts. (Joe Turner Collection.)

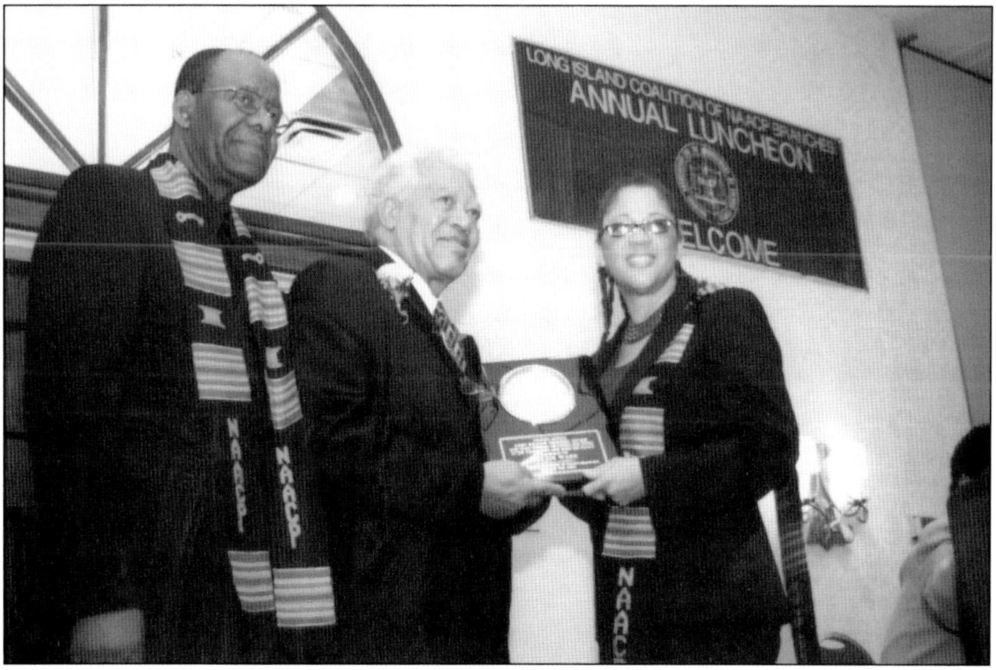

The NAACP Annual Luncheon highlights achievements of local chapter members. The Gary Williams Award is given for community service or achieving high voter registration within the area represented. This award is aligned with the founding principle of removing barriers from the democratic process. Pictured here are Douglas Mayers (left), Lucius Ware, and Maria Williams (right). (Joe Turner Collection.)

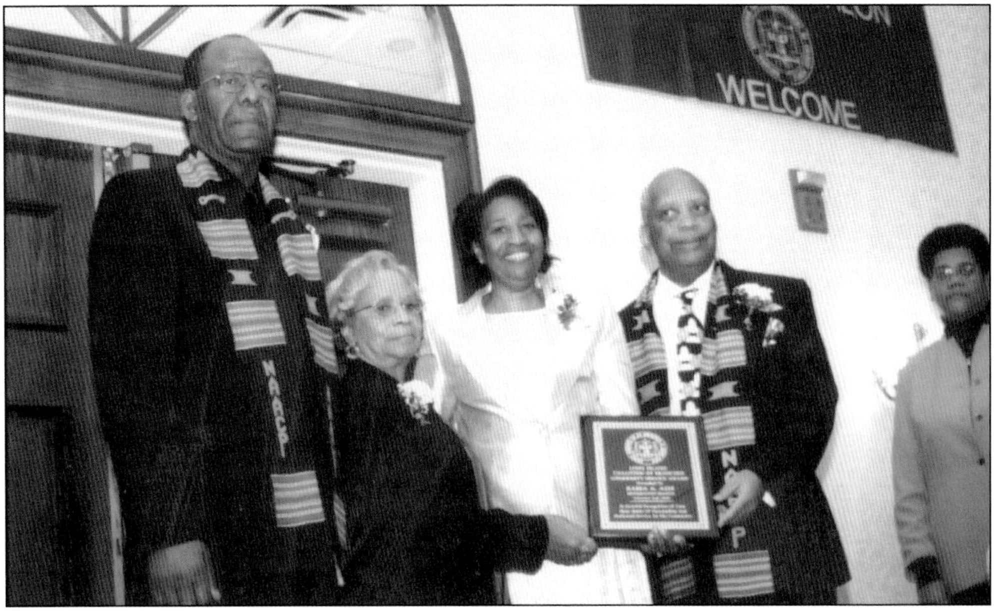

The Community Service Award is given to members who further the NAACP's guiding principles. This 2008 award is being presented to Rabia Aziz. Rabia has worked with the Urban League of Long Island and the Economic Opportunity Council of Suffolk County as chief operations officer. From left to right are Douglas Mayers, Dolores Thompson, Rabia Aziz, and Rev. Beresford Adams. (Joe Turner Collection.)

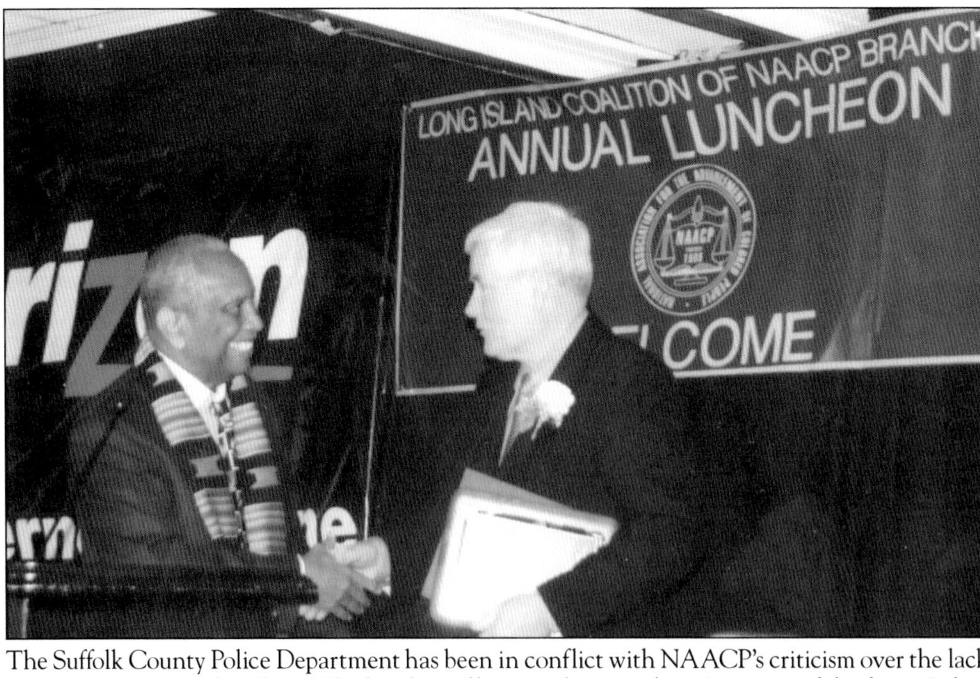

The Suffolk County Police Department has been in conflict with NAACP's criticism over the lack of diversity in the police force. Black police officers make up only 2.5 percent of the force. Police commissioner Richard Dormer was a guest of honor at the NAACP luncheon. The luncheon was an opportunity for branch leaders to collaborate on issues such as hiring practices and community policing. (Joe Turner Collection.)

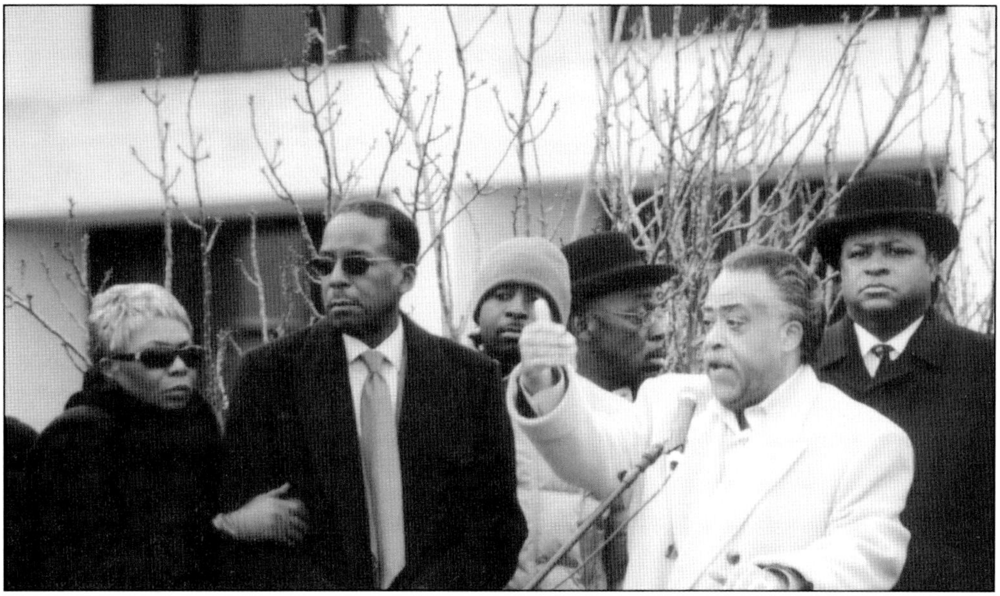

In August 2006, John White, an African American living in Miller Place, confronted two carloads of white teens who were threatening his son Aaron's life. Aaron was one out of four African Americans at Miller Place High School. The two carloads of teens were threatening Aaron over a bogus Myspace threat that was later revealed as a prank. John told the teens to leave, warned them that he would defend his property, and showed them he had a gun. A teen attempted to grab the gun, and it went off and killed a teen. This incident triggered a debate on current racial issues. Pictured above are Sonia and John White at a demonstration with Al Sharpton. (Joe Turner Collection.)

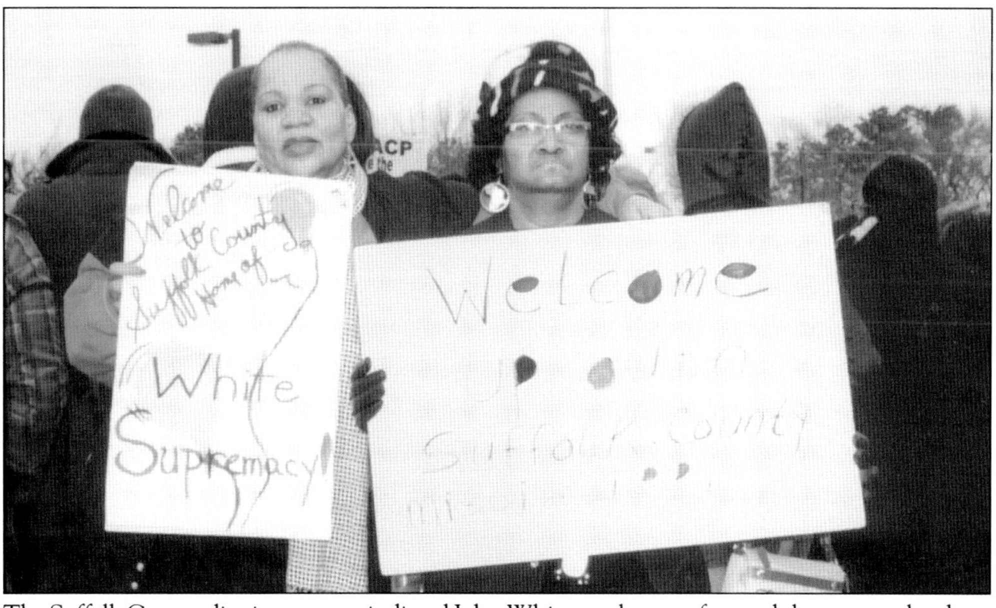

The Suffolk County district attorney indicted John White on charges of second-degree manslaughter. White argued that he was acting in self-defense and that he had the right to defend his property. John went to trial and was convicted of manslaughter. Above, two women attend the demonstration against the charges at Riverhead Courthouse. (Joe Turner Collection.)

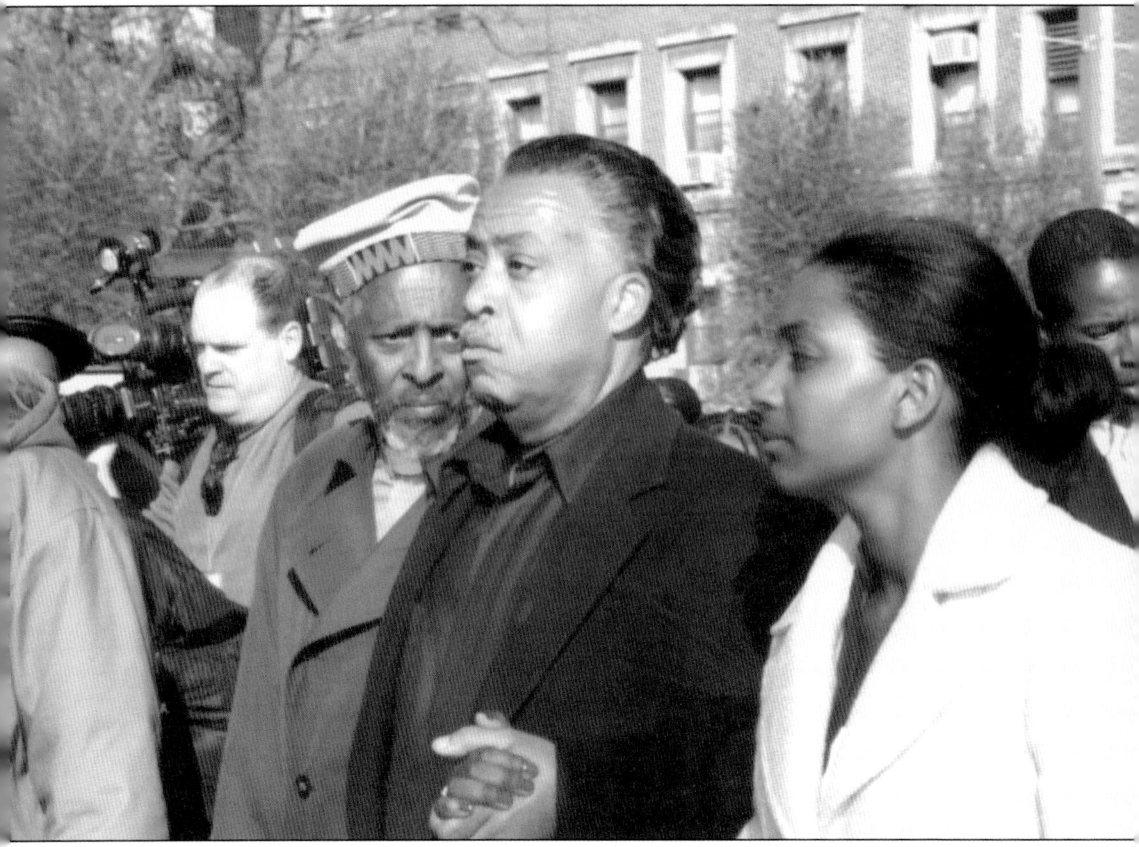

Police within the city and Long Island have had frayed relationships with black communities. Policing tactics within these communities have historically weighed heavily on racial profiling. On the night of November 25, 2006, New York City police shot an unarmed Sean Bell and his friends 50 times on the suspicion that they had a gun. The shooting prompted the New York City and Long Island chapters of the NAACP and the National Action Network to hold a demonstration on the block where Bell was gunned down. From left to right Rev. Herbert Daughtry, Rev. Al Sharpton, and Sean Bell's fiancée, Nicole Paultre. (Joe Turner Collection.)

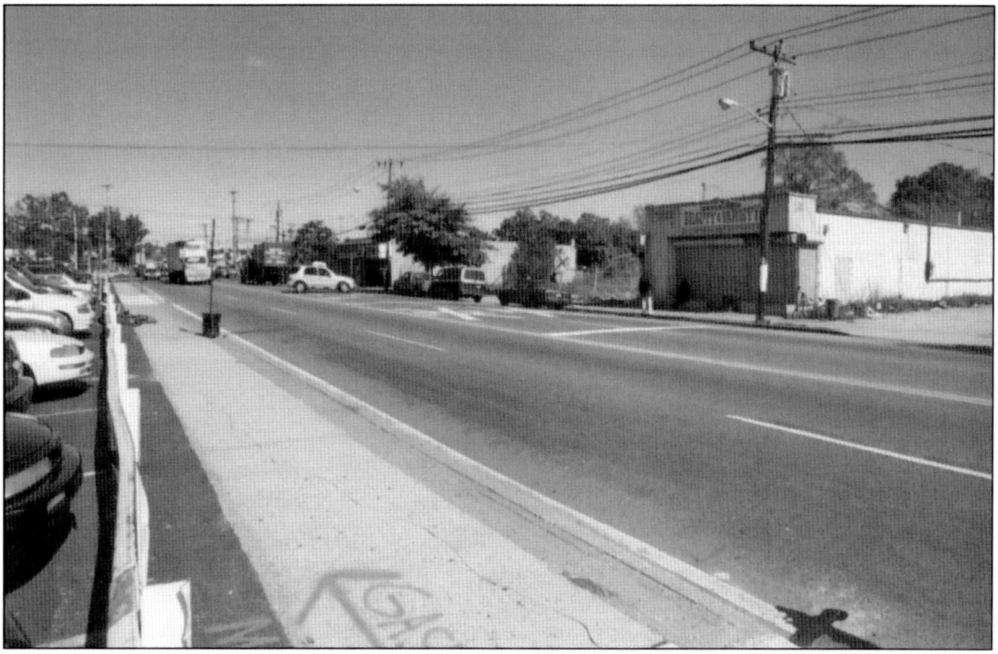

Wyandanch's main road, Straight Path Avenue, is the commercial district of the town. The commercial tax base makes up 40 percent of local Long Island school district funding. For decades, Wyandanch has been plagued with abandoned storefronts. Local and county officials created tax abatements as a fixer against the blight, waiving local taxes for an extended period of time. The community of Wyandanch has suffered economically due to the loss of revenue from the abandoned businesses and the tax abatements. In many cases, when the abatements are up, businesses close or relocate. The outcome is that the school remains financially in the red and employment remains stagnant. (Historic Photograph and Postcard Collection of the Town of Babylon, Office of Historic Services)

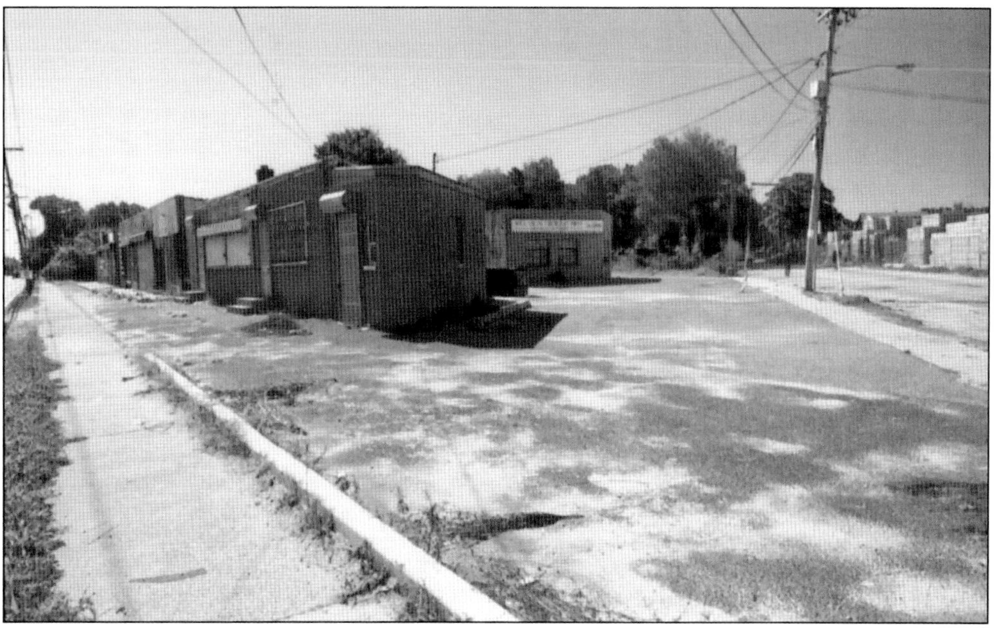

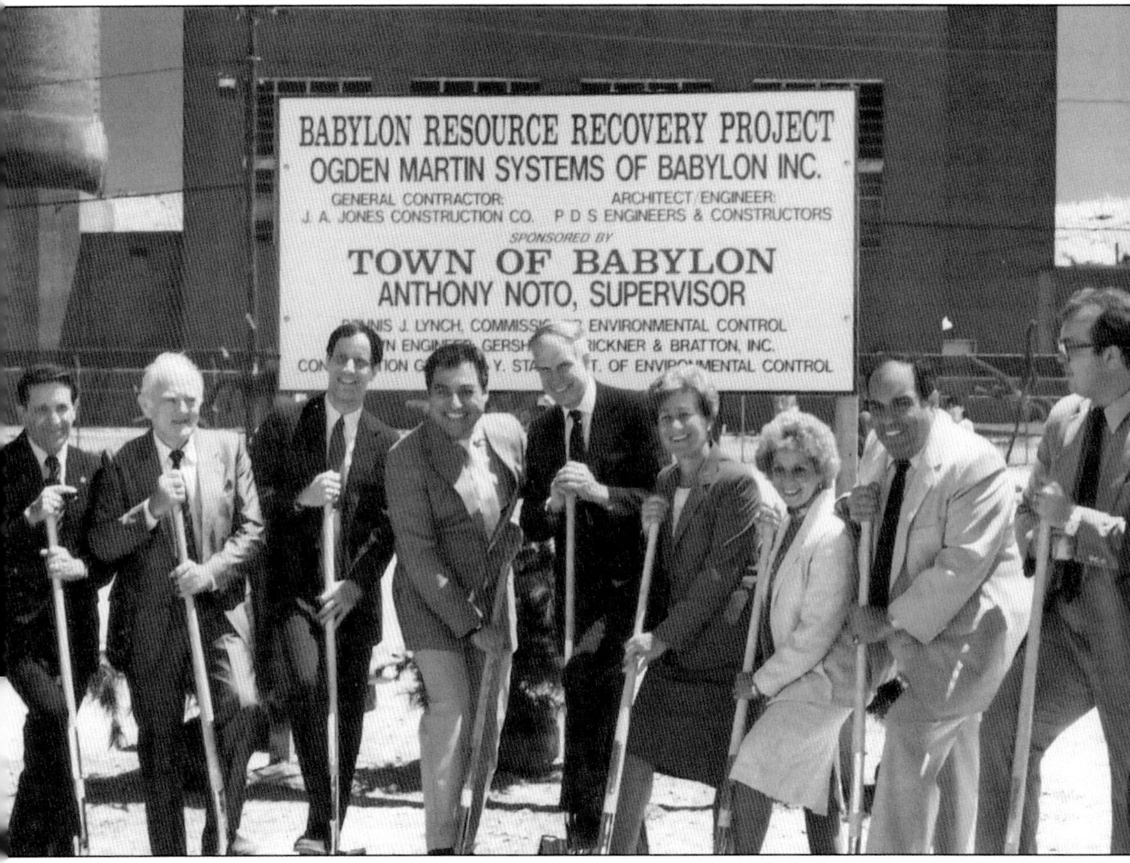

The West Babylon Landfill remains a controversial local issue. A landfill brings many environmental and health problems but provides an exorbitant amount of tax revenue. The landfill is located on Edison Avenue away from most residential homes in West Babylon but close to residential sections of Wyandanch. Locals feel that West Babylon gets all the financial benefits and Wyandanch suffers all the environmental consequences. Here, former Babylon supervisor Anthony Noto and former town council members break ground for the West Babylon Landfill's incinerator. (Historic Photograph and Postcard Collection of the Town of Babylon, Office of Historic Services.)

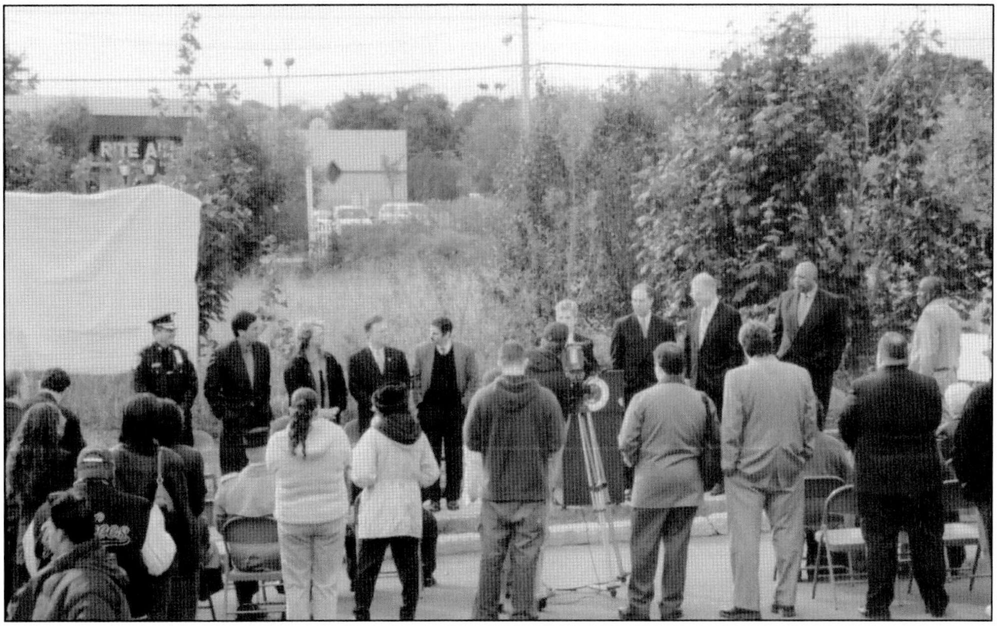

The intersection of Great Neck and Albany Roads in North Amityville is locally known as "The Corner." Since the late 1960s, this plot of land has become known for an open illegal drug market. During the crack epidemic, cars drove up and purchased their drugs with no fear of police. The rezoned commercial district has restored this once-blighted section, but at the potential expense of tax revenue for the schools. The rezoned district gives limited tax abatements to startup businesses. Pictured above are Babylon town supervisor Steve Bellone (behind the podium) and Suffolk County executive Steve Levy (on the right of Levy). In the photograph below, Bellone is behind the podium. (Both, Joe Turner Collection.)

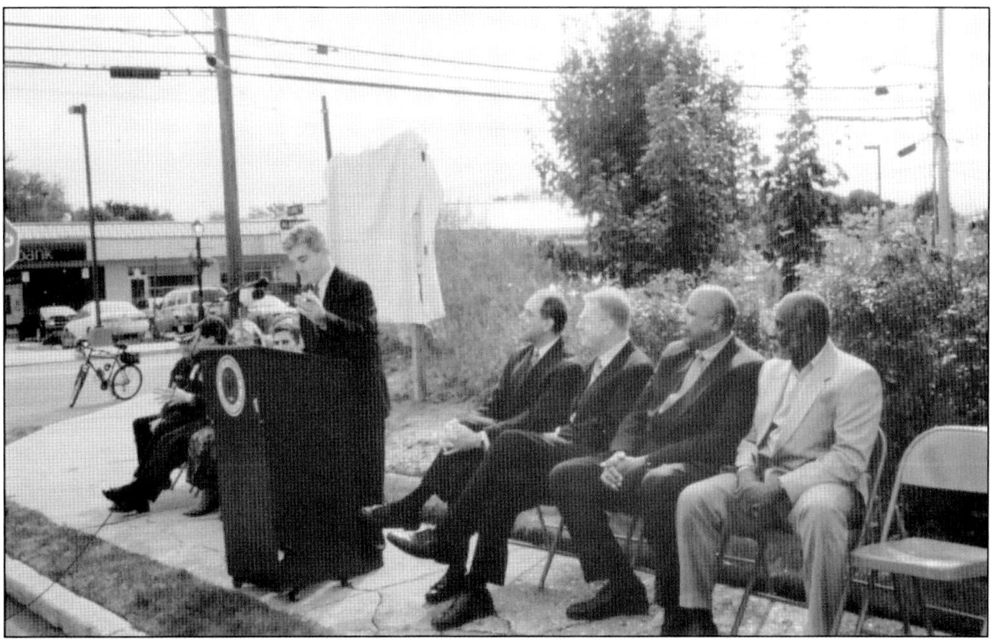

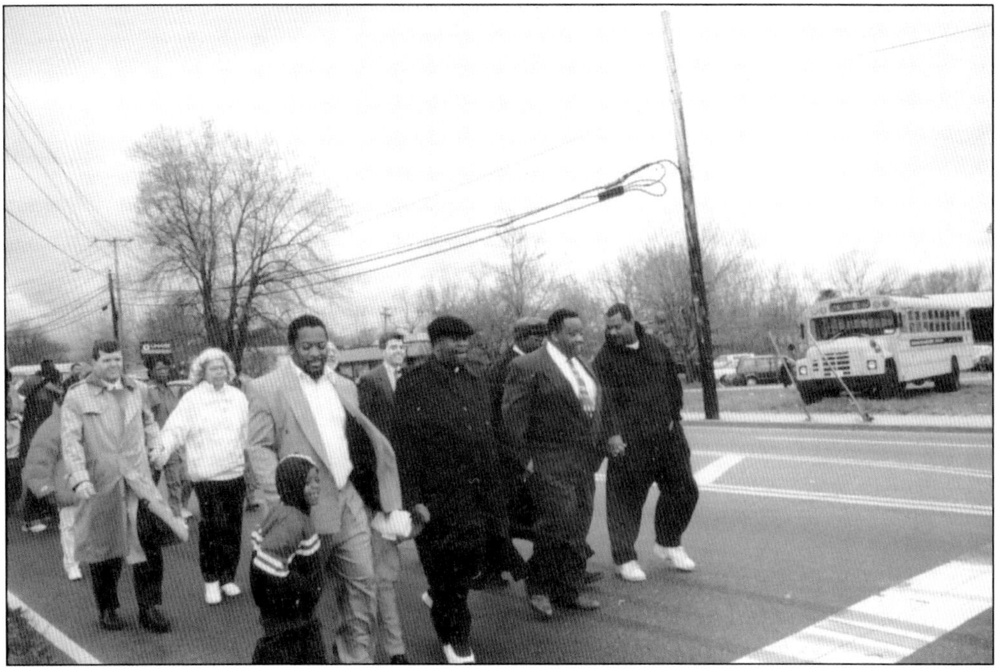

On April 4, 1998, Martin Luther King III came to Wyandanch, Suffolk County, to organize a march down Straight Path Avenue on the 30th anniversary of his father's death. Wyandanch had been plagued with poverty and under-performing schools. This march was to highlight the unfinished work of his father in communities such as Wyandanch. The original main focus for the local activists was to bring awareness to the lack of access to affordable health care. After the march, Martin Luther King III spoke at the dedication ceremony for a free health care clinic. (Both, Joe Turner Collection.)

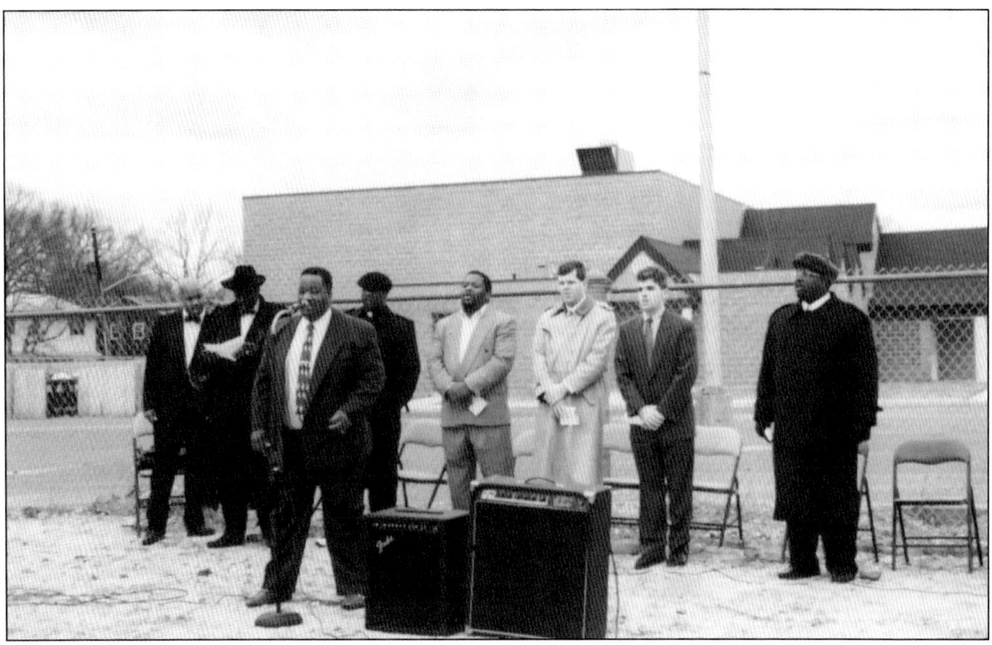

Bibliography

Caro, Robert. *The Power Broker: Robert Moses and the Fall of New York*. New York: Alfred A. Knopf, 1974.

Day, Lynda. *Making a Way to Freedom: A History of African Americans on Long Island*. New York: Empire Books, 1997.

Long Island: Our Story. Hempstead, NY: Newsday, LLC, 1998.

Matarrese, Lynne. *History of Levittown, New York*. Levittown, NY: Levittown Historical Society, 1997.

Purnell, Brian. *Fighting Jim Crow in the County of Kings: The Congress of Racial Equality in Brooklyn*. Lexington: University Press of Kentucky, 2013.